Breaking Down *Breaking Bad*

Breaking Down

Br³⁵eaking Ba⁵⁶d

CRITICAL PERSPECTIVES

EDITED AND WITH AN INTRODUCTION BY

MAtt Wanat and LeoNard Engel

UNIVERSITY OF NEW MEXICO PRESS ☠ ALBUQUERQUE

Library of Congress Cataloging-in-Publication Data
Breaking down Breaking Bad : critical perspectives / edited with an
introduction by Matt Wanat and Leonard Engel.
pages cm
Includes bibliographical references and index.
ISBN 978-0-8263-5683-3 (cloth : alk. paper) — ISBN 978-0-8263-5684-0 (electronic)
1. Breaking Bad (Television program : 2008–2013) I. Wanat, Matt, 1973– editor.
II. Engel, Leonard, 1936– editor.
PN1992.77.B74B76 2016
791.45'72—dc23
2015029022

Cover illustration: © Jim Deaves, www.jimdeaves.co.uk
Cover and interior vector graphics: *Breaking Bad Memorabilia Vector Set*
© benclark32 via vecteezy.com
Designed by Lila Sanchez
Composed in Adobe Garamond Pro; display type is Bundy and Arial

To Tobias Rafael Engel (1993–2012)
Toby—you would have loved *Breaking Bad*

Contents

Acknowledgments

The fascinating, dynamic, and sometimes brutal world of *Breaking Bad* has been an inspiration for this collection of essays. The project has been a labor of love for us, and we are grateful to a number of people who have helped bring it to fruition. First, our thanks to the contributors; they are as enthralled with Vince Gilligan's tragic drama as we are and have shown it through their good work and commitment. Len Engel gives special thanks to Professors Patricia Comitini, Chair of English, and Robert Smart, Dean of the College of Arts and Sciences, at Quinnipiac for their strong support and encouragement. Also, many thanks to Quinnipiac's fine library staff, who have been very helpful, particularly Janet Valeski, Bob Young, and June DeGennaro. Thanks, also, to our patient and very helpful editor Elise McHugh. Finally, Len offers a heartfelt thanks to his wife, Moira, for her love, understanding, and support, especially during the many hours of watching, and vicariously living with, Walt, Skyler, Walt Jr., and the rest—they have touched, at times, the very core of what it means to be human. Matt Wanat would like to thank Jenny Wanat and Brandon O'Neal for introducing him to the series; Judy Carey Nevin and the staff of the Hannah V. McCauley Library at Ohio University–Lancaster; Amber Landis, Scott Minar, Patrick Munhall, Jane Wells, and Ohio University–Lancaster Dean Jim Smith; and his loving family.

Introduction

Matt Wanat and Leonard Engel

Breaking Bad has broken records and won awards—a lot of them. And it has swept across the country like those fleeting images of Albuquerque and its surrounding landscape that Vince Gilligan (*Breaking Bad*'s creator) uses when he wants to dramatize time flying by. The use of Albuquerque and its environs as the focal point for this rich, powerful, multilayered television experience is only one of the brilliant choices he made in this highly popular series. Critics and reviewers have repeatedly commented on the significance of choosing New Mexico, with its nearby pueblos, stark mountain and desert scenery, overwhelming southwestern skies, and, perhaps most important, its proximity to the Mexican border and the violent drug trafficking permeating the Southwest—all of which become dynamic forces in both the interaction of the characters and in the thematic development of the show. Onto this varied landscape come the principal characters: Walter White (a.k.a. Heisenberg); his wife, Skyler; his son, Walt Jr. (a teen with cerebral palsy); his brother-in-law, Hank Schrader (a DEA official in Albuquerque); Hank's wife and Skyler's sister, Marie; Walt's former student and accomplice in crime, Jesse Pinkman; and his crooked lawyer, Saul Goodman—along with many other characters that come and go during the course of the series.

A male protagonist who sets out on a quest to find self, test manhood, and, ultimately, discover things about himself and the world he never dreamed of is a common enough convention in American storytelling—think of *Moby Dick*, *The Adventures of Huck Finn*, and the Nick Adams stories (Hemingway), to name a few. That the hero encounters various forms of evil and sometimes experiences unspeakable horrors along the way is not uncommon in either American or European renditions of this coming-of-age theme, which is categorized by loss of innocence, growth to worldly wisdom, and, in Walter White's case, violence and murder. Gilligan presents a dynamic variant of this quest by posing the question of how far a man facing life-and-death decisions will go in order to achieve a sense of selfhood and some financial security for his family.

Walt's journey begins quietly and in relative innocence as we are introduced to a mild-mannered, financially pressed family man whose brilliance earlier in life contributed to the winning of a Nobel Prize, but he was not acknowledged by the winners. Walt is now an unappreciated high school chemistry teacher who has to work in a car wash part time to support his family. Suddenly thrust into an untenable position with the news that he has terminal cancer, Walt is desperate for a means to support his family after he's gone. Then, by an accidental, fortuitous encounter with former student Jesse, he discovers, through his skills as a chemist, that he can make a high-quality drug—methamphetamine, "blue meth," which eventually becomes widely known all over the Southwest and is sought after by both underworld figures and DEA officials. As the seasons pass, Walt's cancer goes into temporary remission, and he becomes very wealthy, but he also becomes a killer.

The popularity of Walter White, and of the series in general, has raised him to mythic status, and the show has garnered the largest audience in television history. As a common man—an everyman—with uncommon talents, caught in a cruel and tragic situation, Walt's physical and emotional crises resonate with many people; families struggling to achieve the American dream or some version of it also relate to him and his family in very human ways. Attuned to the economic crises in the contemporary American experience of the early twenty-first century, Gilligan explores financial issues that vitally concern many families, especially those affecting the middle class. Intermixed with these economic woes, the show dramatizes the flourishing, violent drug trade in and around Albuquerque and the War on Drugs our government has established in an attempt to obliterate or at least control it.

Many critics and reviewers have weighed in on *Breaking Bad*—on the themes just briefly discussed and, of course, on its brilliant writing, superb acting, exquisite cinematography, and wonderful casting. A brief review of some of this critical commentary might be helpful. On *Breaking Bad*, Liza Cardinale (2012) writes, "Rooting for Walt's criminal success orients the viewer in his or her own shadow, making Walt's moral disintegration easier to connect with. We too are guilty when we hope he gets away with murder, lies and multi-million dollar drug trafficking" (42). It is not surprising that other criticism on *Breaking Bad* has raised similar questions about the moral culpability of characters on the show and the moral complicity of creators and viewers. Consider, for instance, Carlo Nardi (2014), whose primary thesis involves the show's music, but who also notes that "viewers are faced with the deterioration of social bonds as a structural condition of late modernity—viewers share this condition with Walt, who experiences it on the screen, and around this similarity, identification, albeit unsteadily, is built" (185). Just as Nardi considers the show's reflection of social deterioration through a primary thesis about music, others have considered *Breaking Bad*'s moral and ethical character through multiple perspectives, including cultural politics of nation, race, and gender, and also, because one of the existing collections on *Breaking Bad* is part of Open Court Publishing's Popular Culture and Philosophy series, philosophy and ethics as well.

Volume 67 of the Open Court series, *Breaking Bad and Philosophy*, edited by David R. Koepsell and Robert Arp (2012), finds in Vince Gilligan's series multiple occasions for discussions of moral and ethical concerns. Some of the essays in Koepsell and Arp's book veer slightly away from more broadly ethical concerns; for example, Denise Du Vernay offers a more specific and explicitly feminist reading, and Lisa Kadonaga's is a fascinating reading of the show through the lens of changing views of science, wherein Kadonaga asks whether differing scientific world views represented in the show are "signs that formal and 'street' science can be reconciled" (186). Other essays in Koepsell and Arp's book connect ethical concerns to different culture contexts, as Jeffrey E. Stephenson does when he writes, "In the business sphere, people are praised for the extent to which they can make money for shareholders, even if the environment and populace suffer" (211). Most of Koepsell and Arp's contributors, however, focus on *Breaking Bad*'s contributions to long-standing ethical debates within philosophy, with a number of essayists in the book referencing philosophical sources such as Aristotle, John Stuart Mill, and Friedrich Nietzsche. Anderson and Lopez, for example, discuss Mill on liberty, and Brace and Arp use Mill in their discussion, "What's So Bad about Meth?"

Breaking Bad and Philosophy, as its name suggests, ultimately covers a number of philosophical perspectives applicable to the show. Darryl J. Murphy calls Walt's "*materialist* point of view" exactly "the sort of perspective you would want to have if you were ever shoveling the soupy mess of your murder victim into a toilet" (16). Megan Wright reads Walt through Nietzsche. And in separate essays, Sara Waller and Kimberly Baltzer-Jarey explore the existentialism of the series, with the latter writing that "when Walt becomes Heisenberg, the meth cooker and dealer, he becomes an authentic individual—the ideal person Camus and Sartre speak of—finding the balance between defining himself and the role others play in shaping him" (44).

These and other essays in *Breaking Bad and Philosophy* raise many interesting ethical and otherwise philosophical questions about the series. Our collection asks some of the same questions, but our perspective shifts away from the strictly philosophical to more varied lenses through which to view the show. For instance, though Brandon O'Neal's essay in the present collection might agree with Kimberly Baltzer-Jarey that "when Walt becomes Heisenberg, the meth cooker and dealer, he becomes an authentic individual," or with Oli Mould that "for Walt, it may be that his true self actually is Heisenberg's tendency for criminality and a more subversive lifestyle" (175–76), O'Neal's essay reconsiders these concerns of ethics and identity, adding complex layers to previous moral discussions by closely examining the way characters and their actions and personalities are doubled throughout the series. Likewise, Ian Jensen's essay in our collection, by virtue of Jensen's interest in the disturbingly "delicious" quality of the violence on *Breaking Bad*, takes the ethical discourse on the show to another place entirely.

Broader in scope than *Breaking Bad and Philosophy* is David P. Pierson's 2013 anthology, *Breaking Bad: Critical Essays on the Contexts, Politics, Style, and Reception of the Television Series*. As Pierson's subtitle suggests, the essays in his collection look at the series from cultural and critical perspectives, with sections on context, politics, and style. With the advantage of being published at the end of the show's run, some of the essays in Pierson's collection can more confidently extend discussions started in the 2012 Koepsell and Arp collection. For instance, Alberto Bordesco's essay on science in Pierson's collection takes the show's interest in science, already explored by Kadonaga in the previous collection, and applies it to a reading of the evolution, and specifically the moral evolution, of Walt's character across seasons, from initial master of "MacGyverisms" (56) for extricating himself and Jesse from tough situations to "rational-minded scientist who moves in irrational ways, driven by amoral familism and hubris, under the rule of the most fundamental 'uncertainty,' the one about our own mortality" (67).

Ultimately, with essays ranging from Freeley's on time and contemporary multitasking to Anderson's on unruly bodies and Guffey's on the phenomenology of place and space, the Pierson collection offers the first varied treatment of *Breaking Bad*'s cultural contexts and stylistic preoccupations. Our collection adds to this discussion with a number of essays on previously unexplored topics—see, in the present collection, Jeff Severs's essay on psychiatric therapy and Timothy Dandill's fascinating analysis of *Breaking Bad*'s use of Whitman—but our contributors also work nicely in combination with interests explored in Pierson's collection and shared by viewers of the series. For example, Howe's analysis of Latina and Latino characters and Nardi's analysis of *Breaking Bad*'s music, both from Pierson's collection, are extended and enriched by a number of the essays in this collection, including Maria O'Connell's essay on narcotragedy and Cordelia E. Barrera's analysis of *Breaking Bad*'s use of the narcocorrido, treated in only two pages (182–83) of the Nardi essay.

In addition to *Breaking Bad and Philosophy* and Pierson's 2013 collection, readers of this collection also will find interesting Bridget R. Cowlishaw's *Masculinity in Breaking Bad* and Brett Martin's *Difficult Men*. Martin addresses *Breaking Bad* only later in his book, more than 250 pages into a discussion of multiple new millennium shows of what he and others call the "new Golden Age of television," including *The Sopranos, The Wire, Mad Men, Six Feet Under, The Shield,* and *Deadwood*. Nevertheless, the depth of Martin's behind-the-scenes story of what now seems one of the most important eras of television makes *Difficult Men* an indispensable study of the contexts for *Breaking Bad* and other excellent shows of the last fifteen years.

Into this growing field of criticism, we offer original essays on a variety of topics embodied in the series. In these essays, the contributors approach their subjects with new analyses, extensive explorations, and excellent character studies, characterized by fresh insights not found in earlier criticism. In chapter 1, Leonard Engel reminds us that medieval morality plays sent a strong reminder that death is all around us, and that sooner or later we will be forced to face that fact. Therefore, the key question in these plays became *How do we face death and prepare for it, and with what moral certitude*? Vince Gilligan offers a contemporary version of the morality tale as he reveals, in the first season of *Breaking Bad*, the sudden revelation that his everyman protagonist Walter White has terminal lung cancer and, with little time left on earth, had better prepare for death. Gilligan's story reveals Walt's gradual changes. Walt's actions, though limited at first, have serious moral consequences, and what begins as a simple, altruistic motive (apart from the immorality of making the drug)—providing for the future of his family—gradually turns into lying, deceit, robbery, violence, and finally murder. By the end, Walt has become the cause, directly or indirectly, of many deaths. Thus *Breaking Bad* tells the story of a basically good man, a modern everyman, who, faced with a desperate situation, becomes twisted and makes choices that gradually lead to overwhelming tragedy—a narrative that is at the core of the morality play.

In chapter 2, Cordelia E. Barrera argues that *Breaking Bad* dramatizes how Walter White thrives within a western narrative of regeneration through violence in order to underscore a tradition of frontier gothicism. She traces Walt's transformation from Walter H. White, high school teacher of chemistry, into the powerful drug kingpin Heisenberg through a close examination of gothic devices. The narcocorrido "Negro y Azul: The Ballad of Heisenberg," from season 2, episode 7, further highlights gothic elements within a contested Borderlands space. As "Negro y Azul" signifies the ironic shift of corrido hero from a Mexican border dweller to a white male, the ballad both "catalyzes and commodifies Walt's transformation into terror in the flesh." The chapter shows how the gothic mode helps to "trace the development of Walter White / Heisenberg as an alienated, displaced figure who both subverts and redefines the American frontier hero within a new western landscape."

Alex Hunt, in chapter 3, notes the importance of setting the series in New Mexico. With its mountain and desert scenery and big sky, Albuquerque becomes a dynamic force in the visual language and thematic significance of the drama. Throughout its history, however, the city was always less a place than a crossing. During the Mexican and Civil Wars, it had strategic military value, and later it became important as a railroad town, a major stop on the Route 66 migration, the location of the state's main university, and, finally, as a site of Cold War atomic development. In addition, Albuquerque and its surroundings highlight such crossings by their ethnic diversity, proximity to the US-Mexico border, and marked contrast between urban and natural landscapes. *Breaking Bad*, Hunt expertly argues, serves as a critique of the globalized market that promulgates it, yet it simultaneously holds out the possibility of a strong regional identity.

In chapter 4, Jeffrey Severs argues that *Breaking Bad* dramatizes a series of rejections of various therapies and eliminates almost all structures in which the leading characters might productively reflect on their traumas and crimes. By introducing a series of couches that mock the psychiatrist's, *Breaking Bad* incites and justifies further violent behavior rather than curing or curtailing it. Severs traces this symbolism by analyzing the show's contortions of therapy, especially in the pivotal season 4, in which *Breaking Bad* achieves its thematic coherence by replaying Walt's early story of physical illness through to Jesse's more intractable psychological issues of trauma and rage. In his conclusion, Severs suggests that the films of Stanley Kubrick, especially the relentless *Clockwork Orange* (1971), are a key to understanding the way questions of rehabilitation are handled—or, far more often, not handled—in the series.

Brandon O'Neal's argument in chapter 5 focuses on Vince Gilligan's use of the double in both the characters and the plot of *Breaking Bad*. While most of the narrative, O'Neal points out, is driven by Walter White's adventures and mishaps on his way to becoming a feared and respected methamphetamine manufacturer in the Southwest, the secondary plots complement the criminal and law-enforcement worlds of the region with characters connected to the White family. The key plot point of Walt's brother-in-law Hank Schrader as a DEA agent acts not only as dramatic irony but also as the impetus for many of Walt's attempts to skirt justice, as Hank's work leads him along the trail of Heisenberg's pure blue meth. The contrasting nature of Walt and Heisenberg to Hank, and the fact that there is a Walt and a Heisenberg, suggest the importance of the role of the double or doppelgänger. That additional characters participate in the act of doubling or act as doubles for others increases tension in the drama.

In chapter 6, George Mousinho analyzes the elements of discontent in society that create dissatisfaction in individuals and cause them to act against the external world. He does so by focusing on the character of Walter White in the first two seasons of *Breaking Bad*, emphasizing the clash between the interests of the collective and those of the individual. Walt's moment of realization occurs when he sees Jesse climbing out a window in the first episode. Walt realizes he has an opportunity for success but also an opportunity to flirt with transgression against the normalcy of civil behavior. Little is known about him before his fiftieth birthday and the discovery of the lung cancer—the watershed moment that triggers the main drama of the series—but the facts from then on are detailed and socially subversive. Walt turns into Heisenberg, his alter ego, the code name chosen as an introduction to his freer persona.

Maria O'Connell, in chapter 7, points out how the series is a modern take on a classical Greek tragedy. Playing on the gang and drug culture in the southwestern United States and masculine values of violence, honor, and male leadership, the show dramatizes Walter White as a contemporary version of an Aristotelian tragic hero. It is a new form of the old classics, a narcotragedy, and the music chosen in the series becomes a chorus filling in the plot, predicting plot twists, and providing social commentary on the characters' actions. The varied musical styles and the choice to use music in both Spanish and English, including an original narcocorrido called "Negro y Azul: The Ballad of Heisenberg," allow *Breaking Bad* to move the classic tragedy into a present drama about issues in law, morality, power, and borders.

Matt Wanat, in chapter 8 of our collection, explores *Breaking Bad*'s use of genre. In his book *Difficult Men*, Brett Martin writes that, as its premise emerged from Vince Gilligan and the other writers, "*Breaking Bad* fit no discernible genre at all—except quality" (271), but Martin goes on to comment on the show's "wide-open landscapes that are more John Ford than anything a revisionist Western like *Deadwood* could ever allow itself" (276). In other words, though the show cannot be defined by a single genre, it often references specific generic conventions quite well. Wanat's essay begins with the premise that although *Breaking Bad* defies categorization as any single narrative genre, it mixes and exploits existing genres across and within episodes. "Dead Freight" from season 5 offers a fine example of this feature of the series, in this case centering on the caper and in the process manipulating the viewers' conventional expectations about the outcome of the heist.

Considering generic affinities in a different way, Ian K. Jensen's interdisciplinary chapter 9 situates *Breaking Bad* among those "new Golden Age" shows examined in Martin's book by arguing that there is a pleasurable brutality in *Breaking Bad* analogous, at the levels of presentation and reception, less to other shows in *Breaking Bad*'s era of television than to the brutality in death metal music and culture. Applying distinct definitions of experience as *Erfahrung* and *Erlebnis*, with reference to the work of

Benjamin and Gadamer, Jensen considers the specific nature of the experience of brutality while watching *Breaking Bad* and makes the claim that the Erfahrung and Erlebnis distinction is complicated by the communal nature of brutality associated with our viewing of the violence on Gilligan's show. In the process, Jensen not only offers fresh theoretical insights about experience and brutality but also begins to explain the appeal of *Breaking Bad*'s many morally unsettling aspects in an original way that ought to add to the ethical discussion of the show started in *Breaking Bad and Philosophy*.

Following Matt Wanat's lead in discussing subversion of genres (chapter 8), Glenda Pritchett in chapter 10 examines how Vince Gilligan and Quentin Tarantino manipulate genres and much more in their respective works. What these two widely diverse narratives share is a partnership of male characters in which neither can be successful without the other. One element of appeal in the narrative construct is the seeming relationship to the buddy film in which two male characters, often from different backgrounds or races and with every reason to distrust one another, are paired and grow to become friends, overcoming whatever sociocultural obstacles seem to be looming. So Walter White / Jesse Pinkman and Dr. Schultz / Django, inhabitants of entirely different worlds, find themselves paired both by choice and necessity. Django and Schultz develop a harmonious relationship best captured by the astute if harsh observation by Schultz that their respective enterprises—slavery and bounty hunting—are basically "flesh for cash" businesses. But *Breaking Bad* is no *Butch Cassidy and the Sundance Kid* remake. Despite numerous scenes of growing reciprocal understanding and even tenderness between Walt and Jesse, theirs is to be, in the end, no buddy relationship.

In an entirely different vein, Brad Klypchak, in chapter 11, explores identity management and the various forms of duplicity in *Breaking Bad*, with attention to the character of Marie. Sister of Skyler, in-law of Walter, and husband of DEA agent Hank Schrader, Marie represents a variety of identity-manipulative personae—obscuring her kleptomania, denying her husband's self-doubt, ignoring the multitude of dysfunctions tied to being part of the family, and inevitably representing herself through a persona of idealistic suburban security. The false consciousness of such a pursuit becomes conveyed through the narrative, leaving the audience with a sense of the futility embedded within the mythic appeals of suburbia. Klypchak's chapter seeks to explore Marie and her manipulations of identity management through the works of Erving Goffman and Dan Blazer, as representations of the postmodern dissolve of modernist myths of suburban utopia.

In chapter 12, Tim Dansdill claims that *Breaking Bad* matters because it is a story whose "moral" lies in the deepest of all discourse references: that the United States has always been an empire nation. Despite its discourses of rights and laws, US history—from the legal to the literary, from the constitutional to the cultural—is an arc of "breaking bad" in metastatic tension with its arc of "breaking good." The arc of *Breaking Bad* follows the method and pattern of a Whitman poem. With both expansively epic proportions and lyrically compressed intensities, it is a metastatic poem. Furthermore, Walt Whitman and Walter White have many similarities: "both are intellectual pioneers in their fields, their legacies—centuries apart—demanding risk, casting them outside of society, gliding out into the world, liberated from societal constraints. Both strove for perfection in their creations. However we understand 'the arc of "W. W."'—whether of the soul, or of its 'common share' of US manifest destiny's antiheroic arc—*Breaking Bad*, as purveyor of 'imperial selfhood,' cooks up our favorite imperialist psychopomp, Walt Whitman, [and] adds trace elements of . . . William Walker . . . to produce Walter White," one of the most notorious villains we've ever seen on television.

Note

All references to episodes of *Breaking Bad* in this collection provide the season and episode number and refer to the AMC series created by Vince Gilligan that ran from 2008 to 2013.

References

Anderson, Aaron C., and Justine Lopez. 2012. "Meth, Liberty, and the Pursuit of Happiness." In *Breaking Bad and Philosophy: Badder Living through Chemistry*, edited by David R. Koepsell and Robert Arp, 103–20. Chicago, IL: Open Court.

Anderson, Jami L. 2013. "A Life Not Worth Living." In *Breaking Bad: Critical Essays on the Contexts, Politics, Style, and Reception of the Television Series*, edited by David P. Pierson, 103–20. Lanham, MD: Lexington.

Baltzer-Jaray, Kimberly. 2012. "Finding Happiness in a Black Hat." In *Breaking Bad and Philosophy: Badder Living through Chemistry*, edited by David R. Koepsell and Robert Arp, 43–55. Chicago, IL: Open Court.

Brace, Patricia, and Robert Arp. 2012. "What's So Bad about Meth?" In *Breaking Bad and Philosophy: Badder Living through Chemistry*, edited by David R. Koepsell and Robert Arp, 139–49. Chicago, IL: Open Court.

Brodesco, Alberto. 2013. "Heisenberg: Epistemological Implications of a Criminal Pseudonym." In *Breaking Bad: Critical Essays on the Contexts, Politics, Style, and Reception of the Television Series*, edited by David P. Pierson, 53–72. Lanham, MD: Lexington.

Cardinale, Liza. 2012. "Why *Breaking Bad* Is So Good," *Cinemaeditor* 62 (3): 42.

Cowlishaw, Bridget R., ed. 2015. *Masculinity in Breaking Bad: Critical Perspectives.* Jefferson, NC: McFarland.

Du Vernay, Denise. 2012. "Breaking Bonds." In *Breaking Bad and Philosophy: Badder Living through Chemistry*, edited by David R. Koepsell and Robert Arp, 191–201. Chicago, IL: Open Court.

Freeley, Dustin. 2013. "The Economy of Time and Multiple Existences in *Breaking Bad.*" In *Breaking Bad: Critical Essays on the Contexts, Politics, Style, and Reception of the Television Series*, edited by David P. Pierson, 33–52. Lanham, MD: Lexington.

Guffey, Ensley F. 2013. "Buying the House: Place in *Breaking Bad.*" In *Breaking Bad: Critical Essays on the Contexts, Politics, Style, and Reception of the Television Series*, edited by David P. Pierson, 155–72. Lanham, MD: Lexington.

Howe, Andrew. 2014. "Not Your Average Mexican: *Breaking Bad* and the Destruction of Latino Stereotypes." In *Breaking Bad: Critical Essays on the Contexts, Politics, Style, and Reception of the Television Series*, edited by David P. Pierson, 87–102. Lanham, MD: Lexington.

Kadonaga, Lisa. 2012. "You're Supposed to Be a Scientist." In *Breaking Bad and Philosophy: Badder Living through Chemistry*, edited by David R. Koepsell and Robert Arp, 181–91. Chicago, IL: Open Court.

Koepsell, David R., and Robert Arp, eds. 2012. *Breaking Bad and Philosophy: Badder Living through Chemistry*. Chicago, IL: Open Court.

Martin, Brett. 2014. *Difficult Men: Behind the Scenes of a Creative Revolution; From The Sopranos and The Wire to Mad Men and Breaking Bad.* New York: Penguin.

Mould, Oli. 2012. "Been through the Desert on a Horse with No Name." In *Breaking Bad and Philosophy: Badder Living through Chemistry*, edited by David R. Koepsell and Robert Arp, 171–80. Chicago, IL: Open Court.

Murphy, Darryl J. 2012. "Heisenberg's Uncertain Confession." In *Breaking Bad and Philosophy: Badder Living through Chemistry*, edited by David R. Koepsell and Robert Arp, 15–27. Chicago, IL: Open Court.

Nardi, Carlo. 2013. "Mediating Fictional Crimes: Music, Morality, and Liquid Identification in *Breaking Bad.*" In *Breaking Bad: Critical Essays on the Contexts, Politics, Style, and Reception of the Television Series*, edited by David P. Pierson, 173–90. Lanham, MD: Lexington.

Pierson, David P., ed. 2013. *Breaking Bad: Critical Essays on the Contexts, Politics, Style, and Reception of the Television Series*. Lanham, MD: Lexington.

Stephenson, Jeffrey E. 2012. "Walter White's American Vice." In *Breaking Bad and Philosophy: Badder Living through Chemistry*, edited by David R. Koepsell and Robert Arp, 203–13. Chicago, IL: Open Court.

Waller, Sara. 2012. "I Appreciate the Strategy." In *Breaking Bad and Philosophy: Badder Living through Chemistry*, edited by David R. Koepsell and Robert Arp, 125–37. Chicago, IL: Open Court.

Wright, Megan. 2012. "Walter White's Will to Power." In *Breaking Bad and Philosophy: Badder Living through Chemistry*, edited by David R. Koepsell and Robert Arp, 81–91. Chicago, IL: Open Court.

1

Breaking Bad—Morality Play Meets Heisenberg's Uncertainty Principle

"Actions Have Consequences"

Leonard Engel

If religion is a reaction of man . . . it seems to me that it represents a human desire for wrong-doers to be punished. I hate the idea of Idi Amin living in Saudi Arabia for the last 25 years of his life. That galls me to no end. I feel some sort of need for Biblical atonement, or justice, or something. I like to believe there is some comeuppance, that karma kicks in at some point, even if it takes years or decades to happen. My girlfriend says this great thing that's become my philosophy as well. "I want to believe there's a heaven. But I can't not believe there's a hell."

—Vince Gilligan, *New York Times Magazine*, July 10, 2011

Growing out of the religious mystery plays in the Middle Ages, morality plays flourished in Europe in the fifteenth and sixteenth centuries. They usually featured a protagonist who could represent a single individual, a society, a specific section of society, or humanity as a whole. The plays were meant to provide moral guidance in a world of good and evil, examples of which were personified by characters appearing as various vices, such as deceit, cheating, or bearing false witness, and opposed by characters representing virtues such as good deeds, justice, and equity. The core idea of the plays was that God, believing that humanity too easily succumbs to the accumulation of earthly riches, sends a strong reminder that Death is all around us, and that sooner or later we will be forced to face that fact. Therefore, the key issue becomes *How do we face death, and prepare for it,* *and with what moral certitude*? Most plays of the time concentrate on evil, but *Everyman* focuses on good and God's power to help us overcome sin in its various guises.

Vince Gilligan, in the epigraph that opens this chapter, renders a contemporary version of the morality tale as he reveals, in the first season of *Breaking Bad*, the sudden revelation that his everyman protagonist Walter White has terminal lung cancer, has little time left on earth, and, therefore, had better prepare for death. A brilliant chemist who worked on a project that eventually led to a Nobel Prize, for which he received no credit or remuneration, Walter is now a struggling high school chemistry teacher in Albuquerque, New Mexico, who has to work part time in a car wash to support his family. He and his wife, Skyler, have a disabled son in high school, and she is pregnant with their second child. Pressed with his son's medical bills, the cost of his own cancer treatments, and the thought that he will be leaving his family with serious financial debt after he's gone, Walter is desperate. On a whim, he accompanies his brother-in-law, Hank Schrader (a drug enforcement agent), and his team as they surveil a suspected drug house. Their surveillance quickly turns into a drug bust, and Walter, watching from the car, recognizes a former student escaping through a window of the house. This triggers Walt's curiosity and imagination, and eventually he contacts the student, Jesse Pinkman, who happened to be one of his worst chemistry students, and proposes a partnership: he (Walter) would make the drugs and Jesse would handle the distribution and selling. It would be a local and limited operation, securing only enough money to provide security for his family's future. Gilligan could not have chosen a more suitable catalyst for evil in this contemporary morality tale, for drugs have become the modern scourge, the making, taking, and selling of them—paralleling the devastating plagues of the Middle Ages—and have led to massive social problems in our society, not to mention a huge number of deaths.

As the plot develops in *Breaking Bad*, the drug Walt and Jesse produce, methamphetamine, happens to be of high quality, becomes very popular, and doesn't remain local or limited for long. In addition to attracting the attention of the DEA in Albuquerque and particularly his brother-in-law, Hank, this new drug, a high grade of crystal meth, also attracts a host of underworld thugs, which Walt did not anticipate. Gilligan's story reveals Walt's gradual changes: His actions, though limited at first, have serious moral consequences, and what begins as a simple altruistic motive (apart from the immorality of making the drug)—providing for the future of his family—gradually turns into lying, deceit, robbery, violence, and finally murder. By the end, Walt has become the cause, directly or indirectly, of many deaths. Thus, *Breaking Bad* tells the story of a basically good man, a modern everyman, faced with a desperate situation, who becomes twisted and makes choices that gradually lead to overwhelming tragedy—a narrative that is at the core of the morality play.

This chapter will examine the steps that lead Walter White to his destruction; before that, however, we need to look briefly at another aspect of Walt's journey. Once he begins the drug-making operation, he gives himself the name of Heisenberg for the local underworld. In 1927 Werner Heisenberg (the real one) was a professor of theoretical physics and the head of that department at Leipzig University in Germany. In 1932 he was awarded the Nobel Prize for physics for his theory of quantum mechanics, but what he's more famous for in the popular mind is his uncertainty principle. In layman's terms, the principle states that it is "impossible to exactly measure both the position and the speed of a particle, because to measure the position, you'd have to change the particle's speed, and to measure the speed, you'd have to affect its position" (Conradt 2013).

As the principle became more widely known and popularized, its meaning changed—much to Heisenberg's consternation. Its basis in the scientific method (examining material based on reality) shifted to philosophy and theology and developed into what many people considered new rules for moral behavior. In other words, to mass culture, this complex, scientific principle came to mean that morality was indeterminate. Truth is "dependent on the way the individual sees his circumstances" at any given time. That is, an individual can "act one way at one time, and entirely a different way at another, and who is to judge him? Popular misconceptions of the meaning of . . . [the uncertainty principle] eventually produced commonly held concepts . . . and the pop culture mantras, 'You can be anything you want to be' and 'Everything is relative'" (Voshell 2013). (According to scientists who knew him, these meanings were never intended by Werner Heisenberg.) As a result of this popular misconception implying moral indeterminacy, Walter White, a.k.a. Heisenberg, "becomes both victim and perpetrator of moral chaos . . . [and this] gradually destroys not only him, but the social . . . [fabric] he lives with. Family, friends, and all the structures that formerly gave his life meaning and worth explode before his eyes as the 'make it up as you go' morality of the criminal underworld to which he gradually devotes his life takes over" (Voshell 2013). In direct contrast to this view is the Judeo-Christian world view, implied in Gilligan's statement that opens this chapter, which proclaims that consequences follow actions, especially for those who defy the moral law, and as Walt discovers, moral turpitude leads to personal disintegration.

So what is Vince Gilligan implying by giving Walter White the underworld code name of Heisenberg? Is he suggesting that Walt's new status as a drug kingpin allows him to think he is functioning in a moral vacuum that allows him to act as he wishes or as the situation demands? Or is Gilligan hinting at the progression of Walt's desire to provide for his family once he is gone—a desire, as indicated earlier, that begins rather innocently, or at least with good intentions, but soon evolves into a moral morass with each step sinking Walt deeper into more pervasive evil? Perhaps both! But one thing Gilligan is most definitely doing is dramatizing that actions *do* have consequences, that there is a deep "human desire for wrong-doers to be punished . . . [that] there is some comeuppance, that karma kicks in at some point." One of the things that has held fans of the series in thrall is Gilligan's depiction of Walt's inexorable descent into his own underworld, a descent fraught with uncertainty, deceit, guilt, death, and huge financial profit. It is also a descent that includes Walt's shocking statement to Skyler, in the middle of season 4, indicating the apex of his creed of moral relativity (another ironic misinterpretation of Heisenberg's uncertainty principle). When she expresses concern about the danger he may be in, he retorts, "I am not in danger, Skyler. I am the danger! . . . I am the one who knocks!" (season 4, episode 6).

The steps of Walt's descent, as I have stated, loosely follow the framework of a morality play and powerfully illuminate, at times with visceral, bloody imagery, the road to Walt's perdition. Though morally ambiguous at first, these steps invariably lead to one conclusion—the weakening of Walt's humanity and his moral sensibility, followed by his acceptance of, and then embrace of, evil. I will focus on three of the more significant stages in this process: Jane's (Jesse's girlfriend's) death, Gale Boetticher's (Walt's temporary lab assistant's) death, and Gus Fring's (drug lord's) death, while delving briefly into several others in the course of Walt's demise.

Walt has witnessed death before the scene in which Jane dies. In season 1, he and Jesse have an early encounter with Tuco, a small-time drug boss and vicious thug, and they watch in shock and amazement as Tuco gives one of his henchmen bodyguards a severe beating. The beating results in the death of the bodyguard, and while the inexplicability of the brutality and its suddenness clearly unnerve both Walt and Jesse, Walt is an observer, a fearful and visibly shaken one, but still an observer. Earlier in season 1, Walt has entered this brutal world by taking the life of another local drug dealer, Krazy-8, who has been captured by Walt and Jesse and is secured to an iron pole with a bicycle lock in the cellar of Jesse's house, but they don't know what to do with him. Walt knows he should kill Krazy-8 but is reluctant to do it, especially when they converse about people they both know over a plate of food Walt brings (Krazy-8 is the son of a local furniture-store owner from whom Walt has purchased furniture). Finally, Walt, the rational man of science (at least in his own mind) makes two lists: one called "let him live," the other called "kill him." Under the first he writes:

It's the moral thing to do
Judeo/Christian principles
You are **not** a murderer
Sanctity of life
He may listen to reason
Post-traumatic stress
Won't be able to live with your self
Murder is wrong!

Under the second category, "kill him," there is just one sentence—"He will kill your entire family if you let him go" (Bowman 2013, 166). However, Walt's view of himself as "not the bad guy" wins out, and he is about to let Krazy-8 live when he discovers that a sharp piece of broken plate is missing from the debris he picks up after having dropped the plate of food on the cellar floor. Apparently, Krazy-8 discovered the piece and was able to hide it, intending to use it on Walt, or so Walt thinks. This discovery overrides Walt's misgivings about killing him. Yet even in the subsequent, brutal strangling of Krazy-8 with the bicycle lock, Walt repeatedly apologizes to him and is visibly shaken by what he has done. Later, in season 3, he is still proclaiming his innocence, saying to his crooked lawyer, Saul Goodman, "I can't be the bad guy" (Bowman 2013, 166).

While Walt is clearly unnerved by his killing of Krazy-8, his presence at Jane's death (toward the end of season 2) is entirely different. Greatly disturbed by the threats Jane has made to expose their drug-making operation if she isn't given a payoff, Walt goes to see Jesse to talk about the risk Jane poses; he finds both of them drugged out on a bed in Jesse's bedroom. Suddenly, Jane starts coughing, then vomiting, then choking on her vomit. Walt looks down at her, slowly registering what's happening, but does nothing to help her—at this moment he crosses a line. However, in the seconds that follow, his contorted face indicates distress. His sin of omission, consciously letting her die, is not easily dismissed, as his physical being reveals. Nevertheless, at the beginning of season 3, that he is able to recover from his guilt so quickly is remarkable. In the episode "Fly" he talks to Jesse about the odds of his (Walt's) walking into a bar and then, by chance, meeting and talking with Jane's father, Donald, a total stranger, on the very night she dies. Walt then starts to rhapsodize to Jesse on the randomness of life, the Heisenberg uncertainty principle emerging:

> The universe is random. It's not inevitable. It's simple chaos. It's sub-atomic particles in endless atomic collision. That's what science teaches us. But what is *this* saying? What is *it* telling us when, on the very night that this man's daughter dies, it's me who's having a drink with him? I mean, how can this be random? (season 3, episode 10)

So is Walt acknowledging here that things are not random? Science is not the ultimate answer. There is, in fact, some kind of order in the universe according to which, when individuals do things, or, as in Walt's case here, fail to do things, there are, or will be, consequences. In Jane's father's shock and suffering over his daughter's death—and in his stressful job as air-traffic controller—he inadvertently causes a midair collision and the deaths of hundreds of passengers. Walt's randomness-of-the-universe speech to Jesse is a clever articulation, but there's not much evidence that he believes it, or that it makes much difference in his subsequent actions. But suppose he does believe it, and it becomes part of his pattern of lying—in this case, lying to himself—and thus becomes a justification for his actions. He, Walter White, maker of the purest methamphetamine in the whole Southwest and soon to be a drug kingpin, has confronted the chaos of the world and has come out on top (he has won!—as he says later to Skyler, after he engineers the death of Gus Fring). He now has control and is in charge of his fate. If he crossed a line in allowing Jane to die, now, in his own mind,

his control over the randomness of the universe has justified his new position of power. Gilligan magnifies Walt's hubris by having him not only
accept, but capitalize on, the popular misconception of Heisenberg's principle: "You can be anything you want to be! All is relative!" However, as we
shall see, Gilligan will, indeed, have the last word in Walt's demise by his
reverberating, emphatic statement—"Actions [do] have consequences."

Walt's next major stage, Gale Boetticher's death (in season 4), involves
more than his own crossing of a line—he commits a more serious evil by
forcing Jesse to cross a line, too, and commit murder. Gale has been
assigned by Gus Fring to assist Walt in the lab, and despite Gale's skill and
efforts to do everything according to Walt's desires, he cannot please Walt.
Walt has his own agenda: he wants Gale out of the lab and Jesse back in,
so he makes Gale's life miserable. And when his own life is threatened by
Gus, he coerces Jesse into shooting Gale by pleading, "They will kill us if
you don't kill him." Jesse is seriously damaged by what has happened to
Jane (Jesse is unaware of Walt's presence in the room when she dies), and
he blames himself, for he was lying right next to her, passed out from drugs
as she was choking to death. Now, to be forced to kill Gale, who has done
nothing to him, devastates Jesse, but unlike Walt, he is unable to rationalize his actions or mitigate his guilt. He starkly admits his guilt.

Shortly after shooting Gale, Jesse goes to a meeting of Narcotics Anonymous, which he has been attending sporadically, and in response to the
invitation of the leader (a kind of secular Christ figure), he partially unbur-
dens but also severely chastises himself. He tells the group he has just
looked a dog in the eye and shot it. Members of the group try to placate
him, but Jesse won't have it, saying he did it in cold blood. Then some
members show anger toward Jesse, and the leader steps in, saying, "We're
not here to sit in judgment." But Jesse won't have that either; he cries out,

Why not? Why not? The thing is, if you just do stuff and nothing
happens, what's it all mean? What's the point? All right, this whole
thing is about self-acceptance. So no matter what I do, hooray for
me, because I'm a great guy? It's all good, no matter how many dogs
I kill—what, I do an inventory, and accept? (season 4, episode 7)

This outburst is reminiscent of Hamlet's early tortured soliloquies, especially
the one at the end of act 2, when he states, "Oh, what a rogue and peasant slave
am I" (*Hamlet*, 2.2:577). Like Hamlet, Jesse condemns himself. But unlike

Walt, he refuses to rationalize his evil or accept the all-is-relative principle, thus calling into question the randomness of the universe. In begging for punishment, he is attempting to affirm a moral order. There is good and bad in the world, and I know who I am, he says—"I am the bad guy." Vince Gilligan, once again, hammering out his theme: "Actions have consequences."

What I am calling the third major stage in Walt's descent occurs at the end of season 4. As indicated earlier, Walt and Jesse have been working for Gus Fring and have been producing the purest methamphetamine in the Albuquerque area, but they've had a serious falling out with him, and Walt suspects, correctly, that Gus is planning to have them killed. Walt conspires with a former underworld figure, Hector Salamanca, who once worked with Gus but now hates him. Almost totally debilitated and unable to speak, Hector is wheelchair-bound in a nursing home; he is able to move his fingers, however, and at Walt's urging he agrees to kill Gus. Walt sets up a bogus meeting between Hector and Gus and then plans for Hector to have an explosive device hidden on his body. As Gus enters Hector's room and walks toward the wheelchair, Hector triggers the device with his fingers, blowing up both himself and Gus.

Why consider these deaths such a significant step in Walt's descent? Gus and Hector are, after all, two bad guys dispatched simultaneously. In some quarters Walt would be praised for eliminating them. But Walt's decision here must be considered in the context of his earlier actions. In the first two stages—Walt's allowing Jane to die, followed by his coercing Jesse to murder Gale—the results were up close and personal, and both outcomes were devastating for Jesse. Furthermore, Walt's feelings were deeply involved because of Jesse's guilt and subsequent depression. But Jesse has no direct connection with the deaths of Hector and Gus, and Walt has no intimate feelings for them. He wants them dead, especially Gus, and he uses Hector as a suicide bomber. Becoming the master manipulator through this action, Walt announces to the world—to the drug world, at least—that he, Heisenberg, is now in full control. He has defied the chaos and mastered the randomness of the world; he has risen to the top. More important, perhaps his success in eliminating both Gus and Hector convinces *him* that he *is* the kingpin; he has to kowtow to no one. Like Milton's Satan in *Paradise Lost*, who, in defying God, now reigns over the underworld ("Better to reign in hell, than serve in heav'n" [*PL* 1:263]), Walter, in defying chaos and randomness and embracing uncertainty, now commands his own underworld as he sinks deeper into it.

There are at least three additional steps in Walt's descent, less significant than those just discussed but important nevertheless: (1) Todd's shooting the kid on the bike, after the train robbery, (2) Mike's death, and (3) Hank's death at the hands of the neo-Nazis. In the first of these, Walt is still in control, or thinks he is, and he's confident he can talk his way out of trouble. His main task, as he sees it, is to provide support for Jesse, who is devastated by the murder of the kid. For his own safety and sense of selfhood, Walt must keep Jesse in the game, and so he tries condescending smooth talk about how awful the murder of the boy is, how it shouldn't have happened, how it was an accident, how Todd overreacted when he saw him, and so on. When one is involved in dangerous activities, Walt cajoles, sometimes unexpected things happen, and nothing can be done about them. Walt may convince himself with this blather, but he certainly doesn't convince Jesse, and his unctuous tone only serves to deepen Jesse's depression. Walt's manipulations, successful in earlier scenes, are not working here, and cracks in his hubris, in his overweening pride, are clearly in evidence.

On the other hand, Walt's shooting of Mike is the premeditated act of a desperate man who realizes he *is* losing control. He asks, then demands, that Mike give him the names of the prison inmates who have knowledge of his illegal activities. Walt is afraid that these low-life characters, when pressed by the authorities, will "flip" and expose him. The scientific perfectionist who ties up all the loose ends, he wants them killed in prison so there will be no trail leading back to him. But Mike, loyal and true to his own code, refuses to give them up. So Walt shoots him while he's sitting in his car. It's an impetuous act, driven by anger, almost childlike in its audacity, for Walt is not getting his own way. Gilligan highlights the sharp difference between the two men: both underworld figures, killers, in fact, but the level of integrity each displays couldn't be farther apart. Walt, ranting and raving, exuding uncontrolled anger that his command is not obeyed, still thinks he has control of the chaos of the world when, clearly, he does not. Mike, dying but in control of his own integrity, asks Walt to let him "die in peace." Stunningly striking are the brutal childishness of one and the quiet dignity of the other.

That Walt witnesses Hank's death at the hands of the neo-Nazis, one might argue, is his final condemnation. Physically, mentally, and emotionally, Walt has totally lost control, and he knows it. He tosses around in the car like a terrified animal, telling the neo-Nazis to desist and leave, and when they refuse, he begs for Hank's life in a dramatic reminder of how far he has fallen physically and, of course, as an indication of how deep his moral descent is. As in the scene with Mike, Walt's behavior is sharply contrasted with Hank's. Wounded and lying on the ground as he is about to be shot, Hank is defiant to the end, while Walt is an emotional mess, crying and begging for Hank's life.

Season 5 concludes with a hauntingly enigmatic episode, fraught with ambiguity: Gilligan depicts Walt, after a six-month hiatus, as a modern everyman figure in search of redemption. After Hank's death, Walt, driven in a van by one of lawyer Saul's underworld hirelings, escapes to a cold, isolated spot in New England—the antithesis of the hot, dry, bloody Southwest filled with violent characters and high drama. No violent characters or high drama in New Hampshire; nothing but snow and a lot of time on his hands. Walt broods—over what he's done, what has happened, and what might happen in the future. In the long winter that follows, we see him in the ice-locked, silent cabin, desperate in his aloneness. At one point he risks capture or even his life by walking to the nearest town to call his son in Albuquerque. He almost earns our sympathy as we watch him stumble around inside the cabin and outside on the frozen ground. When his driver appears with monthly provisions and newspapers, Walt begs him to stay for a while and even pays him an extra $10,000 for an hour of talk.

We're not sure how much soul-searching Walt does in his seclusion, but when we see him back in Albuquerque he has a confidence and direction he lacked earlier. He now knows what he has to do, especially for the future of his family, and he moves decisively to do it. In an ingenious maneuver, he gains entry to the wealthy home of his former partners, Elliott and Gretchen Schwartz, who had cheated him out of the money and recognition he deserved when he worked with them years before on a highly successful scientific project. In a sense, Gilligan has Walt deal their comeuppance when he forces them to face their earlier corrupt actions. It's a serious yet ironically comic sequence and reveals Walt's control. Not only are they shocked to see him mysteriously appear in their luxurious home, but they are angry and humiliated by his brazen intrusion into their "safe" abode and the total control he now exerts over them—this time to "make things right," as he says just before he leaves. It does appear that his time in the frozen North has changed him, like the long years Odysseus spends on Calypso's island in Homer's *Odyssey*, or the exile that Orestes endures in *The Eumenides* until he is old enough to return to Mycenae and avenge his father's death, or even Hamlet's short exile in England when he averts the death King Claudius has planned for him and has the king's flunkies Rosencranz and Gildenstern killed instead. Hamlet, then, returns to Denmark, emboldened and ready to fulfill his destiny and kill Claudius. Walt's exile, like that of these heroic characters, forces him to strip down and expunge his false outer layers, confront his inner self, accept what he is, discover an authentic self-hood, and embark on a path of partial redemption for the remainder of his short life. His new self now pursues that direction with command, control, and authority. He knows who he is, what he has done, and what he has to do. He's not the "good guy" as he envisioned earlier; he now accepts his fallen nature, admits his evil, and then uses the skills he has learned in the process of "breaking bad" to triumph in the final scene over the *really* bad guys—the neo-Nazis—and, at the same time, to save Jesse.

This self-acknowledgment comes just prior to the violent, bloody finale in the fascist stronghold and lab where the neo-Nazis have been holding Jesse and forcing him to make the blue methamphetamine he and Walt are famous for. Confident in his new self, Walt appears to Skyler where she is living, to say good-bye and to hold Holly one last time. In her sorrow, Skyler pleads that he *not* say that everything he did was for the future of his family. In an unflinching, naked admission, Walt emphatically states, "I did it for me. I liked it. I was good at it. And I was really . . . I was alive" (season 5, episode 16). It's a rare moment of truth from Walt's mouth and an epiphany for his character—a revelation on which the whole series hinges and another ingenious stroke by Gilligan. Walt's statement certainly doesn't make things right, relieve the pain, or reduce the guilt, but it does finally reveal his true motive and clarifies a previously ambiguous situation for both Skyler and him. Walt accepts full responsibility when he unhesitatingly states, "I liked it. I was good at it." It was all about him, he gloried in it, and now he admits it.

As indicated, this admission to Skyler precedes the violent finale in the lab where the neo-Nazis have been forcing a beaten, bruised, half-starved Jesse to continue making the blue methamphetamine. In addition, the finale serves, if not to negate Walt's narcissism in the scene with Skyler, to dramatize another dimension, not only of his character and integrity, but also of the skill he has acquired while navigating the complexity of the dangerous underworld. After carefully constructing an automatic swiveling mechanism with an M60 machine gun mounted on a tripod in the trunk of his car, he connects the device to his keypad so that when he presses a button on the pad, the gun will start firing. Walt then arranges a meeting with the neo-Nazis, ostensibly to return and make methamphetamine for them, but actually to get them all together in a single place inside the building. In order to maximize the effectiveness of the gunfire at this spot, he parks his car in the precise location adjacent to the building where he hopes to have them gathered. For the most part, this complicated plan is successful. A second before he presses the button to initiate the firing, Walt knocks Jesse to the floor (so he won't be shot) while the device, operating like a machine gun, kills most of the neo-Nazis except for Todd (the one who had shot the kid on the bike) and his uncle Jack, the leader of the gang and the one who shot Walt's brother-in-law, Hank. While Todd is staring out a window, trying to determine where the shooting is coming from, Jesse, with chains still around his hands, creeps up from behind and strangles him. Walt, seriously wounded during the shooting, sees that the uncle is still alive and shoots him.

The scene that follows this bloodshed is even more intense: Walt and Jesse are the only ones left alive in the lab, and, as in an old Western shootout, they are standing in a faceoff with Walt holding a pistol on Jesse. Walt then challenges Jesse (who still hates him for all the evil he's done, especially to his beloved Jane) to shoot him, and he slides the gun across the floor to Jesse. After aiming the gun at Walt for an interminable moment, Jesse refuses, crying out, "If you want it done, do it yourself," and he shoves the gun back at Walt. He then runs out of the lab to the parking lot, gets in a car, and drives wildly away. Noticeably weakened by his wound, Walt begins to stagger, and as sirens, increasing in volume, signal the approaching police, Gilligan has a receding overhead camera focus on Walt, claustrophobically framing him as he slowly sinks down on his back with his arms outstretched in a Christlike position—clearly a crucifixion image.

What are we to make of this finale? In "breaking bad," has Walt gone from good to bad, back to good again? Are we to see him now as a redemptive figure, sacrificing himself for his family and for Jesse? It's a complex, intriguing scene. Without providing glib answers, Gilligan forces us to confront issues of forgiveness and redemption, suggesting, perhaps, that redemption isn't easily gained; it may come, but at a high price. Despite a large measure of unpredictability and chaos, ruthlessness, and tragedy during the lengthy course of the series, Walt does, by the end, receive his punishment, and the final scene clearly reminds us of Gilligan's statement at the beginning. We are not governed by moral relativity or a so-called uncertainty principle; there is, ultimately, some degree of moral determinacy in the world. We do have free will to make choices, and the choices we make produce actions, and these actions sometimes have severe consequences.

Prior to his frozen exile in the North, Walt had committed a lot of evil, which he admitted and took responsibility for (in the final scene with Skyler), and he certainly gets his "comeuppance." But after returning to Albuquerque, Walt also does a lot of good: forcing the Schwartzes to get their "comeuppance" (for their past deeds) and, at the same time, securing his family's future with a financial plan that will allow them to receive at least some of his money without governmental intervention. He also saves Jesse.

Thus, it should be clear in this contemporary morality drama that there are no easy answers, no simple resolutions to sin, guilt, sacrifice, forgiveness, and redemption. The imagery Gilligan uses powerfully reinforces this conclusion. That these themes have touched many people in the world today can be attested to by the immense popularity of the series and the many awards it has won. By tapping into a medieval genre, depicting a modern everyman trying to live while facing an impending death sentence and confronting good and evil daily, Gilligan has provided exciting entertainment—touching a chord that resonates with the very essence of what it means to be a human being in a complex, sometimes brutal and unforgiving world.

References

Aeschylus. 1977. *The Eumenides*. Translated by Robert Fagles. New York: Viking Penguin.

Amitin, Seth. 2012. "*Breaking Bad*: 'Buyout' Review." *IGN Entertainment*, August 12. http://www.ign.com/articles/2012/08/20/breaking-bad-buyout-review.

———. 2012. "*Breaking Bad*: 'Gliding over All' Review," *IGN Entertainment*, September 3. http://www.ign.com/articles/2012/09/03/breaking-bad-gliding-over-all-review.

Atwood, Blake. 2013. *The Gospel According to "Breaking Bad."* Dallas, TX: AtWords Press.

Bowman, James. 2013. "Criminal Elements." *New Atlantis*, no. 38: 163–73.

Brodesco, Alberto. 2013. "Heisenberg: Epistemological Implications of a Criminal Pseudonym." In *Breaking Bad: Critical Essays on the Contexts, Politics, Style, and Reception of the Television Series*, edited by David P. Pierson, 53–72. Lanham, MD: Lexington.

Conradt, Stacy. 2013. "Beyond *Breaking Bad*: Meet the Real Heisenberg." *Mental Floss*, September 27.

Homer. 1998. *The Odyssey*. Translated by Robert Fitzgerald. New York: Farrar, Straus, & Giroux.

Koepsell, David R., and Robert Arp, eds. 2012. *Breaking Bad and Philosophy: Badder Living through Chemistry*. Chicago, IL: Open Court.

Kuo, Michelle, and Albert Wu. 2012. "In Hell, 'We Shall All Be Free': On *Breaking Bad*." *Los Angeles Review of Books*, July 13. https://lareviewofbooks.org/essay/in-hell-we-shall-all-be-free-on-breaking-bad.

Milton, John. 2005. *Paradise Lost*. Mineola, NY: Dover.

Nussbaum, Emily. 2012. "Child's Play: *Breaking Bad*'s Bad Dad," *New Yorker*, August 27, 82–83.

Pierson, David P., ed. 2014 *Breaking Bad: Critical Essays on the Contexts, Politics, Style, and Reception of the Television Series*. Lanham, MD: Lexington.

Roberts, Kyle. 2012. "*Breaking Bad*: Why Society Still Needs 'Sin' Language." *Patheos Cultivare* (blog), August 16. http://www.patheos.com/blogs/cultivare/2012/08/breaking-bad-why-society-still-needs-sin-language/.

Segal, David. 2012. "The Dark Art of *Breaking Bad*." *New York Times Magazine*, July 6, 18–23.

Shakespeare, William. 1998. *Hamlet*. Edited by Sylvan Barnet. New York: New American Library.

Thomas, June. 2012. "Hank's Eureka Moment." *Slate*, September 3. http://www.slate.com/articles/arts/tv_club/features/2012/breaking_bad_season_5_/week_8/breaking_bad_review_hank_does_some_bathroom_reading_.html

Thornton, Jack. 2012. "*Breaking Bad* and the Problem of Sin." *Word on Fire*, September 29. http://www.wordonfire.org/WoF-Blog.

Voshell, Fay. 2013. "*Breaking Bad* and the Uncertainty Principle." *American Thinker*, September 29. http://www.americanthinker.com/articles/2013/09/breaking_bad_and_the_heisenberg_uncertainty_principle.html.

"Negro y Azul"
The Narcocorrido Goes Gothic

Cordelia E. Barrera

The gothic has a long history in American literature, generating fear and anxiety in readers and viewers. Its hauntings—sites of moral and mental terrors—can unsettle the very idea of the United States. If the country is built on national mythologies that underscore individual promise and faith in progress, American gothic undermines these idealized myths by focusing on threats and anxieties related to race, class, gender, and the historical repression of dispossessed "Others." Influenced by the tradition of frontier gothicism, the popular AMC series *Breaking Bad* dramatizes Walter White in a western narrative of regeneration through violence. Closely examining gothic devices, this chapter will trace Walt's transformation from a mild-mannered chemistry teacher to the powerful drug kingpin Heisenberg.

The narcocorrido "Negro y Azul: The Ballad of Heisenberg," from season 2, episode 7, of *Breaking Bad* further highlights gothic elements within a contested borderland space. As "Negro y Azul" signifies the ironic shift of a corrido hero from a Mexican border dweller to a white male, the ballad reinforces Walt's transformation. Narcocorridos are historically tied to border ballads, or corridos—traditional folk songs of resistance against Anglo encroachment. Therefore, the positioning of a white male as a protagonist set against a Mexican rival, or rivals, subverts both the corrido and the narcocorrido form. This shift is significant for two reasons. First, it addresses the broader psychic disintegration of the Anglo male in the twenty-first-century borderlands. Second, it culminates in a gothic apocalypse that shows how the hope that lies behind the myth of frontier regeneration collapses in on itself. The gothic mode described here is a flash point by which to trace the development of Walter White / Heisenberg as an alienated, displaced figure who both subverts and redefines the American frontier hero within a new western landscape.

Borderlands, Frontiers, and New Western Landscapes

Brett Martin argues that *Breaking Bad* is "by far the most visually stylized show" of what he calls the Third Golden Age of television.[1] A tightly focused serial that reveals a continuous, unresolved mode of storytelling as opposed to single episodes that can easily be rearranged and sold into syndication, *Breaking Bad* employs the kind of cinematography audiences are apt to expect from big-budget Hollywood movies. This is a show obsessed with vast deserts, interminable parking lots, and domes of endless blue sky. Extreme long shots, high-speed time-lapse montages, and wide-open landscapes root *Breaking Bad* in a twenty-first-century New Mexican landscape. It is also a show obsessed with the concrete and the literal, as well as the nature of what things *are*. Often the camera lingers on unusual, yet meaningful, objects, such as the missing eye of a stuffed bear, a box cutter, or a pair of broken eyeglasses. The show's lifeblood is chemistry. In the first few minutes of the pilot, Walter White gives a lecture to his high school chemistry class. "Chemistry is the study of change," he says to his mostly bored students. "It is growth, then decay, then transformation." This is the show's main preoccupation: the nature of change, namely Walt's transformation, as creator Vince Gilligan has publicly stated in at least one interview, from "Mr. Chips to Scarface." Processes, too, writes Martin

(2013, 276), take center stage: the pulse of a chemical as it inches through a tube, the calculated disassembly of a dirt bike after its young owner has been fatally shot, Walt soberly shaving his head.

When we examine the series as a cultural form, an artifact of American culture in the twenty-first century, we are confronted with the still-unresolved conflicts and tensions bound within a history of conquest in the US Southwest. Because Walt's transformation personifies a modern reimagining of the myth of the American dream within a historically contested borderlands landscape, we must look to narratives and "myths" of Anglo America that have often romanticized the cruel realities of Euro-American conquest. Furthermore, as a white male in the twenty-first century, Walt encapsulates the struggles of masculinity that reflect what some might call the deterioration of the US meritocratic system into one of plutocracy. A focus on entwined narratives central to an American imaginary throughout the series allows us to engage the drama in its broader context. First, it highlights the conversation on political and national concerns of the US Southwest in order to disclose the ways in which the series is in dialogue with western narratives about the American landscape and Americans themselves. Second, it allows for an examination of defining tropes associated with the literary gothic in America, a subject I will take up in the next section of this essay.

The US Southwest mirrors the narratives and permutations of the US West, but with the inclusion of a borderlands space. It is a regional space that contains all the mythic elements associated with the West and with frontiers, but it is bound within a landscape that Gloria Anzaldúa (2012) defines as a "third country" in a constant state of transition (25). This "third country" at once separates and joins at least two cultures and nations. Further, it is bound by imagery of conquest over a wild, hostile landscape, as well as a wild, hostile, racial Other (Spurgeon 2005, 6). A hostile landscape and a hostile Other are entry points for new western historians, such as Patricia Nelson Limerick (1987), who reorganizes western history as a study of place to shed light on the boom/bust instability of capitalism. A main facet of western history is that it revolves around an ongoing competition for legitimacy among groups of people who compete for the right to claim themselves as legitimate beneficiaries of western resources (Limerick 1987, 26–29). At the heart of Walter White's struggle in *Breaking Bad* is his razor-sharp focus on establishing himself as *the* supreme player in a struggle for legitimacy against the Other in the American drug imaginary:

the Mexican cartel. As he and his accomplices jockey for absolute control of the available resources and capital to be had in the regional methamphetamine trade, they play out a story aligned with much of western history: theirs is a contest for dominance charged with the drawing of lines and border disputes that fuses the roles of victim and villain.

For Walt/Heisenberg, progress is a calculated move associated with territorial expansion in the Southwest. Whereas traditional western histories often underscore the frontier as a finite stage of American progress and development for Euro-Americans, new western histories foreground historical and moral complications associated with the conquest of indigenous peoples and the landscape itself. The focus is also on the dominant role of capitalism and the convergence of multiple peoples in a hostile, contested landscape. The symbolic and metaphoric thrust of *Breaking Bad* is entrenched in the historically contested desert landscape of New Mexico, but the drama teems with gothic elements: secrets and lies, psychological haunting and doubles, imprisonment and crawlspaces, and, most important, an ominous suburban sterility that plays upon our suspicion that even the most ordinary house or family has something to hide. With its unscrupulous characters who glory in orchestrating violent and often grisly stratagems of masculine power and authority, *Breaking Bad*'s concerns mirror gothic forms to produce a ruthless anti-Western or revisionist Western. Susan Kollin (2000) writes that anti-Westerns disrupt the confidence of national narratives by examining how western mythologies repress the underside of US development. *Breaking Bad* is critical of national myths that present the US West as a place of promise and hope, as the series complicates still-unsettled conflicts surrounding American mythologies and the American dream in an increasingly globalized world.

Patricia Nelson Limerick (1987) maintains that the "origin myth" of Anglo America romanticized the brutal reality of Euro-American conquest.[2] This is the cruel reality—the often unspoken or silenced history of the Other—that Mogen, Sanders, and Karpinski (1993) argue "speaks" from the landscape (16). In this space, the American dream turns into nightmare. Although indigenous cultures and African Americans figure prominently in both the origin myth of the United States and American gothic forms, in *Breaking Bad* the Other is further represented by a new breed of unhappy, entrapped Others: suburban methheads. These are not devil worshipers or those associated with the natural world, as in classic gothic tales by Brockden Brown or Nathaniel Hawthorne, but a marginalized underclass of addicts aligned with grinding poverty, police brutality, and the slow disintegration of family values. Here, then, is another specific locus of fear in the series that is closely attuned to unbroken twenty-first-century anxieties throughout the United States and exacerbated by the War on Drugs in the US Southwest.

Gothic Frontiers and Western Gothicism

Breaking Bad employs gothic devices and tropes to highlight political and national concerns in order to subvert the codes of American mythologies that have historically dramatized what Richard Slotkin (1992) describes as its "moral consciousness" (5). In so doing, the series rethinks and redirects the contours of American gothic forms in order to transform the landscape into a tragic, fallen space in the wake of white settlement and globalization. By season 2, the fallout from Walt's actions to dominate the methamphetamine business in the Southwest increases and the death toll mounts. In the season's finale, "ABQ," the image of airplane wreckage and bodies raining down on Walt's house becomes a signifier of what has been sacrificed to the forces of progress and development in the West. Just as the methamphetamine business will rend asunder Walt's home and family life, so too has it become a destroyer of the suburban dream.

At the heart of *Breaking Bad* are the repressed urges that account for much of the psychological weight of the gothic unspeakable, as the series is preoccupied with the unspoken realities of the increasingly dissolving American dream in the United States. Where the European gothic works have historically focused on issues of class and gender, American gothic forms address the optimism entwined in new world ideals and values. The series exposes central contradictions of the American dream while it subverts and interrogates national mythologies that presuppose the innocence of its Euro-American victors. Walter White is not haunted by his past; he escapes it, journeys far beyond it, and in so doing his actions invoke terror and horror in viewers, as they, too, are induced to confront their own (repressed) nationalistic demons. This is not a story of guilt, as Leslie Fiedler (2003, 143) so eloquently argues lies at the heart of the gothic in the United States, but of bloody redemption on the borderlands, a redemption that discloses the ethical contradictions of our shared violent history.

Teresa A. Goddu (1997) stresses that the gothic is deeply engaged with historical concerns and so must be read in terms of its cultural context. Addressing various sites of historical horror such as massacres of Native inhabitants and the means by which the legacy of slavery haunts American gothic forms, Goddu interprets the gothic as a distorted, rather than disengaged, version of reality. Although British gothic forms have been seen as escapist, American gothic forms are not. American gothic is a regional, mutable, "uncertain" form, obsessed with transgressing boundaries (3–5). Furthermore, although some scholars have claimed that the United States does not have the history necessary to sustain the gothic's challenge, Goddu disagrees.

According to Goddu (1997), "specific sites of historical haunting, most notably slavery" (10) sustain the gothic's challenge in the United States. She claims that American gothic forms reveal sites of cultural contradiction that undermine narratives of American literary history to "unsettle the nation's cultural identity" (10). These contentions are central to my argument. First, in that the US Southwest is a space of conflict and negotiation, a historically contested, postcolonial borderlands site, Goddu's premise is fitting because the Southwest is a landscape steeped not in the horrors of slavery but in the massacres and extermination of indigenous peoples. Native Americans in the US Southwest signify a ruined and conquered past. Second, because "the Gothic tells of the historical horrors that make national identity possible" (10) but are often repressed within the gothic mode, we can look to this mode to expose artificial foundations on which individual American identities are precariously balanced. In this respect, I argue that *Breaking Bad* encapsulates a specific site of historical horror, one that, as a society, Americans continue to grapple with—the horrors of the twenty-first-century War on Drugs that still ravages entire communities in the Southwest.

Walt pursues a Euro-American narrative of manifest destiny not in the light of day, but under cover of secrets and lies, in the twilight zone of methamphetamine addicts and grotesque drug lords like Tuco Salamanca and Gus Fring. His transformation explodes the heart of the indigenous frontier story that D. H. Lawrence (1971) suggests is an intrinsically gothic space both enticing and terrifying, the violence of the wilderness experience. Significantly, the power of the gothic frontier for Lawrence is a source of creative imagination as well as annihilation, a space that has a "powerful disintegrative effect on the white psyche" (Lawrence 1971, 56). The gothic frontier is a realm of paradox and persecution for white men who must exorcise Native ghosts and demons that yet menace the landscape. Even now, the histories of unappeased, unplacated Others yet reside in this landscape, which becomes "no longer a locale" (57) but a vast space where a harrowing transformation of consciousness is reflected as an ongoing wilderness experience.

Two triggers immediately manifest Walt's transfiguration of consciousness, which, in time, will engender an actual *physical* change in his persona. In the first fifteen minutes of the pilot, his wife, Skyler, throws Walt a fiftieth birthday party at his home. The scene (and much of the pilot itself) is rife with cues that signal Walt's eroded masculinity as the father of a disabled teen and a browbeaten husband who must struggle desperately at two thankless jobs in order to provide for his family. When Hank Schrader, Walt's testosteronic brother-in-law, commandeers the group to watch the local news story of a methamphetamine bust that he and his fellow DEA agents recently made—a bust that yielded more than $700,000 in cash—Hank does more than impose a masculine script intended to reflect the imbalance of power and physical prowess that he continually lords over Walt. He helps seed an idea in Walt's mind. "It's easy money . . . until we catch you," jeers Hank. Significantly, this seed is sown *before* Walt learns that he has cancer.

The New Mexico desert and suburban Albuquerque that factor so heavily in Walt's transformation are emblematic of a uniquely American gothic landscape. Mogen, Sanders, and Karpinski (1993) argue that much of the "range and power of the gothic frontier" can be found in the promise that, as Lawrence (1971) suggests, Americans can "get away from everything they are and have been" (15). It is an escape from the confinements of a civilization associated with Old World European values, yet ultimately an escape from self: "To open out a new wide area of consciousness means to slough the old consciousness . . . [that] has become a tight-fitting prison" (Lawrence, 57–58). Contrary to Robert Louis Stevenson's classic gothic tale, *The Strange Case of Dr. Jekyll and Mr. Hyde* (1886), Walt does not create an elixir to mask the repressed evil within his body in an attempt to reconcile warring aspects of his personality. In the pilot, Walt undergoes chemotherapy, a modern process that virtually destroys the body's cells—both malignant and viable. Does this chemical process make him a "new man"? Hardly. As a place of confrontation with nature that is both nightmarish and visionary, the frontier offers startling possibilities for regeneration and revolutionary possibilities for the self.

Unlike Fiedler (2003), who suggests that frontier heroes engage in retreat and evasion, Lawrence (1971) suggests that the myth of the frontier, and subsequently the frontier experience, involves a regressive movement, from old age toward youthful bloom and promise. The frontier experience asks for a "great and cruel sloughing first of all. Then it finds a great release into a new world, a new moral, a new landscape" (54). In *Breaking Bad*, this new landscape comprises a new value system for Walt. A scientist to the core, Walt lives in an absurd and godless world. According to Sara Waller (2012), Walt's love for his family, at least at the outset, is "the meaning that he gives to his life in a world that has otherwise been rather meaningless for him" (129). After he "awakens" and confronts Jesse Pinkman with his idea to cook methamphetamine, Walt relinquishes his ties to that faithless, godless world where he has lost all personal power and masculine efficacy. Money "becomes the new family value" (130) capable of rectifying Walt's family's—and his own—vision of himself by his intellectual prowess, an aspect of his personality that had been crushed by circumstance but hardly extinguished. Here, then, is the "true myth of America" that Lawrence suggests is a regressive movement "from old age to golden youth." Beginning as "old, old, wrinkled and writhing in an old skin," which it gradually sloughs off, it emerges "towards new youth . . . the myth of America" (60).

Here, too, we find James K. Folsom's (1993) western landscape, which he argues is both a projection of our most abiding fears and a reflection of our American ideals. Folsom's western gothicism is a locale where, to the consternation of its inhabitants, the landscape "metamorphoses into something unanticipated and therefore terrible" (36). Thus, when Walt first hears about all that money and the seed takes root, we see his transformation taking shape. The landscape—both the suburbs and the desert—has metamorphosed to lay bare "the terrible opposite side which lies hidden beneath its apparent benevolence" (36–37). The landscape has become "an apt vehicle for gothicism" (37), rife for profits born of the underworld. This is where Walt's dreams can grow to fruition. Not in the light of day, not in the corporate world of Gray Matter Technologies—the highly profitable pharmaceutical company begun by Elliott and Gretchen Schwartz—where the rich only seem to get richer at the expense of an underclass of workers, but under cover and alongside the Others who rule the nighttime world of the suburban gothic: the drug lords, the methheads, the small-time pushers. In this space, the panorama of the West becomes "emblematic of interior states of mind . . . of internal concerns" (40). Here, then, thrives Folsom's western "gothicism," in that dark place where the face of the enemy is none but our own.

The gothic frontier is a space of attraction and revulsion. It promises escape from the confines of civilization and the ruins of Old World European experience toward a future that holds the promise of regeneration through violence. It is significant that this promise reflects an escape from self. Folsom (1993) argues that, in the tradition of western gothicism, both the landscape and those inhabiting it are "primarily projections of internal states of mind as well as reflections of external states of being" (30). The landscape reflects internal rather than external truths, where "evil is actively pursued, albeit the searcher may not know precisely what he is seeking" (31). This points to a central trope of the American gothic, reflected in its reliance on the archetypal story of the quest, a journey to discover the "duality at the heart of human nature," and suggesting that ultimate freedom may be found not in civilized society but in nature itself. This underlying pattern reveals an American obsession with "what things *are*" (Folsom 1993, 35; italics in original). This obsession, revealing the Puritan preoccupation with who were among the elect or the damned, is a central theme of the series, as evidenced in the first few minutes of the pilot, when Walt first discusses the nature of chemistry as one of change and transformation for his students. "That's all of life. It's the constant . . . the cycle," he says. Walt is an unrepentant antihero who *chooses* to journey into evil. His movement through the series is absolute and severe; he intrigues us in the way he carries the power of chemistry to its ultimate limits by tapping into the creative well of his darker, shadow self. What's most chilling is that, as he remarks in the final episode of the series, he likes it.

Suburban Dreams Run Amok

In the episode "Peekaboo" Walt gives a lecture about the invention of synthetic diamonds by the American physical chemist H. Tracy Hall. Hall, he says, "made GE [General Electric] a fortune . . . incalculable. How was he rewarded?" Walt asks. "A ten-dollar US savings bond." On the surface, this is a lecture about carbon, but it's really about Walt, and an entry into his obscure break from Gray Matter. Although we never know for certain exactly why Walt left Gretchen that Fourth of July weekend in Newport, we know that he harbors an intense disdain for both Gretchen and Elliott. At the core of the restaurant scene in which Gretchen confronts Walt about the lie he has told Skyler—a lie that has led Skyler to believe Gretchen and Elliott have been paying for Walt's cancer treatments to date—there lurks the current of an ideological impasse that stems from the politics of class difference. When Gretchen asks, "What happened to you, Walt? This isn't you," an infuriated Walt counters by asking Gretchen about her presumptions about him, adding that "waving your checkbook around like some magic wand will not help me forget how you and Elliott cut me out. . . . My hard work!" he growls, "My research . . . and you and Elliott made millions off it!" Before Walt walks away from the conversation with a seething "fuck you" aimed at Gretchen, he adds that she is "a rich girl, just adding to [her] millions." What was it that made Walt pack his bags that weekend and never want to look back? Yet he did look back; he was always looking back. This explains his apathy before he awakens. But why does a life with Gretchen and all that her money might offer not fit into Walt's reality? Why *must* he walk away from Gretchen and, ultimately, the riches promised by Gray Matter?

I believe the answer lies in Slotkin's (1992) premise that the "complete" American is one who has "defeated and freed himself from both the 'savage' of the western wilderness and the metropolitan regime of authoritarian politics and class privilege" (11). After he is diagnosed with cancer—indeed, after he realizes the capital to be had in the global market that lies at his fingertips and just outside his suburban home—Walt discards any illusions about his past. He no longer appears disoriented in his present. He signifies human nature in vitro, a kind of experimental twenty-first-century Adam. Once a man of logic and science, Walt's daily encounters with a host of shifting adversaries demand more primal, instinctual responses, much like the reactants he lectures about in the episode "Crazy Handful of Nothin'." He tells his students that "the faster reactants change, the more violent the explosion." Just as the show itself is narratively ruthless, so must Walt—an otherwise harmless substance—become pure ego, pure ruthlessness. When people come to respect his work, Walt's sense of power and ego become decidedly inflated. As a symbolic new Adam, one dispossessed of the American dream of promise and prosperity during a period of recession and economic upheaval for the middle class, he becomes highly emotional and highly volatile. As Rob Tannenbaum (2013) puts it, Walt's not "used to dealing with his emotions, so like a child, things get messy very quickly" (65). His cancer and the $700,000 methamphetamine arrest are catalysts, but they represent, in the literal and symbolic language of the series, a rupture in time.

For years, Walt has led his dull and complacent life of conformity in the New Mexico suburbs. Frozen into his monotonous and highly predictable way of life, in the opening scene of the pilot episode Walt exercises on an elliptical trainer, his movements a reflection of his aimless suburban existence: going through the motions, sweating all the while, but going nowhere. The camera pans toward a plaque on the wall of his dim bedroom, imaging the movement of his eyes. His once terrifically bright future has been reduced to a plaque that reads, "Science Research Center, Los Alamos, New Mexico, hereby recognizes Walter H. White, contributor to research awarded the Nobel Prize, 1985." According to Oli Mould (2012), when Walt "awakens," his nature "*unveils*" (172; italics in original). Mould discusses Walt's transformation in the section "Constructed Reality versus the Real" to argue that Walt's constructed reality is divorced from "the real," in the Lacanian sense. Our constructed realities are like defense mechanisms we erect to move about our daily lives; "the real," by contrast, takes the form of death, traumatic events, or terrifying ecstatic experiences. For Mould, Walt's constructed reality is cleaved in two by "the real" after his cancer diagnosis. His constructed reality is heavily entwined in the American dream, a fleeting myth in the twenty-first-century suburban nightmare that has suffocated Walt for years. Mould concludes that Walt's "true self" (175) may reside in Heisenberg's criminal tendencies. If this conclusion is correct, then when Walt "awakens," in effect, he must acknowledge that his suburban lifestyle is a constructed reality. Walt is now in a position to move beyond constructed reality into "the real" where he can achieve "a kind of nirvana state of awareness" (175).

If Walt's constructed reality is a soporific, his explosive entry into the world of methamphetamine is his salvation—and his doom. Bernice M. Murphy (2009) argues that the suburban gothic reflects the shadow side of the American dream of progress and optimism, one that perceives suburbia as "the physical personification of all that [is] wrong with American society, a deadening assembly of identikit houses and a breeding ground for discontent and mindless conventionality" (5). The author asserts that the subgenre of the suburban gothic can tell us much about the social, economic, and cultural transformations that have shaped US society, as it has always "served as a counterbalance to the myths of progress and optimism by which the nation from the outset defined itself" (199). The suburban gothic extols the unacknowledged guilt and anxiety buried deep in the national psyche and is committed to revealing the dislocation and the chaos beneath the apparent order. Louis S. Gross's (1989) articulations mirror D. H. Lawrence's (1971) when he writes that a protagonist's gothic journey offers "a darkened world where fear, oppression, and madness are the ways to knowledge, and the uncontrolled transformation of one's character the quest's epiphany" (1). It is important to note that Gross (1989) concludes that the protagonist's gothic quest ends in the shattering of his or her image and legacy. This finish reminds us of the final episode of the series, when Walter Jr. and, indeed, the world, learn that Walter H. White is the one-man dynasty Heisenberg.

The gothic's range of possibilities, for Gross, is circumscribed by what he calls a "narrowly defined mode of perceiving the world" (1989, 89). The gothic imprints upon its pages, and in the case of *Breaking Bad*, within its visual and symbolic codes, a mode of perception in which terror lies at the heart of the institutions of family, church, and state. Walt's logic is cold and based in science; it does not stem from faith in a godhead or community. In fact, I would argue that much of Walt's distress emanates from the fact that he never actively contributes to a community and his actions are determined by the narrowly defined limits of one family—his own, which, as we will see, is as lost as he is. When these limits are coupled with the added anxieties associated with a borderlands landscape that has historically invited combat, a landscape in which early Euro-Americans became transformed by the wilderness experience into new persons, the New Mexico desert of *Breaking Bad* becomes not a place on a map, but, as Gross argues, a "place of the mind" (89), founded on an idea, and therefore the living embodiment of that idea. Writers and artists who engage the gothic mode entwine images of terror that share a common thread: "the singularity and monstrosity of the Other" (90). In the series, Walt confronts the shadow image he has unsuccessfully repressed. Rather than continue to be haunted by his Other, as he has since he broke from Gray Matter Technologies, he feels his shadow—Heisenberg—strengthening him with all the horrors the twenty-first-century borderlands can deliver.

The Gothic Landscape of "Negro y Azul: The Ballad of Heisenberg"

An equally pernicious Other sets in motion Walt's inescapable downfall: the Mexican. In the narcocorrido "Negro y Azul" Walt is presented as the protagonist, the hero outlaw with whom listeners—according to the nature, language, and structure of the ballad—are asked to identify.[3] On the flip side stands the Mexican cartel, positioned as the enraged, vengeful antagonist who is being disrespected. This ironic shift unsettles both corrido and narcocorrido forms. Furthermore, it speaks to the psychic disintegration of the Anglo male in the twenty-first-century borderlands, as it culminates in a gothic apocalypse in which the white male—unbeknownst to him—is already dead.

In his influential work *With His Pistol in His Hand*, Américo Paredes (1996) examines border corridos in detail. At the heart of the border corrido are conflicts that arise with the meeting of two cultures—a border hero who fights for his rights as a citizen and sentimental outlaw figures who rob the rich to give to the poor. Border outlaw corridos, however, "make a very definite distinction between the hero of border conflict and the mere outlaw" (143). Corridos featuring border outlaws represent such men as rogues—"realistic, selfish, and unusually unrepentant." Such men, writes Paredes, do not "repent on the scaffold in moralizing verses" (143–44). The corrido of border conflict historically assumed its most characteristic form during the late nineteenth and early twentieth centuries, when its subject dealt with the conflict between border Mexicans and Anglo Texans. These corridos often depict the Mexican—outnumbered and pistol in hand— defending his right against the Texas Rangers. The corrido of border conflict follows a general pattern, and border ballads that have been most widely accepted contain three durable and defining features: a ballad structure related to the eighteenth-century Spanish romance, a theme of border conflict, and a hero who defends his right against an encroaching adversary (Paredes 1996, 147–50).

Corridos are historically autochthonous forms, localized products of a border community that strive to memorialize a culture hero. By contrast, narcocorridos, writes Mark Cameron Edberg (2004), are a twentieth-century, commercialized musical genre that often originate with boastful drug traffickers themselves or record companies seeking profits. Although Edberg describes these narcocorridos as offshoots of original corrido forms, there are significant differences.[4] I am concerned with two that coalesce gothic elements in "Negro y Azul": the *despedida*, or farewell, and the character of the hero, structural elements that Paredes (1996) cites as among the most resilient and defining features of the corrido.

Traditional corridos celebrated and often eulogized the heroic values of those whose principal offense was a response to an oppressive social system. Corrido heroes (such as Gregorio Córtez, a peaceful, hardworking man forced by circumstance to defend his rights by violent means and the subject of Paredes's study) often hail from the working class or an otherwise subordinate social position in a certain locale. How, then, has the "cultural persona" (104), as Edberg (2004) calls it, of the narcotrafficker inculcated itself into the classical form of the corrido? The answer is complex and steeped in the ways dispossessed persons function within a system of social stratification in the United States and Mexico. Those who have studied narcocorridos as discursive, cultural forms, including Edberg, avoid presenting them as merely symbolizing "resistance to the oppression of the class system in Mexico, global capitalism, and the United States" (104). Edberg adds that narcocorridos represent a counter discourse of resistance. The cultural fluidity of the US-Mexico border region will undoubtedly continue to stimulate morphing of the genre. The shift, then, from peaceful border hero forced to fight against a background of poverty and social and economic instability to a narcotrafficker who celebrates and perhaps even regulates a system of violence in an era of ever-increasing globalization is not hard to fathom.

The graphic documentary *Narco Cultura*, directed by Shaul Schwarz (2013), is a chilling depiction of Mexican and Mexican American youth who see the violence of the narcotrafficker as an acceptable, even desirable, means of social mobility. The film depicts record labels and musical groups, such as the Twins Culiacan, who write and produce narcocorridos for drug dealers in Mexico and the United States. At one point in the documentary, the artist El Komander travels to Culiacan, the largest city in the state of Sinaloa, Mexico, and the home of the Sinaloa cartel. El Komander idolizes the cartel, stating that he likes to "feel narco" and that money and happiness are the same thing; "money is respect," he says proudly.

In the film, narco culture is described as "an anti-system rebellion that's making a hero out of someone that operates outside the law." At one point, Schwartz's film takes us inside a Mexican prison and introduces us to a captured member of an unnamed drug cartel. He states plainly how narcos "can show no weakness. . . . you must turn cold . . . no compassion." Here is a picture of Walt, then: a cold, calculating man who operates outside the law and whose new family value is money, enough money to gain respect and dominate an entire region. But Walt is an Anglo male, and Anglo males don't ordinarily surface as protagonists in narcocorridos. When the outlaw is a shadow of one's persona, however, as in Walt's case, the demon created by his own terror in the face of all that is slipping from him as a middle-class American becomes an aspect of a gothic landscape, a dark world that is itself an engine of uncontrolled metamorphosis.

Despite its morally compromised key white players, *Breaking Bad* is an American production and expects viewers to favor these flawed characters who repeatedly triumph over Mexican enemies. Walt is not goaded into violence by twenty-first-century circumstances that have emasculated his patriarchal authority to earn a respectable living wage in which his health and the health of his family is assured. Walt *chooses* violence. The tale of "Negro y Azul" is one of white patriarchal authority deposed. There is a despedida, a farewell to the hero, but it is an ironic farewell that foreshadows the continuing disintegration of the white psyche and articulates the fragility of masculine authority in the twenty-first-century borderlands. If Walt triumphs in *Breaking Bad*, his manhood and masculine authority are not regained in the domestic suburban sphere but rather within the globalized world of commerce and the marketplace of the War on Drugs. As with all narcos, Walt's rise to power is likely to be short-lived and excessively violent.

His power rests in the systems that created him: the legal, political, economic, and cultural systems that abandoned him yet nonetheless reflect an anguished national mood intensified by financially devastating current events. The great economic upset of the twenty-first century that left many formerly secure middle-class Americans "feeling like desperate outlaws in their own suburbs," the palpable methamphetamine epidemic in the United States, and the increasing violence of the Mexican cartel along the US-Mexico border provide a backdrop for the series (Martin 2013, 272). But the ironic turn that announces Walt's real-world loss of control and ultimate demise is stated directly in "Negro y Azul," as the lyrics proclaim outright that no one ever escapes the cartel's fury. Walt, in the language of the narcocorrido, is a dead man walking. Whereas in early American gothic writing indigenous cultures are understood as doomed to vanish with the arrival of white settlers, in *Breaking Bad* it is the white man and, by extension, the American dream of progress and fulfillment that are at risk. The series critiques US expansionist ideologies within a gothic discourse, but it does so with an eye toward the palpable destruction that the wake of globalizing forces has wrought along the US-Mexico borderlands.

The quest motif in which the protagonist who sets out on a journey and subsequently encounters various forms of evil along the way is found in both American and European strains of the gothic. Secrets, lies, and evil abound and are not confined to the external foes Walt encounters. Initially, he resists succumbing to evil, and his actions suggest the possibility of redemption. In time, however, his exaggerated ego mirrors the grotesque manifestations that abound amid the nightmare landscape the War on Drugs has wrought in the US Southwest. Walt's actions, as Fiedler (2003) has suggested, "correspond in quality to our deepest fears and guilts as projected in our dreams or lived through in 'extreme situations'" (155). As a character and a man, Walt dissolves in a way that lends credence to the symbolic landscape of the gothic. Thus, *Breaking Bad* and Walter White / Heisenberg have achieved a kind of mythic status in contemporary US culture. The huge popularity of the series can be credited to superb writing and acting and powerful, often eerie, cinematography. But questions posed by the series are still present. Where, exactly, is the monster? Does it lie in global market systems that value profits and capital above all? Or is the monster Walt, who is, after all, a reflection of our own fears and desires? Perhaps the answer lies in what each of us is capable of doing in the face of certain death. To what length would we go to secure financial well-being for our families? As in all gothic forms, the boundaries between good and evil are intentionally blurred. Certainly the atrocities Walt commits equal, if not exceed, the atrocities committed by the naturalized demons of the drug war: drug lords like Tuco and the Salamancas. Gross (1989) explains that the key area gothic forms exploit is the fear of losing one's relationships with our families, our communities, and our beliefs—what he calls "the monstrousness of singularity" (8), the chaos beneath the apparent order of our lives. Maybe we like to envision ourselves as Skyler or Hank, or even Jesse; but we can't help but fantasize about being Walt. Fear, after all, is the motivating and sustaining emotion of all gothic forms, and what we fear most is ourselves—unhinged perhaps, but ourselves just the same.

Notes

1. Martin acknowledges three Golden Ages of television, the first being the flowering of creation during the early days of the medium, the second represented by a short period of network excellence in the 1980s, and the third represented by the generation of cable drama that lasted roughly from 1999 through 2013. For more, see chapter 1 of Martin (2013).

2. Limerick (1987) argues that for white Americans the most popular origin myth of the United States concerns the frontier. This, our nation's most popular "creation myth," helps explain US exceptionalism. For more, see Limerick (1987, chapter 10).

3. In compliance with copyright restrictions, all lyrics in this paper are paraphrased. The lyrics to "Negro Y Azul" can be found, in both English and Spanish, at http://breakingbad.wikia.com/wiki/Negro_y_Azul:_The_Ballad_of_Heisenberg.

4. The differences in form are beyond the scope of this paper. For more, see Edberg (2004, chapter 1), Wald (2001), and McDowell (1972).

References

Anzaldúa, Gloria. 2012. *Borderlands / La Frontera: The New Mestiza.* 4th ed. San Francisco, CA: Aunt Lute Press.

Edberg, Mark Cameron. 2004. *El Narcotraficante: Narcocorridos and the Construction of a Cultural Persona on the U.S.-Mexico Border.* Austin: University of Texas Press.

Fiedler, Leslie A. 2003. *Love and Death in the American Novel.* Champaign, IL: Dalkey Archive Press.

Folsom, James K. 1993. "Gothicism in the Western Novel." In *Frontier Gothic: Terror and Wonder at the Frontier in American Literature*, edited by David Mogen, Scott P. Sanders, and Joanne B. Karpinski, 28–41. Madison, NJ: Fairleigh Dickinson University Press.

Goddu, Teresa A. 1997. *Gothic America: Narrative, History, and Nation.* New York: Columbia University Press.

Gross, Louis S. 1989. *Redefining the American Gothic: From Weiland to Day of the Dead.* Ann Arbor, MI: UMI Research Press.

Kollin, Susan. 2000. "Race, Labor and the Gothic Western: Dispelling Frontier Myths in Dorothy Scarborough's *The Wind*." *Modern Fiction Studies* 46 (3): 675–94.

Lawrence, D. H. 1971. *Studies in Classic American Literature.* New York: Penguin.

Limerick, Patricia Nelson. 1987. *The Legacy of Conquest: The Unbroken Past of the American West.* New York: W. W. Norton.

Martin, Brett. 2013. *Difficult Men: Behind the Scenes of a Creative Revolution; From The Sopranos and The Wire to Mad Men and Breaking Bad*. New York: Penguin.

McDowell, J. H. 1972. "The Mexican *Corrido*: Formula and Themes in a Ballad Tradition." *Journal of American Folklore* 85: 205–20.

Mogen, David, Scott P. Sanders, and Joanne B. Karpinski. 1993. *Frontier Gothic: Terror and Wonder at the Frontier in American Literature*. Madison, NJ: Fairleigh Dickinson University Press.

Mould, Oli. 2012. "Been through the Desert on a Horse with No Name." In *Breaking Bad and Philosophy: Badder Living through Chemistry*, edited by David R. Koepsell and Robert Arp, 171–80. Chicago, IL: Open Court.

Murphy, Bernice M. 2009. *The Suburban Gothic in American Popular Culture*. New York: Palgrave.

Paredes, Américo. 1996. *With His Pistol in His Hand: A Border Ballad and Its Hero*. Austin: University of Texas Press.

Schwartz, Shaul (director). 2013. *Narco Cultura*. New York: Ocean Size Pictures, DVD.

Slotkin, Richard. 1992. *Gunfighter Nation: The Myth of the Frontier in Twentieth-Century America*. New York: Atheneum.

Spurgeon, Sara L. 2005. *Exploding the Western: Myths of Empire on the Postmodern Frontier*. College Station: Texas A & M Press.

Tannenbaum, Rob. 2013. "The Last Word on *Breaking Bad*." *Rolling Stone* 1192: 63–65.

Wald, Elijah. 2001. *Narcocorrido: A Journey into the Music of Drugs, Guns, and Guerillas*. New York: Rayo / Harper Collins.

Waller, Sara. 2012. "I Appreciate the Strategy." In *Breaking Bad and Philosophy: Badder Living through Chemistry*, edited by David R. Koepsell and Robert Arp, 125–35. Chicago, IL: Open Court.

3

Breaking Bad as Critical Regionalism

Alex Hunt

Breaking Bad was initially to be set in Riverside, California, before cost factors led to the choice of Albuquerque, New Mexico (*Breaking Bad Wiki* n.d.; Martin 2013). Commentators and critics have remarked that the ultimate choice of New Mexico is significant, more so than the static notion of "setting," with its roots in theater stagecraft, implies. Indeed, Albuquerque, the surrounding indigenous pueblos, the mountain and desert scenery, and the big Southwestern skies become dynamic forces in the visual language and thematic significance of *Breaking Bad*. To use the traditional language of regionalism and place studies, the show would be far different, or some other show, for numerous reasons, if set in California or Texas or New York. Ensley F. Guffey (2013) has shown the extent to which the invocation of place, home, and houses serves

Breaking Bad as a powerful narrative tool. Yet the importance of place itself is insufficient to appreciate fully the dynamic impact of Albuquerque and New Mexico. Considering *Breaking Bad* as an exercise in critical regionalist form reveals the degree to which the operations of place and space are integral to the show. The interplay of local and global factors in a regional space is the essence of place as it is the essence of capitalism. Perversely, the methamphetamine trade, from production to distribution, becomes a metaphor for the possibility of place and community itself in the contemporary era.

Critical regionalism has been theorized by numerous scholars, in particular Paul Ricoeur (1965), Kenneth Frampton (2002; chief popularizer of the term), and Fredric Jameson (1994). Ricoeur raised the question about the possibility of partaking in both local culture and universal civilization (277). This question was taken up by architect Frampton, who in his writings on critical regionalism advocated an architecture of the resistance of regional forms against homogenizing global forces. In Frampton's critical regionalist architecture, regional culture ideally partakes in global technologies and aesthetics while maintaining a degree of autonomy in its expression of heterogeneous local or global identities and traditions. A critical regionalist architecture, Frampton argued, must not be reactionary or parochial but must be an engagement: what he described as a play of reciprocal influence and an uneven synthesis that must remain in tension. While seemingly intrigued by the possibility of such local forms, Jameson remained unsure of what critical regionalism would look like in various media and expressed the concern that regional identity would be subsumed in a kind of Disney-fication of the regional or local.

In discussing *Breaking Bad* as regional we are well down the path of Jameson's concerns. The AMC cable television program is much more akin to the commodification of the regional than it is to Frampton's examples of regional architecture. Yet to borrow more from Frampton, the question is not whether the show is a commodity—clearly it is—but whether its engagement with the regional is "scenographic" (that is, superficially decorative) or structural in nature, integral to composition and theme, and whether the engagement of local and global are harmoniously hybridized and thus normalized or an engagement in which local and global remain in tension (Jameson 1994). To the degree that the show's topic of the methamphetamine trade and its chosen location of Albuquerque function on multiple levels of investigation of global economics and local communities,

I argue, *Breaking Bad* serves self-reflexively as a critique of the very global-ized market that promulgates it and holds out the possibility of regional identity and form, ameliorating the impact of neoliberal economic global-ism (Pierson 2013, 16).[1]

Places and Spaces

Albuquerque was always less a place than a crossing. Just as today it is a hub where Interstates 40 and 25 cross, it was at its 1706 founding a conve-nient location along the Rio Grande and the Camino Real where Spanish colonists, after the reconquest of Santa Fe in 1692, sought agricultural opportunities between Socorro to the south and Santa Fe and the indige-nous pueblos—Acoma, Jemez, Zia, and many others—that drew Spanish military and ecclesiastical attention (Sánchez, Spude, and Gómez 2013). Later, it was a place of strategic value in the Mexican-American War and the US Civil War, a railroad town, a major stop on the Route 66 migration, the location of the state's main university, and a site of Cold War atomic development. As much as we might wish to seek the essence of a place, as in the pure air and blue skies of the Land of Enchantment, in truth every place has its origins in movement; place is an intersection of histories. Albuquerque and its surroundings highlight such crossings by their ethnic diversity, proximity to the US-Mexico border, and marked contrast between urban and natural landscapes.

As for *Breaking Bad*'s treatment of place, the visual representation of New Mexico is iconic: the Sandía Range and southern Rockies, towering cumulus clouds against cerulean skies, deserts, and grasslands. Such scen-ery often implicitly invokes language of the Western genre, as when Walter White and Jesse Pinkman find isolated scenes of canyon and prairie, nota-bly To'hajiilee, in which to cook methamphetamine. It does so explicitly at times as well, as when Walt and Gustavo Fring meet gunfighters in a big, empty cinematic space in "Full Measure" (season 3, episode 13). Yet the show's self-conscious citation of the genre is part of what marks it as a "postwestern," as Neil Campbell (2013) has termed it. Post-Westerns are typically engaged in the contemporary (rather than mythic/historic) West and in the West as a place of shifting boundaries and categories, geograph-ical, ideological, and otherwise.

The representation of New Mexico in *Breaking Bad*, however, works to avoid the Western genre more often than it invokes it. Most obviously, the urban Albuquerque and inner-city shots of the Drug Enforcement Administration (DEA) headquarters, ghettos and drug houses, and mundane suburban neighborhoods (notably including the Walt and Schrader homes) are new western and part of the antimythic West in character (Robb 1997). The Simms building in downtown Albuquerque used as DEA headquarters is a historic building, the city's first modern international-style, glass-and-steel monument to cosmopolitan placelessness. Walt's home is a generic, suburban, ranch-style home, making no claim to an identifiable place. By contrast, the Schrader house is a perfect example of new West in its pseudo-adobe suburbanism, the commercialized fantasy of the Land of Enchantment. Only Pinkman's home, originally his Aunt Ginny's house, might be called a gracious Southwestern-style house with its red-tile roof, stucco walls, and arches—a responsive sense of space and light. Yet that house is the scene of repeated nightmares and almost unspeakable moral depravity.

Other memorable locations seem chosen to avoid western association. Consider, for example, the strip mall that houses Saul Goodman's bustling office or the Crystal Palace Crossroads Motel where the prostitute Wendy S. subsists or the truly hellish home of Spooge and his lady. But even shots of western landscapes and Indian reservations are inflected with an antimythic feel of dirty realism that self-consciously deconstructs its own visual language. Take as an example the scenes at the Big Chief Gas Station, where we meet the young Native American clerk, Cara, who is briefly drawn into Hank's investigation. *Breaking Bad* continually invokes post-Western sites like Route 66 junk shops, atomic-bomb museums, terracotta-and-turquoise highway overpasses, the Georgia O'Keeffe Museum, desert rehabilitation clinics. The relative ease with which Walt and Jesse can drive their RV out of the urban space of the industrial scrapyard and into the open desert highlights the frontiers of nature and culture, the crossings of civilization (in this case truly corrupt) and nature. The representation of place in *Breaking Bad*, in short, is complex, referential, and contradictory.

Places are the intersections of histories, and those histories are ultimately and inevitably larger than the place itself. Places are formed by their outside even as we are often inclined to define them from the inside. In *Breaking Bad*, Albuquerque is not represented as an innocent locale where the cartels and the DEA have arrived to do battle. It was never an Eden. Instead, the locale is intimated and implicated in the history of methamphetamine, which, after it was first criminalized, was a locally produced, home-cooked narcotic. The techniques of methamphetamine cooking spread in grassroots fashion through social communities (Weisheit and White 2009). Methamphetamine production, along with marijuana growing, is often folklorically associated with the production of moonshine.[2] If associated with the nomadism of motorcycle gangs, it is also characterized as a drug that traditionally was produced and consumed in place rather than being imported (Weisheit and White 2009).

Jesse Pinkman, the self-styled "Cap'n Cook," in a sense epitomizes Albuquerque as a corrupt crossroads. A middle-class white boy driving a Chicano-style lowrider, blaring rap music, Jesse is a small-time methamphetamine cook who is known for his "signature" recipe of adding the spice of Southwestern cuisine, "chili-p," to his methamphetamine (as in season 1, episode 1). His new partner, Walter White, the California Institute of Technology–educated chemist, brings Jesse over to his scientific method, which, he proudly asserts, will produce "a chemically pure and stable product that performs as advertised." Jesse and his brand represent a local production, amateur yet charmingly regional, while Walt, especially when he adopts the synthesis of blue methamphetamine—using methylamine rather than pseudoscience derived from antihistamines—represents the desire for a highly marketable product that can be mass-produced and will find a wider economy. Although Jesse might well have come to a bad end on his own, Walt repeatedly brings Jesse into danger as the two face difficulties—difficulties seldom involved with the actual process of producing high-grade methamphetamine but that rather concern where to produce it (place, site) and how to market it (space, globalism).

Late in the series' second season much of this issue of place and space comes to the forefront. Having been freed from the deadly association with Tuco and having failed miserably, in the death of Combo, at running their own network of dealers, Walt and Jesse authorize the incomparable lawyer Saul Goodman to arrange a deal with Gustavo Fring, who has the reputation, at least, of rational professionalism. Hank Schrader, a DEA agent and Walt's brother-in-law, already thoroughly obsessed with Heisenberg and Blue Sky methamphetamine, is initially puzzled by the sudden disappearance of the blue methamphetamine from Albuquerque. He discovers, however, that the product is appearing in Texas, Arizona, Colorado, and Nevada—in other words, all around New Mexico, but not in New Mexico itself. Heisenberg is still at work in Albuquerque, Schrader proudly asserts, but has learned "not to shit where he eats"; Heisenberg "has gone regional, only he's still right here in town" (season 2, episode 13). Of course, Heisenberg's apparent ability to "go regional" is owed to Gustavo Fring's distribution via his chain of Los Pollos Hermanos restaurants.

This turn of events, going from local to regional, is one among several other intriguing, geographical, or spatial narrative elements coming into play at this point. Most important is the air disaster. On one immediate thematic level, the fact that the accident was caused by Donald Margolis, the air-traffic controller stricken with the death of his daughter (and Jesse's girlfriend) from an overdose, underlines the show's theme that individual actions have wide and often-tragic consequences. On a more general level, such a horrific event, which costs 167 lives and leaves debris and human remains strewn over parts of the city, adds to the sense of impending violence and ruin imminent for Walt, Jesse, and their families. Regarding its spatial significance, we should notice that the accident was a collision. More specifically, it was a crash between a Boeing 737 Wayfarer Airlines jet and a small regional or commuter plane, a turbo-prop flying from St. George, Utah, to Amarillo, Texas—a collision of national and regional "vectors" over Albuquerque. Another intriguing factor here is Walt Jr.'s website, SaveWalterWhite.com. Walt Jr.'s desire to help his family pay for his father's cancer treatment is touching, which makes all the more sleazy Saul Goodman's plan to have a computer hacker in Eastern Europe launder Walt's drug money through the site, to which Walt agrees. Virtual space is important here, as hacked "zombie" computers from all over the United States and Canada are used to send small amounts of money to Walt Jr.'s PayPal account. *Breaking Bad* plays on sense of place, regional and national scales of space, and virtual space.

Significant in the dynamics of place and space is the matter of race, ethnicity, and nationality. It should be noted that our main protagonists are white and pink men in a land where most residents, including many of the gang members, drug addicts, innocent bystanders, DEA agents, and others we meet are Hispanic, Latina and Latino, Chicana and Chicano, or Mexican. Gustavo Fring, the Chilean, is of African ancestry. Numerous minor characters are Native American, Navajo or Pueblo. Others are African American. The indomitable Saul Goodman, as he explains it, is not actually a Jew but adopted his name because his customers prefer a Jewish lawyer. He has an affinity for Eastern European and Vietnamese immigrant women because, as he puts it, they are "just so grateful to even be here" (season 3, episode 2). Albuquerque is a mixed-up world, a cosmopolitan space of immigration.

The Globalization of Space

Most noteworthy as the series went on into its third season is the transnational fact of the drug trade, as exemplified by the approaching Salamanca cousins and the strained relationship between Fring and the Juárez cartel. Ostensibly to make peace after the cousins' disastrous visit to Albuquerque, Fring and Mike Ehrmantraut bring Jesse to Mexico, where the three men are taken, blindfolded, to a super-lab where Jesse is to teach the Mexicans how to cook the blue stuff. After Jesse produces a batch more than 96 percent pure, it is revealed that Fring sold Jesse to the cartel. This is a ruse, however, as becomes clear when we see Fring's real plan unfold. Taking long-awaited revenge and, in effect, taking over the Juárez cartel territory, Fring poisons and kills the entire leadership of the cartel and the three shoot themselves out, though not without casualty (season 4, episode 10). The cartel had flown the men into Mexico in a small plane, but getting back is a different story, as Fring explains to Jesse: "There are many good ways south. Unfortunately, only one way north. Six miles to Texas. I've got a man there who will drive us the rest of the way" (season 4, episode 11). They walk.

Also significant from the transnational standpoint are the cousins. First mentioned by Tuco in season 2, episode 2, but not seen until the opening of season 3, the Salamanca cousins are the most terrifying aspect of the Juárez cartel, with which Walter White, Jesse Pinkman, and Gustavo Fring are entangled. When we first see them, they take part in a Santa Muerta cult ritual and they are represented as soulless, cold killers. A significant counternarrative to the cousins' movement north from Mexico to Albuquerque is Schrader's DEA promotion and transfer from Albuquerque to El Paso. At the border, Schrader is met with skepticism and is derided by fellow agents (justifiably, considering the nature of the job) for his inability to speak Spanish. The violent events that undo Schrader and send him back to Albuquerque involve a creative beheading that, it turns out, was performed by the cousins; they most memorably dramatize the transnational violence of the drug trade. In effect, Walt and Jesse are caught up in a turf battle between the Juárez cartel and the displaced Chilean, Gus

Fring, who is using Walt to break with the cartel and supply his own southwestern US territory. It is interesting that, when Mike, Fring's enforcer, kills four cartel gunmen in Albuquerque, he finds them holed up in Golden Moth Chemical, a company patronized by Fring, where they have taken its Chinese proprietor, Duane Chow, as a hostage.

If season 2 sees Walt's product going from local to regional and seasons 3 and 4 concern the transnational drug trade of the US-Mexico border, season 5, the final season, goes global with the development of the Madrigal connection. Madrigal Electromotive, a multinational corporation headquartered in Hannover, Germany, is first mentioned in season 4, when it is uncovered by Hank Schrader as the true owner of Los Pollos Hermanos and the source of an extremely expensive and sophisticated air exchanger delivered to Albuquerque (in fact, to Fring's underground methamphetamine lab). But in season 5 we learn more of Madrigal as Mike renews a partnership with Lydia Rodarte-Quayle, who had worked with Fring from her Houston-division office. In fact, Mike had been on his way to kill the highly strung Lydia (who had been engaged in her own attempt at murderous self-preservation in the wake of Fring's death) before a failure of resolve and his need to procure methylamine moved him to spare her life.

Madrigal serves as the face of globalism within *Breaking Bad*'s escalating scales of geographical reference. Lydia's position as head of logistics at Madrigal enables her to offer Walt (who, having no further need for her, was, like Mike, planning her execution) an enticing business opportunity. She explains to Walt that the Czech Republic has the greatest demand for methamphetamine in Europe:

> Five percent of its ten million people, which is roughly the population of the Southwest from western Texas to Phoenix, are using meth. You keep your market here, but by adding overseas sales you can more than double your current profits. And I checked: the average purity is only about 60 percent. They've never seen anything like your product. (season 5, episode 8)

Walt expresses doubt that Madrigal, now under DEA investigation, is safe, but Lydia makes an argument of invisibility because of the corporation's size. It is primarily the restaurant division that is under investigation, but "we have 46,000 employees spread across 14 divisions." Both in fear for her life and impassioned by her faith in the strategy, she assures Walt, "This is what I do, you understand? I move things from point A to point B all over the globe. 1.2 million metric tons a month. And all of it right at my fingertips. A laptop click away." And, in a point that no doubt relates to Walt's family concerns, Lydia cites geographical scale as an avenue of safety: "There are considerable advantages to diversification of distribution, like putting six thousand miles between you and your product." Lydia estimates that they can net $2 million a week, adding that she should have a 30 percent cut.

The Unsettling of Place

An aspect of critical regionalism is its unsettling of place, and in the case of *Breaking Bad*, it is easy to find. Another aspect of critical regionalism, however, is its championing of regions in their resistance to globalism and expression of distinct regional culture. In its dark treatment of a grim subject in *Breaking Bad*, it is difficult to find positive attributes of place, community, and identity—a sense of regionalism—that survives the carnage of the drug trade. Jesse Pinkman's "chili-p" signature methamphetamine exemplified the regional in one way. And Jesse, for all the damage he does, demonstrates one minor good as he gives money to Andrea to move herself and her son to a better neighborhood and finally removes himself as a danger to their safety (unsuccessfully, in the end). Methamphetamine is corrosive to communities, neighborhoods, families—realities Jesse knows well.

Another layer of critical regionalist analysis requires that we examine the relationship between the show and its locale. In other words, how has *Breaking Bad* affected Albuquerque? Perhaps there was little choice in the matter, but it is striking how much the city has embraced the show. As one commentator put it, the show was so good that "it made Albuquerque look good being bad" (Krueger 2013). In the first place, of course, city officials enticed the producers away from California by reinstating a law that raises tax subsidies for television productions (Martin 2013). As the show gained popularity and in the aftermath, the city has helped promote *Breaking Bad* tours through the Chamber of Commerce website. There one can learn about trolley car, RV, limo, and bicycle tours of *Breaking Bad* locations (Albuquerque Visitors and Convention Bureau n.d.). There is Blue Sky Rock Candy for sale as well (Contreras 2012). And, of course, the T-shirt business is thriving. Yet it is not surprising that the Chamber of Commerce burble fails to mention the serious issue of the methamphetamine trade or comment on the presence of methamphetamine laboratories, drug houses, or street killings—as if these events were a fiction portrayed against the backdrop of Albuquerque rather than a reflection of realities of Albuquerque (which they certainly are). So where is a more critical engagement between city and show rather than a celebratory commodification?

A couple of examples of *Breaking Bad*'s positive effect on Albuquerque are a funeral fundraiser and a rehabilitation scholarship program. The widely reported funeral of Walter White was held by the Albuquerque Foundation and raised $17,000 for Albuquerque's HealthCare for the Homeless organization (Grow 2013). Two addiction-treatment scholarships were offered through collaboration between Sage Neuroscience Center (a rehabilitation facility) and HealthShire.com ("New Mexico Clinic" 2013). More substantive or enduring effects, however, are difficult to find or foresee. And, as the *Los Angeles Times* has reported, not all find *Breaking Bad* a boon:

> "Meth use among the young hasn't dropped," said Katrina Hotrum, director of the Bernalillo County Department of Substance Abuse Programs. "We're going to be seeing this drug here for a very long time." All the publicity from the show hasn't meant more drug treatment funds for her department, she said.
>
> Law enforcement has no interest in keeping the "Breaking Bad" bandwagon rolling. The federal Drug Enforcement Administration, which was represented in the series by the character of Agent Hank Schrader, will no longer comment on drug stories that mention the show. The Homeland Security Department and local U.S. attorney's offices also refused comment.
>
> "Our drug problem here is more serious than most cities our size," said Dist. Atty. Kari Brandenburg, an admitted fan of the show. "These agencies don't want to be accused of buying into that culture."

The article goes on to note that the city's younger drug users and dealers have adopted *Breaking Bad* as a mark of distinction and a bragging point for Albuquerque as a place "on the map" for "bad-ass" criminality, vying with Los Angeles (Glionna 2014).

Breaking Bad begins and (in a sense) ends in a particular place: To'hajiilee. To'hajiilee Indian Reservation, once Cañoncito, some thirty miles west of Albuquerque, is a noncontiguous part of the Navajo reservation, most of which is farther west and north. Walt and Jesse go to To'hajiilee when they cook their first batch in the RV (season 1, episode 1). And it is also where, in the episode bearing the place-name (season 5, episode 13), Walt buries $80 million but is tricked by Jesse and the DEA into revealing the location. He has also arranged to meet Jack Welker and his neo-Nazi gang at the same place, but then he realizes, too late, the disastrous mistake he's made when the two sides confront each other, the DEA agents (Hank Schrader and Steve Gomez) and the neo-Nazis. Schrader and Gomez are killed by the gang and are buried in the same hole where Walt had planted his cash, which has now been stolen by the gang. "To'hajiilee" or "Tó Hajiileehé" literally means "where people draw up water by means of a cord or rope one quantity after another," as, for example, drawing water from a well (Analytical Lexicon n.d.). The place, for Navajos, has significance as a landscape and as a historical habitation. It seems unlikely that the show's producers chose the location for the meaning of its Navajo name, or that the Navajo place-name influenced the plot; nonetheless, the name carries fortuitous thematic resonance. Perhaps it is Walt's nostalgia for his early work with Jesse that leads him back to the location; the buried cash means Walt's survival just as the well means survival for desert dwellers, and it is his need to go to the well one too many times that leads to his downfall. Here, too, is a strikingly ironic confluence of players. Onto sovereign Native land come the feds (operating without prior notification, as would be properly legal), neo-Nazis with automatic weapons, and our now fully estranged antiheroes Walt and Jesse for a shootout in a landscape that recalls Sam Peckinpah's *Wild Bunch*. Mythic, cinematic, fictional, and real places merge here in a specifically cited place that bookends the story of *Breaking Bad*.

If place is space humanized, to summarize the argument of cultural geographers, here we have moved from space to place before place is again returned to abstract space. When Walt and Jesse first come to the canyon in To'hajiilee, it is because it is open space, uninhabited (Jesse climbs a cliff and reports seeing only a "cow house") and free from eyes. While we cannot know why Walt chose to return and bury his money at To'hajiilee, the spot is now significant through his relationship with Jesse and their history. This is where he first cooked methamphetamine, faced a gun, and killed a man. This desert is not abstract space but a place. Then, however, in a characteristically rational fashion, Walt marks the coordinates of his buried treasure with a GPS. The coordinates are heavily repeated for viewers: we see the numerals on the digital display of the GPS, Walt repeats them as he commits them to memory, he repeats them again to Jack Welker, who writes them on his hand, and, subsequently, there are several closeup shots of the lottery ticket bearing the coordinates that Walt purchases and later gives to Skyler so that she can use it as a bargaining chip with the DEA (still looking for their agents' bodies).[3] Just as Walter White's initial motivation and highest value—as a dying man seeking to provide for his family after his death—is replaced with a large value of cash (quantifiable, $80 million), so is a place of rich personal memory reduced to coordinates. Here at this place Walt loses everything: his wealth (or the great majority of it), his freedom, his family, and his partner.

It is too reductive to assert that space in its abstraction and quantification, associated with economics and globalism, is the evil in opposition to which place and associated human values are the good. But the treatment of To'hajiilee in its transformation between place and space recalls the idea that critical regionalism finds the highest value in defining a region as a double mediation between local and global, place and space. And thus in considering To'hajiilee, the point is not that deserts are spaces devoid of memory, the constant against the ephemeral human action. Rather, it is that deserts are, in their apparent emptiness and voidness of character, powerful reminders of the ghostly nature of memory and history—present even if invisible in the landscape. The violence that characterizes this place as place in *Breaking Bad* reminds us that space and place, global and local, are not dialectical but are in a constant process of becoming and being undone.

One of the most thought-provoking moments of *Breaking Bad* in this sense occurs in the brilliantly titled "Ozymandias" episode as Walter White is rolling his one remaining barrel of cash against the desert floor of cholla and bunchgrass to arrive at the home of a Navajo elder. The house is weathered, hewn sandstone and wood, a bull skull displayed on the fence. The man looks traditional, in braids, carrying a walking stick, his wrinkled face and square jaw appearing hewn out of stone as well. Walt makes clear his desire to buy the man's ancient truck. "It's not for sale," says the man. Walt holds out a bundle of cash, and in the next scene he is loading his barrel in the back of the truck (season 5, episode 14). Should we lament the corruption of the Navajo elder by Walt's ill-gotten cash, or should we instead applaud the man? He is going to have himself a new truck soon. If *Breaking Bad* is tragic, it is also comic; life goes on.

Finally, more than depicting negative or positive aspects of the region, and more than its negative and positive impact on the place it depicts, *Breaking Bad* is itself a critical engagement with regionalism. To the high degree that the show makes us ask hard questions about place, it performs a kind of critical regionalism that makes it far more than merely an example of regionalist representation. *Breaking Bad* is not simply set in a place; the show makes its viewers think about place in relation to the larger world. "Region" or "place" do not participate in the category of good versus the evils of global capitalism, Walt's escalating ego and desire for a methamphetamine empire demonstrate the increasing violence that accompanies larger economies of scale. Places, whether Albuquerque or Prague (and note that the places are now increasingly distant from the actual place of production), are increasingly threatened by globalized economies. *Breaking Bad* represents Albuquerque as at once a regionally unique place, a multicultural and multinational interface, and globalized space. This depiction of Albuquerque operates through imagery of place and the visual mapping of the city in relation to the broader Southwest, the northern Mexican borderlands, and the world. It is of course methamphetamine that recenters Albuquerque as a hub in the new world order of the borderlands, where the DEA and multinational cartels do battle. *Breaking Bad* shows methamphetamine, in keeping with its effect on the nervous system, as an explosive commodity that has a frenzied impact on places and peoples and shows how growing markets affect a place. In a way, such phenomena are nothing new; the borderlands have long been a place of trade and hybridity. But the focus, intensity, and velocity of change and violence are unprecedented. *Breaking Bad* is a somber consideration of worlds in collision. In that sense, methamphetamine's corrosive effect on the Southwest is a synecdoche for places and regions subject to global capitalism.

Notes

1. Pierson (2013) argues that *Breaking Bad* as a series interrogates "neoliberal ideology" that mandates "that the market should be the organizing agent for nearly all social, political, and personal decisions" (16).
2. For example, in the James McMurtry song "Choctaw Bingo" or Steve Earle's "Copperhead Road" or "Calico County."
3. Angela Watercutter (2013) has noted that the show's fans discovered the coordinates to be those of Studio Q, where *Breaking Bad* was filmed in Albuquerque.

References

Albuquerque Visitors and Convention Bureau. n.d. "Breaking Bad in Albuquerque." http://www.visitalbuquerque.org/albuquerque/arts/breaking-bad/.

Analytical Lexicon of Navajo. n.d. http://interglacial.com/d/navajo/entry?LO%27#G_32.

Breaking Bad Wiki. n.d. http://breakingbad.wikia.com/wiki/Pilot.

Campbell, Neil. 2013. *Post-Westerns: Cinema, Region, West.* Lincoln: University of Nebraska Press.

Contreras, Russell. 2012. "NM Shop Sells 'Meth Candy' to Honor *Breaking Bad.*" *Albuquerque Journal*, August 23. http://www.abqjournal.com/125416/abqnewsseeker/nm-shop-sells-meth-candy-to-honor-breaking-bad.html.

Frampton, Kenneth. n.d. "Rappel à l'Ordre: The Case for the Tectonic." http://suw.biblos.pk.edu.pl/resources/i5/i4/i8/i8/r5488/FramptonK_RappelOrdreCase.pdf.

———. 2002. "Towards a Critical Regionalism: Six Points for an Architecture of Resistance." In *The Anti Aesthetic: Essays on Postmodern Culture*, edited by Hal Foster, 16–31. New York: New Press.

Glionna, John M. 2014. "*Breaking Bad* Is Still Cooking in Albuquerque." *LA Times*, January 31. http://www.latimes.com/nation/la-na-c1-albuquerque-breaking-bad-20140131-dto-htmlstory.html.

Grow, Kory. 2013. "Walter White Laid to Rest in *Breaking Bad* Charity Funeral." *Rolling Stone*, October 21. http://www.rollingstone.com/movies/news/walter-white-laid-to-rest-in-breaking-bad-charity-funeral-20131021.

Guffey, Ensley F. 2013. "Buying the House: Place in *Breaking Bad.*" In *Breaking Bad: Critical Essays on the Contexts, Politics, Style, and Reception of the Television Series*, edited by David P. Pierson, 155–73. Lanham, MD: Lexington.

Jameson, Fredric. 1994. *The Seeds of Time.* New York: Columbia University Press.

Krueger, Joline Gutierrez. 2013. "Why We Love, and Miss, *Breaking Bad.*" *Albuquerque Journal*, October 29. http://www.abqjournal.com/290497/upfront/why-we-love-and-miss-breaking-bad.html.

Martin, Claire. 2013. "Breaking Up with 'Breaking Bad' Is Hard for Albuquerque." *New York Times*, September 28. http://www.nytimes.com/2013/09/29/business/breaking-up-with-breaking-bad-is-hard-for-albuquerque.html?pagewanted=all.

"New Mexico Clinic to Offer *Breaking Bad* Free Rehab." 2013. *MSN News*, October 1. http://news.msn.com/pop-culture/new-mexico-clinic-to-offer-breaking-bad-free-rehab.

Pierson, David P., ed. 2013. *Breaking Bad: Critical Essays on the Contexts, Politics, Style, and Reception of the Television Series.* Lanham, MD: Lexington.

Pierson, David P. 2013. "Breaking Neoliberal? Contemporary Neoliberal Discourses and Policies in AMC's *Breaking Bad*." In *Breaking Bad: Critical Essays on the Contexts, Politics, Style, and Reception of the Television Series*, edited by David P. Pierson, 15–33. Lanham, MD: Lexington.

Ricoeur, Paul. 1965. "Universal Civilization and National Cultures." In *History and Truth*, 271–84. Evanston, IL: Northwestern University Press.

Robb, James J. 1997. *Atlas of the New West*. New York: W. W. Norton.

Sánchez, Joseph P., Robert L. Spude, and Art Gómez. 2013. *New Mexico: A History*. Norman: University of Oklahoma Press.

Watercutter, Angela. 2013. "What's the Meaning of *Breaking Bad*'s Lost-esque Lottery Numbers?" *Wired*, August 19. http://www.wired.com/2013/08/breaking-bad-lottery-numbers/.

Weisheit, Ralph, and William L. White. 2009. *Methamphetamine: Its History, Pharmacology, and Treatment*. Center City, MN: Hazelden.

On the Red Couch

Breaking Bad and the Refusal of Therapy

Jeffrey Severs

Who needs therapy? Nearly every character on *Breaking Bad* could clearly use it, and nearly all receive or aggressively resist some form of therapy, which the show defines flexibly as both mental and physical. Walter White submits to chemotherapy after much haranguing, and at the start of season 2 he outwits a hospital psychiatrist to continue his methamphetamine production. Hank Schrader, another macho resister of "shrinks," refuses to see a psychiatrist after trauma in El Paso has clearly crippled him psychologically. In addition, he only reluctantly works with a physical therapist in seasons 3 and 4 after he is shot, redirecting himself into an addiction to minerals (which the show associates with the "glass" of methamphetamine and, more important, the obsessiveness that populates so many "bad" tracks). More panic attacks follow in season 5 for the untreated Hank. His kleptomaniac wife Marie goes to therapy (clearly ineffective, as season 4 shows), and in season 5 her therapist is an object of mockery. Jesse Pinkman—a fitting patient for trauma after finding Jane dead next to him and, later, shooting Gale Boetticher—is the show's self-medicating character, one who recurrently points out the quasi-therapeutic, life-destroying effects of the drug use that drives this world's economy. Jesse also spurns a therapeutic setting by using his Narcotics Anonymous group as a market for methamphetamine, then openly mocking its leader. Season 4 suggests throughout that trauma's victims (Gus Fring is yet another, forced to witness the sudden death of his "brother" at a poolside) end up not cured but, in fact, bonded to criminal enterprise and cycles of revenge. Thus we know therapeutic solutions in *Breaking Bad* primarily by their absence and denigration. Once one breaks bad, there seems to be no path to rehabilitation and recovery.

In this essay, I examine what fills the vacuum left by these rejections of therapy. Swerving away from its master influence, *The Sopranos*, *Breaking Bad* maintains its twisted conceit of a suburban chemistry teacher's meth-amphetamine production by eliminating almost all structures within which the leading characters might productively reflect on their traumas and crimes. In charting psychological developments, in lieu of expository scenes with therapists, *Breaking Bad* provides a physical set of signs for the characters' inner struggles, including a series of couches that mock the psychiatrist's by inciting and justifying further violent behavior rather than curing or curtailing it. By tracking this symbolism, I provide a map to the show's contortions of therapy, especially in the pivotal season 4, where *Breaking Bad* achieves some of its thematic coherence by replaying Walt's early story of physical illness through Jesse's more intractable psychological issues of trauma and rage. In the conclusion I suggest the films of Stanley Kubrick, especially the relentless *A Clockwork Orange* (1971), as a key to understanding the way questions of rehabilitation are handled—or, far more often, not handled—in this series. The ultraviolent *Breaking Bad* often sounds the same notes as Kubrick's Alex, who in a dystopian hospital concludes the film with a sarcastic line about psychiatrists' efforts to change his psychotic ways: "I was cured all right." *Breaking Bad*'s main players are cured all right too.

In sociological terms, *Breaking Bad*'s aversion to therapy is surely a sign of its times and of its reactionary masculinity. As Brian Faucette (2014) argues, Walt and others, reflecting "a perceived crisis of masculinity" and male authority in the new millennium, "embrace older models of masculinity based on violence, intimidation, and control in order to re-masculinize themselves" (74). But on an aesthetic level, the rejection of therapy expresses *Breaking Bad*'s anxiety of influence and its search for original material. When *The Sopranos* premiered in January 1999 and its pilot gave viewers scenes between a Mafia don and his therapist, the implicit joke testified to just how common therapy had become for the American bourgeoisie by the late 1990s—for even a mafioso sees a counselor. *Breaking Bad* would become the most successful of the several shows that tried to replicate the *Sopranos* model of the criminal family man who kills in one scene and resolves domestic drama in the next (and later sits musing by a backyard pool). As creator Vince Gilligan said succinctly after the death of James Gandolfini, "Without Tony Soprano, there would be no Walter White" (*Hollywood Reporter* 2013). *The Sopranos*—product of David E. Kelly, a creator much invested in romanticism—often bore the traces of a spiritual outlook: Tony lacked Carmela's interest in Catholicism, but Dr. Jennifer Melfi's office was nonetheless a sort of confessional for him. *Breaking Bad*, by comparison, offers an utterly pragmatic, zero-illusions atmosphere, a Machiavellian vision that it puts to the test again and again through Walt's schemes. As I suggest later in this essay, the show also recasts the therapist Melfi as a corruption-enabling, neoliberal counselor of a different sort, Saul Goodman.

Breaking Bad repeatedly suggests that violence and criminality have therapeutic effects for Walt. The pilot sets the tone: Walt encounters emasculation and tragedy on his fiftieth birthday, with his cancer diagnosis and humiliating experiences at his car wash and teaching jobs ushering him toward his methamphetamine plan. The pilot illustrates Walt's transformation with scenes that might, in a different scenario, occur on either side of sessions with a therapist: In an awkward summary of their routine sex life, Skyler strokes a stressed-out Walt under the covers (apparently a failed venture) while she bids on an online auction item. At the pilot's end, after he wields a phallic gun in his underwear out in the desert, Walt returns to the marital bed newly aggressive and with no erectile problems, leading Skyler to ask, "Walt, is that you?" The suggestion of his recovered sexual powers continues in "A No-Rough-Stuff-Type Deal" (season 1, episode 7), in which Walt seeks other forms of transgression, stimulating Skyler under the table at a meeting with school authorities about the equipment he himself stole. Later the couple go from the meeting to the backseat of their car, mischievous teenagers at play.

Season 1 also begins a more sustained, deeper story of Walt's flouting of the authority embodied by therapists, best illustrated in "Crazy Handful of Nothin'" (season 1, episode 6)—in my estimation the episode where the series begins to come fully into its own. While a newly bald Walt's first showdown with Tuco provides the main action, on the domestic side the Whites attend a family support group for cancer victims, where Skyler reacts to the effects of Walt's chemotherapy as well as his long afternoon absences from home. The female group facilitator, the first of many counselors who will be mocked throughout the series, joins Skyler in prodding Walt: "Now's the time to share." Walt, claiming that he likes to go on nature walks after work, redefines the term *therapy* with his lies: "I really enjoy the nature," he says. "The cacti, vegetation, that kind of thing. It's really very therapeutic." His speech blends with a scene of desert nature soon revealed to have the RV nearby, midsynthesis. Inside, we see Walt at work before, overcome by coughing, he stumbles out.

Chemotherapy and what we might call Walt's chemistry therapy are commingling here, for both are cures that work (if they do work) by introducing new sickness into the system. Chemotherapy, in effect, makes a patient sick in other ways in order to impair cell division and combat cancer, while in a grand analogy especially important to the first two seasons, Walt's methamphetamine scheme responds to his physical sickness with a moral sickness, a force that continues metastasizing long after his cancer has gone into remission. "Crazy Handful of Nothin'" makes these links symbolically through abject images of red: In the RV scene just cited, as Walt describes his therapeutic walks, he is seen, weak from chemotherapy, pouring reddish liquid into a flask. This image of liquid red is meant to match with later shots in this episode of intravenous injection in the chemotherapy ward and Walt's blood-tinged urine flowing into the toilet at home. Red, of course, is also the show's rather obvious code for both murderous rage and the moral contagion that Walt sets loose by way of a drug that itself infects the user's bloodstream. In just one example of a potent symbolic system that extends throughout the series from clothing to cars and the paint job in Gus's lab, in "Cat's in the Bag . . ." (season 1, episode 2) Jesse wears a red hoodie while struggling to follow Walt's orders and dispose of Emilio's body, efforts that end with red blood running all over his house. Jesse will naturally be wearing a red shirt when he shoots Gale at the end of season 3.

One of the great plotting challenges of *Breaking Bad* is sustaining the tension and motivation that initially make Walt's cooking project plausible, especially after his cancer fades away as a narrative device. In this process, the show resets itself in later seasons by transferring the plot of recovery from Walt to the other male leads. Thus, in seasons 3 and 4, a bedridden Hank, obsessed with minerals and ultimately agitating to return to work, offers parallels to the once debilitated Walt. Such plotting, keeping Hank grounded, allows Gilligan to defer for many more episodes the climactic outcome that seems almost inevitable from the pilot forward: the shrewd DEA agent finally avoiding yet another near miss and figuring out that his own brother-in-law is Heisenberg. But in terms of therapy's failures, the grounded Hank gets to express the show's essential stances: always resist treatment, always repress, and always regard bullheaded work, whether cooking or policing, as the only possible cure.

But more important than Hank's recapitulation of Walt's recovery is the arc of Jesse. In season 4, Gilligan and company seem to sense the need to reset Jesse's dilemmas as well, giving greater emotional texture to the motives and desires of a character Gilligan famously said he had planned to kill off at the end of the first season (but one who clearly grew into a coprotagonist with Walt).[1] Jesse, in metaphorical terms, takes over the illness plot line and anger issues of Walt by being diagnosed, in the wake of Gale's shooting, with a "rage virus." In accordance with the show's basic principles, the diagnosis is obscured and far from heeded. In seemingly meaningless banter early in "Thirty-Eight Snub" (season 4, episode 2), Badger and Skinny Pete argue over video games and zombies' running speed while snorting methamphetamine, an activity Jesse is now getting back into. "Dude, that's because they're not even zombies!" Badger says to Skinny Pete, critiquing the enemies in the game Left 4 Dead. "They're just infected. They got, like, this rage virus. Amps them up like they've been smoking the schwag!" Jesse sits nearby doing more drugs, the zombielike face he was wearing earlier in the scene now marked by drug-induced trembling and agitation.

The implication is clear: they are talking about Jesse's own infection with a rage virus. He is the "Nazi zombie" Badger refers to elsewhere in the video-game discussion. As he uses drugs and social life to repress his memories of shooting Gale, Jesse is indeed getting "amped up" in multiple senses: he decides to throw a days-long house party with punishingly loud music, and providing the mind-numbing noise is a stereo system with blue amplification indicators that he seems to fetishize, particularly in the moving scene of his breakdown at the end of "Thirty-Eight Snub" (perhaps the stereo signifies his own mechanization and noise-rattled head). Jesse's rage issue is intertwined with the posttraumatic stress he clearly suffers from: At the beginning of "Problem Dog" (season 4, episode 7), he is seen playing a shooting game and flashing back to Gale's face; tellingly, the game is called Rage (Dayton 2011). The rage virus is Jesse's cancer, metastasizing within him, and eruptions of uncontrollable anger will mark him in the final two seasons, up through and beyond the moment in "Confessions" (season 5, episode 11) when, having figured out how Brock was poisoned, he pours gasoline all over Walt's house.[2] Jesse, in season 3, has already been equipped with a family that recapitulates Walt's, complete with an especially vulnerable son. Jesse will, like Walt, attempt to give Andrea and Brock his methamphetamine proceeds while keeping them insulated from the business's grave dangers, a precarious project that fails completely by the series end. As Faucette suggests, being a provider for one's family, a primary marker of manhood in *Breaking Bad*'s vision of masculinity, is used as justification for the most heinous acts; and thus Jesse can grow up, on the show's terms, only by gaining an instant family of sorts (Faucette 2014, 76, 77).

The fact that Jesse will not solve his problems by going to therapy or otherwise seeking help may be a foregone conclusion by season 4, but the writers nonetheless carefully weave into the rage-virus leitmotif suggestions of the overarching motif of refusal of therapy and its distortion. During the zombie debate in "Thirty-Eight Snub," Jesse sits alone on an important piece of furniture new to his home in season 4: a red futon couch. In a few shots, as he sits glumly snorting, he is framed in a way that anticipates the iconic scene from "Hazard Pay" (season 5, episode 3), made famous in advertising, that embodies the show's masculine swagger: Jesse and Walt looking out from a couch, garbed in their yellow jumpsuits and gas masks. Sitting and staring at the camera is a position of power, ambition, and anger for this series: consider the image of Walt sitting alone amid stacks of methamphetamine and cash, under the heading "All Hail the King," in ads for season 5. In season 1, red was, as I suggested earlier, the color through which the show coupled Walt's cancer and his drug production. In later seasons, though, red is converted into the color of rage, a looser metaphor that binds Walt to Jesse in sickness: the childlike Pink-man, a figure Gilligan has called "fundamentally innocent," grows irrevocably red and full of rage under the influence of Walt.[3] Jesse's red couch is the leading edge of a series of scenes that will turn his entire house, especially the living room, into a manifestation of his chaotic internal state. Although he needs to get on a psychiatrist's couch, all this world offers him are further vehicles for his rage and criminality.

"Problem Dog," at the midpoint of season 4, draws many of these themes together. First, as Walt seduces him back into a plot to kill Gus, Jesse stands on a ladder, painting over the graffitied walls of his house—or, in my reading, covering over the complexities of his tormented mind. The graffiti shows through Jesse's multiple coats, and he goes over and over only a small portion of the large wall: Here too he is mimicking his old teacher, taking on the Walt White whitewashing technique of psychological cover-up. But the inchoate scribbles of his trauma over the murder show through. Notably, too, this is the wall that the red couch sat along in previous scenes. Jesse ends the negotiation by saying to Walt, "I'll do it. . . . I'll kill him first chance I get"—a promised actualization of the violent repetitions in his mind.

In the scene that gives "Problem Dog" its title, Jesse is seen in his Narcotics Anonymous group, where he echoes Walt's lies about "very therapeutic" nature walks in season 1. Jesse is, in his own way, trying to inch toward a partial psychological resolution by translating therapy into his own contentious terms. The attempt fails, though, beginning with his botched metaphor—putting down a "problem dog"—for the killing of Gale. The whitewash metaphor unravels into arguments with other members of the group and Jesse's indictment of the entire moral economy of therapy, its prescribed regimen of "not judging" and "accepting" oneself. "So, no matter what I do, hooray for me, because I'm a great guy?" Jesse shouts scornfully at the group leader's offer of comfort. "It's all good? No matter how many dogs I kill, I just, what, do an inventory and accept?" To the leader he adds, "I mean, you back your truck over your own kid and you, like, accept? What a load of crap!" Jesse, always the show's voice of buried guilt, cries out here for a moral guide in the amoral world that he has been helping Walt construct for three and a half seasons. The metaphor of a problem dog itself accords with the show's generally nihilistic logic of what it means to break bad: once it is infected with a virus, there is no rehabilitation or recovery for the human animal; there are only extremes of murder, death, and vengeance.

According to the symbolic economy of couches I have identified, "Problem Dog" is also about Walt's rejection of conventional therapy in favor of a more sinister form of counselor—Saul Goodman. Before Jesse's therapy outburst, Walt retreats to Saul's office after acting out his own adolescent rage by gleefully driving and then blowing up the symbolically red sports car he bought for Walt Jr. At the start of the scene in Saul's office, Walt appears, in a close-up of his head, leaning back into the couch as the lawyer yells into his phone about Walt's contrition (a term of religious reconciliation) over blowing up the car. The moment suggests that Walt has used Saul throughout as a therapist. There are interesting reflections here of the spiritual and economic themes in the show and its artistic lineage. Saul's office bears resemblances to Dr. Melfi's on *The Sopranos*, suggesting *Breaking Bad* wants to make the link: an odd white light comes from behind characters' heads in both—from the long rectangular windows along the walls of Melfi's office and from the inexplicable porthole-like windows in Saul's. The shows use Goodman and Melfi as vehicles of exposition and self-observation, such as they are in these worlds. But where Tony and Dr. Melfi eventually find a vocabulary for discussing his life crises that partly synthesizes psychoanalytic explanations and their mutual Italian Catholic background, Saul is a figure of amoral incitement for Walt: he uses legal manipulations to protect Walt from the consequences of his decisions. There are clear religious resonances in Goodman's name: he is neither a good man nor due for any conversion like that of St. Paul, who was a Saul before being struck down by God's blinding light on the road to Damascus (*Breaking Bad* plays often with images of moral sight, from eyeballs to glasses and cracked windshields).

In more concrete terms of political economy, though, Saul's role accords with the neoliberal logic that David Pierson (2013) shows to be driving *Breaking Bad*. Drawing on its portrayals of public education, health insurance, and, especially, illegal entrepreneurship, Pierson demonstrates that *Breaking Bad*, treating criminality as "one market among others" (21), explores and even valorizes the "harsh brutalities, risk/benefit calculations, and winner-take-all ethos best associated with neo-liberalism" (30). The sales pitch Jesse hears in being delegated to kill Gus is only one of the many ways Walt's drug business exemplifies the infiltration of metrics of market efficiency into American life under neoliberalism, which codifies a view of the subject as an exploiter of capitalist advantage on every level, from the psychological and ethical to the civic and political. In such an environment, Walt instinctively chooses a counselor who signifies the wholesale liquidation of the legal-political into the economic—the inflatable Statue of Liberty on Saul's office roof and the Constitution reproduced on his walls mark the reduction of democratic ideals into cheesy advertising. "Yeah, there's no deep-seated issues *there*," Saul says sarcastically in "Phoenix" (season 2, episode 12) when Walt resists using charity for money laundering, and Saul, throughout the series, serves as more than a mere legal adviser, facilitating Walt's ruthless repression of emotions and moral qualms in favor of total aggression in the neoliberal marketplace.

In "Mandala" (season 2, episode 11), Saul says to Walt and Jesse as they argue, "Guys, guys. Who do I look like, Maury Povich? I'm not your marriage counselor. You're professionals. Act like it." And yet there is a strange sense in which Saul does function as a marriage counselor—yet another form of therapist—to Walt in his relationship to Skyler. In the first few episodes of season 3, Walt takes Saul's advice that he bring his crime-world manipulations into the intimate sphere and thus pushes his way back into his family home. Examining some of these scenes, E. Diedre Pribram (2014) points out that *Breaking Bad* treats "marriage as an emotional institution as well as an economic and legal one" (205), and Saul's discourse is crucial to that view. "You're professionals. Act like it": Saul's neoliberal solution to all problems is to invoke the code of business, and in seasons 4 and 5, we notice that, with their lawyer's guidance, Walt and Skyler's marital relationship is reanimated along business lines. Through the car wash, Skyler handles money-laundering intricacies while Walt continues methamphetamine production. Their bond becomes one of shared entrepreneurial (and criminal) risk.

Let me close with an idea about where all this disfigurement and rejection of psychiatry comes from: Kubrick. Gilligan, a self-described Kubrick fanatic, credits the film director's idea of "non-submergible moments"—images that remain in the mind long after "you forget all the specific plot elements"—for many "Holy crap" scenes in the series (Keller 2010). Specific Kubrick homages run throughout the show: The ax-wielding Salamanca twins recall Jack Torrance running around the Overlook Hotel with an ax, and when they murder a police officer, the radio call the officer is making is "KDK-12 to dispatch," the code Wendy Torrance uses in radio communications throughout *The Shining* (1980).[4] The shots of spilled blood on the red laboratory floor in "Box Cutter" (season 4, episode 1) owe something to Kubrick's climactic scenes at the Overlook as well. As Jesse fixates on the sound quality of his stereo in "Thirty-Eight Snub," the turning point for so many of the developments I have outlined here, the show evokes Alex in *A Clockwork Orange*, purveyor of ultraviolence and obsessed with his Beethoven records and stereo. Walt's black hat, its brim pulled low and donned at moments of menace, is primarily a Western reference but also an ongoing allusion to Alex and his droogs' black bowlers, while *Breaking Bad*'s shots of men staring out from couches with steely gazes owe a debt to Kubrick's framing and to *Clockwork*'s iconic milk-bar scene. And the dim and boorish Badger and Skinny Pete fill in nicely for Kubrick's rendering of Georgie, Dim, and Pete.

Breaking Bad's nods to Kubrick are yet more extensive and a subject for another entire essay, but on the deepest levels the filmmaker seems most important to Gilligan and his cocreators as a source of the view of the subject as inherently, irreparably given to evil impulses, around which psychiatric solutions can only feebly dance—or devolve into forms of sadism. In effect, *Breaking Bad* imports into twenty-first-century New Mexico an attitude toward the doctoring of the mind inspired by the dystopian aversion therapy, called the Ludovico Technique, on which *Clockwork* culminates. Although there are no eyelids pinned open in *Breaking Bad*, Jesse is an object of prolonged torture in season 5, and his link to Alex is clinched in the series finale (season 5, episode 16) as young Pinkman, yelling, drives away from the final shootout—the shot of him through the windshield closely mimicking the scene of Alex maniacally driving a stolen sports car in *Clockwork*. In the series, this is the recovery—escaping from the scene of further violence and trauma, with issues unresolved—that has to suffice.

Of the ending, Gilligan says that, although he does want viewers to be free to decide Jesse's fate, "I prefer to believe that he got away, and he's got a long road to recovery ahead, in a sense of being held prisoner in a dungeon for the last six months and being beaten to within an inch of his life and watching Andrea be shot. All these terrible things he's witnessed are going to scar him as well, but the romantic in me wants to believe that he gets away with it and moves to Alaska and has a peaceful life communing with nature" (Snierson 2013). Imprisoned, scarred, traumatized, "long road to recovery"—all the signs are here that Gilligan might be ready to suggest for his character a little rehabilitative time on the couch. And yet all this dissolves in the space of a sentence into the show's essentially romantic, magical, and rather childish vision of how one might break a little better: the wild, untamed subject, communing with nature off the grid, finding an alleged peace.

Notes

1. Gilligan discusses his initial plan to kill off Jesse at the end of the first season (he calls it the "bad pitch") in an interview about the series finale (*Breaking Bad Insider Podcast* 2013).
2. A tune titled "Gas Can Rage" is the soundtrack here. The song is named in *Breaking Bad Wiki* (n.d.).
3. Gilligan makes this comment about Jesse in Keller (2010).
4. I am indebted for this insight to Margaret Lyons (2012). Lyons also discusses similarities in the treatment of Skyler and Wendy Torrance.

References

Breaking Bad Insider Podcast. 2013. "Episode 516." September 30. http://www.amctv.com/shows/breaking-bad/insider-podcast-season-5.

Breaking Bad Wiki. n.d. "Confessions." http://breakingbad.wikia.com/wiki/Confessions.

Dayton, Lee. 2011. "What Was That Video Game That Jesse Was Playing, Anyway?" *Breaking Bad Blog*, August 31. http://blogs.amctv.com/breaking-bad/2011/08/learn-more-about-rage/.

Faucette, Brian. 2013. "Taking Control: Male Angst and the Re-emergence of Hegemonic Masculinity in *Breaking Bad*." In *Breaking Bad: Critical Essays on the Contexts, Politics, Style, and Reception of the Television Series*, edited by David P. Pierson, 73–86. Lanham, MD: Lexington.

Hollywood Reporter. 2013. "Vince Gilligan: Without Tony Soprano, There Would Be No Walter White." June 26. http://www.hollywoodreporter.com/news/james-gandolfini-death-vince-gilligan-574556.

Keller, Joel. 2010. "Vince Gilligan Is Rethinking 'Breaking Bad' Season 3 Cliffhanger—TCA Report." *HuffPost TV*, August 5. http://www.aoltv.com/2010/08/05/vince-gilligan-is-rethinking-breaking-bad-season-3-cliffhanger/.

Lyons, Margaret. 2012. "What *Breaking Bad* Owes to *The Shining*." *Vulture*, August 30. http://www.vulture.com/2012/08/breaking-bad-the-shining.html.

Pierson, David P. 2013. "Breaking Neoliberal? Contemporary Neoliberal Discourses and Policies in AMC's *Breaking Bad*." In *Breaking Bad: Critical Essays on the Contexts, Politics, Style, and Reception of the Television Series*, edited by David P. Pierson, 15–33. Lanham, MD: Lexington.

Pribram, E. Diedre. 2013. "Feeling Bad: Emotions and Narrativity in *Breaking Bad*." In *Breaking Bad*: *Critical Essays on the Contexts, Politics, Style, and Reception of the Television Series*, edited by David P. Pierson, 191–207. Lanham, MD: Lexington.

Snierson, Dan. 2013. "*Breaking Bad*: Creator Vince Gilligan Explains Series Finale." *Entertainment Weekly*, September 30. http://insidetv. ew.com/2013/09/30/breaking-bad-finale-vince-gilligan/.

Doubling Down on a Handful of Nothin'
The Role of the Double in *Breaking Bad*

Brandon O'Neal

One of these men is Genius to the other;
And so of these: which is the natural man,
And which the spirit? Who deciphers them?

—William Shakespeare, *Comedy of Errors*

Vince Gilligan's crime drama *Breaking Bad* follows the transformation of mild-mannered high school chemistry teacher Walter White into ruthless meth lord Heisenberg. Although most of the narrative is driven by White's countless adventures and mishaps on his way to becoming the most feared and respected methamphetamine manufacturer in the US Southwest (possibly the world), the secondary and tertiary plots flesh out and complement the criminal and law-enforcement worlds of the region with characters connected to the White family socially and professionally. Static characters are few and far between as alliances and vendettas enjoy a constant fluidity, providing unnerving tension between players and suspense for viewers, who observe how the forces of coincidence and irony act as fuel for the narrative. Indeed, the key plot point of Walt's brother-in-law

Hank Schrader as a Drug Enforcement Administration agent acts not only as incredibly effective dramatic irony but also as the impetus for many of Walt's decisions and his attempts to skirt justice as Hank's work leads him on the trail of Heisenberg's trademark 99-plus-percent-pure blue methamphetamine. The contrasting nature of both Walt and Heisenberg to Hank and the very fact that there is a Walt and a Heisenberg beg us to analyze the role of the double or doppelgänger within the series and to examine other works that may aid in this analysis. That many additional characters participate in the conscious or unconscious act of doubling or act as doubles for others only intensifies the examination.

Much of the literary tradition of the double is rooted in the work of the German Romantics, who were primarily influenced by both folklore and early psychological theories, namely Franz Anton Mesmer's theories of dual consciousness (Tymms 1949, 28). Grillparzer's dream-play *Der Traum ein Leben* (1934) features Rostan, a protagonist quite reminiscent of Walt in that he has an ambitious Napoleonic nature that grows in strength and begins to supplant his habitually peaceful and contented tastes as he becomes an ambitious criminal (81). Literary theorist Ralph Tymms posits that because all the play's action happens in a dream—the place in which the second self is often revealed to its full extent—Rostan is able to realize his true nature without incurring the guilt of his crimes: "the dreams do not create the wishes, they awaken those already there, and the seed of what the morning now scares away lay hidden within you" (81). Unfortunately for Walt, his crimes do not take place in a dream, and his second self is not something that comes and goes each night; it is an active part of himself whose role in his decision-making and moral reasoning increases the longer he continues to lead a double life. Heisenberg differs from most doppelgängers in that there is neither a completely separate personality that struggles for dominance over Walt's consciousness nor a disparate entity, typically identical to the original character and usually having a similar background but being of a dissimilar nature. It doesn't appear that Walt has doubled himself in the sense that he has created an entirely different persona; to be sure, his primary personality changes as well, initially most notably with his sexuality— he becomes "frisky," as Skyler points out—but later in the way he takes things too far when sharing a drink with Junior, and eventually by taunting Hank with the notion that Gale, whom Hank has taken to be Heisenberg, had merely been a copycat, cooking with the formula of a much smarter individual, a comment that puts Hank back on Heisenberg's trail.

In order to determine the exact nature of the Heisenberg double we must first analyze its origin and purpose, which, although similar in many respects to other postmodern-era doubles, does differ in significant ways. Heisenberg, more than anything, is Walt's decision to live life on his own terms, to take and do as he sees fit, often for the betterment of his family financially but many times for the sheer thrill of it. Walt first uses the pseudonym when speaking with Skinny Pete while Jesse lies unconscious in the hospital, having been beaten and robbed of methamphetamine by Tuco. In a series of events foreshadowed by Walt's lecture on fulminated mercury, Walt shaves his head (beginning the Heisenberg look) and goes to see Tuco, demanding money for their methamphetamine and for Jesse's pain and suffering. When Tuco is uncooperative, Walt explodes the mercury in order to shock Tuco and make it known that he has the fortitude to back up his impeccable methamphetamine cooking skills with violence and chaos. The plan works and they set up a regular production schedule, the first meeting of which has Walt donning the porkpie hat, thus completing his Heisenberg look later seen in the sketch carried by Tuco's cousins. The persona may be Walt's way of coping with the harsh realities of being diagnosed with cancer, and later the trauma of the drug industry, for his cancer precedes his decision to cook, though he creates the distinct alias within which to operate in his second life only after encountering violence.

It may even be fruitful to view Heisenberg as an extension of Walt's personality prior to leaving Gray Matter and settling down with Skyler. Throughout the series, particularly in the fifth season, though as early as the opening scene of the pilot, which reveals a plaque awarded to Walt for research contributing to a Nobel Prize, we learn of a Walt who was responsible for founding and building what would become a multibillion-dollar company, although he took a buyout of $5,000 long before it took off. In the end, his methamphetamine empire is his second chance at leading the successful, exciting life he missed long ago, and it is all that he has left, as he relates to Jesse when Jesse and Mike want to sell their share of the methylamine they have procured from a train robbery. Gretchen and Elliot of Gray Matter consistently embody Walt's missed opportunity, especially when they assert on television that Walt's only contribution to the company's founding was naming it. The conjunction of their assertion with hearing from Walt Jr. that the family doesn't want his money gives Walt the second wind to carry out his final plan, which uses Gretchen and Elliot to deliver the money to his family.

Two films are especially relevant in aiding our analysis at this point: *Fight Club* (1999) and *The Dark Half* (1993). Both feature individuals with doppelgängers who redress their own physical, emotional, sexual, and spiritual shortcomings. Tyler Durden (Brad Pitt) and George Stark (Timothy Hutton) exhibit the traits that both films' protagonists wish to possess. (Although both are adapted from novels, the films alone are referred to here for brevity.)

> All the ways you wish you could be, that's me. I look like you wanna look, I fuck like you wanna fuck. I am smart, capable, and most importantly, I am free in all the ways that you are not.
> (Tyler Durden to Narrator)

> Part of me has always admired George Stark. I admired his simple violent nature. A man who doesn't stumble over things, who never looks weak or silly. A man with a straight sharp answer for everything.
> (Thad Beaumont [the writer doubled by Stark])

Like Heisenberg, Tyler Durden is created out of the desperation of a quiet, scared, boring, nameless individual (Edward Norton). Stark, however, recalls the most reproduced form of the doppelgänger, the one who takes the form of a physically separate individual who looks uncannily similar to his genius (with both played by Hutton), but who is quite unlike him in personality and habit. Stark is the result of a spirit that entered an undeveloped twin dormant inside Thad's brain when he began writing as a child. The tumor's removal produced a horrific flock of sparrows that swarmed the hospital, acting as psychopomps for Stark, and later return when Thad reveals that he is the author of Stark's books. They eventually pick him apart when Thad finally overcomes his need for a dark half to live out his unconscious desires, which, in the form of Stark, are threatening his family. Durden, on the other hand, is a dissociative double: a separate personality who does not resemble the Narrator—the Narrator hallucinates him as another entity altogether—but who completely takes over his consciousness for long periods of time. Both narratives offer variations on the common ending of protagonist killing his double only to find himself mortally wounded: Stark cannot kill Thad or he also will die, and he isn't finally killed himself until Thad lets his dark side go; similarly Durden only dies when the Narrator shoots himself in the mouth in a self-sacrificing yet surprisingly nonlethal way, after he finds that shooting and hitting Durden are futile because he is only hitting himself or the air.

Establishing that Heisenberg has Walt's personality and connection to reality, as well as his physical body, is paramount for contextualizing their relationship within the history of the double as a narrative device and psychological event. The lack of paranormal phenomena in *Breaking Bad* lends realism to the doubling and further corroborates our identification of the show's doubling as frequently being the "allegorical" version of the theme, in Tymms's term, which loses the supernatural, external doppelgänger in favor of an internal struggle between good and evil (Tymms 1949, 120). In fact, improbability is the most abnormal (and certainly not paranormal) element within the series; Walt and others are often seen reeling with random and unlikely events that both save and destroy lives indiscriminately. The most notable of these events occurs in the bottleneck episode "Fly," in which Walt reflects on what would have been the perfect time to die, specifically the night Jesse's girlfriend Jane died when Walt, ironically and unknowingly, had a conversation with her father in a bar. With a protagonist whose alter ego is named after the father of the uncertainty principle, it is quite fitting that the series' characters are constantly relying and reflecting upon the uncertain and improbable actions of others and of the universe itself—as in the case of Skyler's impromptu lie about Walt having earned his money gambling using a mathematical probability system. The believable and often mundane actions of the characters help to anchor the fantastic happenstances occurring within the narrative. Other examples are Walt's participation in school events; Jesse's problems with his family as his social life evolves; and Walter Jr.'s fairly commonplace existence, unnoticeable except for his disability. The point is that the series is consciously rooted in a realistic, material world, and Walt is completely connected with all aspects of his personality and persona and not subject to delusion or dissociation—proven by his employment of a fugue state as an excuse for being gone from the home for days and his later "admitting" to a psychoanalyst that he just wanted to get away.

A brief exploration of an evolution of psychological theories is useful for us to understand exactly where these doubles come from. In *Das Doppel-Ich*, Max Dessoir draws upon the findings of late nineteenth-century experimental psychologists, positing that dual personality to some extent is a normal phenomenon, emanating from two spheres of consciousness, one that performs automatic actions without conscious mental effort (Tymms 1949, 106). This work confirms much of the romantic and Mesmeric notions of the double, and "following Jung's interpretation, psychologists have described 'emotionally stressed complexes' as being 'bundles of psychic energy' that have become inaccessible to the normal consciousness, and exist only in the subconscious mind; through the re-agency of emotional crises, however, these split-off parts of the psyche may once more become accessible to the normal consciousness, and even dominate it, as if a second personality were ruling the mind" (107). This theory certainly holds true for Durden and (almost too literally) Stark; and it appears to be the case that the emotional crisis of being diagnosed with terminal cancer and having nothing to leave his family is the initial cause of Walt's actions. In the case of Heisenberg, however, we don't appear to be dealing with a malignant double who seeks to harm or taunt Walt or necessarily overtake his personality. In fact, Heisenberg appears to be highly beneficial for Walt as he breaks free from his dull exterior and becomes a virile, dominating individual who takes charge of what little life he has left. Heisenberg is a call to the life that Walt has always wanted for himself, after living so long as a quiet, meek individual; as he states to Jesse when handing him all his money to buy an RV for them to use as a rolling methamphetamine laboratory: "I am awake," implying that up to this point he had been in a slumber consisting of the banality of his overly average life, which is reinforced several times by Hank's various comments to Marie about Walt's boring, marginal personality and life. At one point Walt recalls being kept awake at night before his cancer diagnosis, lying in bed afraid of what might happen to himself and his family, but after receiving his diagnosis, sleeping like a baby.

Pinpointing the exact event that has led Walt to embark upon a second life as a methamphetamine cook operating under a pseudonym may not be entirely necessary for our analysis; after all it's clear enough that it is some combination of his diagnosis, the opportunities in life that he has missed, and the financial state of his family—which is the excuse Walt himself gives for his actions until his final scene with Skyler in which he confesses he did those things because he enjoyed them. To this end, in addition to the theories of Dessoir and Jung, which represent the psychological realist observing in actual practice the signs of an analogous dualism within man's personality, it is important that we also examine the views of the allegorist starting out from a purely theoretical and preconceived moral hypothesis of man's ethical dualism (Tymms 1949, 114). The allegorist Werfel formulates his views in his explanation of his play *Spiegelmensch*:

> The human personality embraces as its most powerful extremes two persons, . . . the *actual* self and the *apparent*, or *mirror* self. At the moment when man begins to criticize his consciousness (awakening of spirituality) he splits up: i.e. these two persons come to life, to battle with one another. Actual-self pines for absolute, complete, unimpeachable reality; apparent-self lures one towards the enjoyment of mirror-reality (unreality). (Quoted in Tymms, 114)

Werfel uses this mirror-symbolism to build an allegory of the "self-conqueror," or *Selbstbekrieger*, who saves his life by losing it and, by freeing himself from his evil self, finds harmony by a "miracle" (116). Walt's character and his double aren't subject exclusively to either an allegorical or a realist analysis, but the concept of the mirror-self is prevalent in the series. The relationship between Walt and Heisenberg is one of a once-lost passionate, brilliant, and vital personality that is resurfacing in a dark, antagonistic way, replacing the years of status quo and the mundane that laid the groundwork for Walt's mirror-self. Walt's "awakening," which began with his diagnosis, is the initial crack in this mirror-self, the image he has shown the world and even himself for so long, and very quickly it takes him to a place where he is a criminal pretending to be a normal person for the sake of his family, rather than a normal person who is pretending to be a criminal to secure their future after he is gone. Indeed, the few successful lectures he gives at school revolve around his own transformation: the fulminated-mercury lecture precedes his use of it on Tuco; the lecture about the inventor of the man-made diamond being given a small savings bond by the General Electric Company for a product that made them many millions of dollars is clearly reflective of Walt's involvement in Gray Matter; and most important, his lecture on chirality—the ability of things to look identical but behave differently because of extremely minute differences in their composition—is self-reflexive of his double life and echoes a lot of our own mirror-self conversation.

It's not difficult to see that many characters in the show have their own mirror and true selves, some more obviously than others. Gustavo Fring may be the most blatant example, a former military figure from Chile who hides in plain sight, having immigrated first to Mexico and then the

United States on the premise of being a fast-food entrepreneur, but who in reality is a distributor for the cartel. Fring's rigid, polished manner helps to secure the weight his mirror-self must be able to hold, being a public figure. The few times he appears to show emotion or concern are often deadly and always part of a deeper ruse. In fact, the relationship Gus has with Mike reflects Walt and Jesse's initial brains-and-street relationship, and another is the original partnership of Gus and his "brother," a highly trained chemist who mentions that the chirality of his methamphetamine creates a much different product from what was currently available, again very reflective of Walt and Jesse. Saul Goodman also hides in plain sight as an obnoxious buffoon of a criminal attorney, when in reality, as Jesse points out, he is a *criminal* attorney, quickly forming a partnership with Walt and Jesse and being instrumental in countless criminal activities, always with an eye on the bottom line and his own welfare. Ironically, and possibly self-reflexively, Marie, ostensibly one of the most static characters in the series (symbolically reiterated by her purpl-ing of everything she owns and wears), in one incident begins attending open houses with a series of assumed identities and complex back stories. Calling Marie static is not to say that she is without her skeletons in the closet, but hers is not a dynamic existence; she's forever the neurotic sister who engages in petty crime, seemingly as comic relief for the major crimes and life problems of everyone else. The two most important men in her life (Hank and Walt) are undergoing the two biggest personality crises in the series, and she deals with her stress from being stuck at home with Hank by playing pretend with realtors.

The remaining characters who are experiencing the same kind of *Selbstbekrieger* journey that Walt is on are Jesse and Hank, who, not surprisingly, function as Walt's two most important doubles in a broader sense of that term. Jesse and Walt enjoy a relationship reflective (coincidentally) of Jean Paul Richter's twin brothers Walt and Vult, who are of contrasting appearance and temperament but share a strong emotional bond that is an extension of their complementary personalities (Tymms 1949, 31). Their unlikely partnership is frequently put to the test by their own personalities, but it is one they're never fully able to escape even when they try to leave the other behind and, eventually, when Jesse tries to bring Walt down and Walt tries to kill him. Walt, constantly nitpicky and fatherly, often causes them both trouble by giving Jesse orders without further explanation, most notably in the disposal of Emilio's body with hydrofluoric acid, which Jesse was supposed to undertake in plastic tubs but doesn't, resulting in plenty of gore and a giant hole in the floor. Jesse's erratic behavior and drug addiction also stress the relationship and reinforce Walt's role as the dominant father figure and Jesse's as the troubled child, which makes sense because Jesse's own true self is that of a young boy, in spite of the mirror self-image of criminal drug dealer he so frequently tries to portray.

The evidence for the childlikeness of Jesse's true self exists not only in things we see Jesse say and do, but more frequently in things that happen to him, namely that his own fate, and to a great extent the entire narrative, is highly influenced by his interactions with young boys. For example, at the beginning of "Peekaboo" (season 2, episode 6) we find Jesse standing by train tracks playing with a cockroach, letting it crawl over his hands, echoed by a similar scenario at the beginning of "Dead Freight" when Drew Sharp plays around with a tarantula before capturing it in a jar. In "Peekaboo," as Skinny Pete arrives to meet Jesse, Skinny Pete instinctively squashes the bug, echoing Hank's speech about criminals being like cockroaches to be stomped out without thought that he makes at the end of the previous episode, but also, in the context of the connection to Drew Sharp, tying the bugs and their fate to the fate of the young. Jesse spends the majority of "Peekaboo" trying to recover methamphetamine (or money to replace it) from Spooge and Spooge's Lady, a junkie couple who also have a small boy, clearly neglected, as he is filthy and underfed. Jesse identifies with the boy because he himself has recently been evicted, lost both his vehicles, and at one point was covered in sewage from a portable toilet. Jesse tries to care for the boy and eventually, after Spooge's Lady kills Spooge, frees him by calling the police and telling him to have a good life.

Though the incident shows Jesse's concern for the young boy, it also leaves him with a reputation for violence, which gives him the confidence to expand the operation, which, in turn, leads to Combo's being shot and killed by Tomás, another young boy. Combo's death has the initial consequence of retriggering Jesse's use of methamphetamine, which leads to his and Jane's using heroin together and her eventual death, and it is also the impetus for finding Fring. Later, after finding out that Tomás was the one responsible for Combo, Jesse confronts Fring about using children in the organization, which he agrees no longer to do. But here, too, Jesse's concern for a child mixes with escalating conflict, since Jesse's intervention results in the murder of Tomás, and Walt and Jesse never recover from the strain put on the relationship with Fring caused by Walt's killing Tomás's killers. Consequently, while trying to assassinate Fring, Walt poisons Andrea's son Brock in order to get Jesse actively involved and back on his side, claiming that Gus used the ricin Jesse is missing to get Jesse to kill Walt. After telling Andrea about the ricin, Jesse is detained by the police and has time to recall his visit to Salamanca with Fring, giving Walt a window to kill Gus.

In another series of events that cause Jesse's compassion for the young to have violent consequences, during the train heist in "Dead Freight," Jesse, while trying to avoid bloodshed, makes comments that lead Todd to kill Drew Sharp as thoughtlessly as Pete killed the roach. This action leads to Jesse's feud with Todd and to Jesse and Mike's plan to sell their end of the methylamine to Fring's competitor Declan. In addition, Jesse's concern for Brock's welfare precipitates more violence when, later, after finding out that Walt was behind Brock's poisoning, Jesse colludes with Hank to bring him down. This, ultimately, leads to the deaths of Hank and Gomez by Todd's uncle Jack and his gang, as well as the end of both Walt's career as a meth lord and his relationship with his family. Eventually Jesse, while being held captive, is forced by Jack's gang to cook methamphetamine in order to save the life of another child, Brock. Later, Brock's mother Andrea is murdered by the gang as retribution for Jesse's failed escape attempt. In each of these cases, while trying to aid children, Jesse unwittingly steers the course of the narrative to more violence and death.

Opposite Jesse, as Walt's other frequent double, is Hank. Throughout the series Hank becomes obsessed with bringing the notorious meth lord Heisenberg to justice, sacrificing his own career, his health, and, finally, his life. In the family setting Hank doubles Walt as a foil, and a sharp contrast exists between their mild and *muy caliente* personalities from the very first time we see them together. So, too, is Hank a foil for Heisenberg in the drug world—the tireless but frequently unsuccessful DEA agent always pursuing Heisenberg's trademark blue methamphetamine. Their mirror and true selves are also dissonant: Walt, faced with death, grows stronger while developing his Heisenberg persona, beating cancer, and making millions of dollars; on the other hand, Hank, after the shootout with Tuco, begins having panic attacks and flashbacks that increase after he narrowly avoids a bomb that kills several agents in El Paso. After beating Jesse and hospitalizing him, Hank confesses to Marie that he has lost his virility, that he's done as a lawman, which is only confirmed when the

Salamanca cousins cripple him in an assassination attempt orchestrated and purposely botched by Fring in order to gain control of the industry. This reciprocal arc between the rise of Heisenberg and the fall of Hank is mirrored by Walt's successful battle with cancer and Hank's becoming disabled. In fact, after Hank begins to reestablish his personal hunt for Heisenberg via Gale and Fring, Walt finds himself in danger of being killed by Gus. At one point they are both trying to bring down Gus, Walt by killing him and Hank by gathering evidence with Walt as his driver, until Walt injures both of them by causing a traffic accident in order to avoid going to the laundromat where Fring's methamphetamine laboratory is housed. Eventually Walt, after killing Fring, finds himself jobless and penniless, while Hank is walking again and being promoted to Assistant Special Agent in Charge. Walt has to rebuild his methamphetamine business, meeting with failure and tragedy every step along the way, but he eventually succeeds precisely at the time when Hank is reprimanded for his continued pursuit of Heisenberg. Hank, however, continues to pursue Heisenberg, whom he eventually identifies as Walt, and Walt, no longer in remission, is once more dying of cancer.

This systematic arc between Walt and Hank is echoed by the use of a classic tragic cycle in which the two men employ a similar model of behavior and each becomes a nemesis of the other. In a theoretical sense, there is a possibility that Walt's entire decision to become involved in the methamphetamine trade was triggered by events surrounding Hank's brash challenge for him to come on a ride-along to a methamphetamine bust. In fact, that event, which takes place at Walt's birthday party, employs a common tragic device: Hank, in an act of hubris, diverts the attention of the crowd from Walt and onto his own televised methamphetamine bust, which also allows Walt to see the amount of money one could make from cooking the drug. Having emasculated Walt jokingly in front of everyone, including Walter Jr., Hank continues the cycle on his path into ate (which is distinct from the manly pride connotation of hubris), characterized by blind, arrogant acts that anger the gods—which Hank achieves by toasting Walt with further joking insults and, most important, taking Walt's beer out of his hand and drinking it at the toast. Heisenberg is the nemesis created by Hank's participation in the classical equation hubris → ate → nemesis. This dynamic would explain why the virility of the one man seems to come with the weakening of the other, their connection highlighted when they are treated at the same hospital, as Walt points out, and why Hank's retribution comes at the hands of Tuco's cousins, who were originally seeking to kill Walt.

The preceding explains the first half of the cycle, but what could explain Hank's reemergence to health and Walt's downfall? The initial urge is to look at the poisoning of Brock, which does create a nemesis of Jesse in the end, but Hank had already been investigating Fring by that point. In fact, it is the night that Walt, having been removed from Hank's crosshairs by the murder of Gale (who everyone is convinced is Heisenberg), proceeds to get drunk and challenge Hank. He begins by speaking ill of Gale, saying that from what he saw in the notebook Gale is no great scientist, that there doesn't appear to be any clear deductive reasoning in the notes, just a recipe written by what is probably a much smarter individual. He goes on, at the frightened astonishment of Skyler, to posit that Hank's Heisenberg might still be out there, effectively saying, "Try to catch me; I'm right in front of you and you don't even know it." Of course, Hank responds the next morning by reopening the case and recommitting himself to his search and his physical therapy, thus becoming Heisenberg's nemesis.

After Hank dies and Walt loses his family, there is little left for Walt to do but hide out and regroup, withering away from cancer in a cabin in New Hampshire. Miraculously, he does return to New Mexico and is able to make a way for his money to reach his family. Walt ultimately sacrifices himself in the *Selbstbekrieger* tradition, and although his motives aren't completely clear, he does destroy what has become of his methamphetamine empire, further ensuring the safety of his family and freeing Jesse from his bondage to Jack's gang. There is a clear self-determined redemption in his actions, but he has no remorse or justification for them, as we can see when he tells Skyler that he did everything because he liked it. This fact is also clear when he coldly tells Lydia that he has poisoned her, and when he fearlessly hands Jesse the gun, telling Jesse to kill him. Rejecting Walt's offer, Jesse speeds off into the night, leaving Walt lying on the floor of the destroyed methamphetamine laboratory, succumbing to a hidden wound from the Elmore Leonard–esque oscillating machine gun he devised to kill Jack's gang.

> Once he has freed himself from his false and evil mirror-self by the
> voluntary death of the better self, the man can awaken to a new life,
> in which he has no reflection; for in this Nirvana, in which conflict
> and effort have ceased, he is no longer divided into real and false

selves: he no longer sees his selfish ego projected into everything around him, and his vanity is cured. Harmony (the synthesis of "comprehension") has brought his spiritual *Doppelgangertum* to an end. (Tymms 1949, 116)

References

Fincher, David (director). 1999. *Fight Club*. Los Angeles, CA: 20th Century Fox.

Rank, Otto. 1971. *The Double: A Psychoanalytic Study*. Chapel Hill: University of North Carolina Press.

Romero, George A. (director). 1993. *The Dark Half*. Los Angeles, CA: Orion Pictures.

Tymms, Ralph. 1949. *Doubles in Literary Psychology*. Cambridge, UK: Bowes and Bowes.

Civilization and Its Discontents and Walter White's Individual Disorder in Seasons 1 and 2 of Breaking Bad

George Alexandre Ayres de Menezes Mousinho

The human conflicts in the AMC's television series *Breaking Bad* stem from several distinct motivations and frustrations that coexist mostly around the protagonist Walter White. The series introduces several characters that either are troubled by psychological or material pressures or are located outside the sphere of emotional conflicts—that is, members of law enforcement. In tackling controversial themes such as terminal diseases, narcotics trafficking, and family disruption and distrust, *Breaking Bad* works with both the social and the individual imaginaries to construct its narrative around contemporary dilemmas. As the television seasons come and go, it becomes more apparent that the chain of problematic events becomes ever more distant from the initial issue presented (terminal disease) and progressively infiltrates Walt's very behavior. The way in which he relates to the different strata of human contacts is how the series is guided most of the time. The spectator is given Walt's perspective, and it is through that perspective that his family, his workplace, and his frustrations are seen and measured; his judgments undermine or emphasize the many instances of anguish and disappointment befalling his persona throughout the narrative.

Walter White is the patriarch of a middle-class family in Albuquerque, New Mexico. He carries on a double-job life, working as a chemistry teacher at a local high school and as a cashier at a car wash. His wife, Skyler, is in early pregnancy at the beginning of the first season, and they seem to have an emotionally stable home life. The first episodes seem to focus repeatedly on the predicaments of Walt's daily life, the vexations of his jobs, and on how minor his roles—especially as a teacher—seem to the people who receive his services and sometimes to friends and family members. Students mock him and disregard his classes and teaching; and Bogdan, his employer at the car wash, puts Walt in charge of services he was not supposed to perform. In addition, the financial difficulties force him to stay in these contexts of humiliation, because the couple did not intend for Skyler to become pregnant, and because her pregnancy prevents her from working, Skyler cannot help Walt pay the bills. After finding out that he has lung cancer and that there is possibly a bleak future ahead, Walt fears for his family's well-being after he is no longer alive. These frustrations allow him to justify what happens next: his expertise in chemistry plus an accidental meeting with a former student, who is now a low-level drug dealer, make him believe he has a better chance at providing for his family's future if he embarks on the production of methamphetamine.

Sigmund Freud, in his work *Civilization and Its Discontents* (1962), argues about the clash between the individual and the society, the former's desires to express his or her inner feelings and to act freely, and the latter's contingencies that constantly keep those desires at bay. Freud proposes that a considerable part of the individual's anguish in life comes from the moral and organizational barriers imposed by the collective conventions. Subsequently, a myriad of subjective discontents arise in members of a disturbed society, each discontent with its own sources and constraints. Therefore, society increases the repression of individual interests and desires that would lead to the formation of new values and goals. When an individual violates a tenet of societal organization or progress, the consequences might be penal confinement or worse, such as mob threats.

Freud elaborates that the individual then feels "the urge for freedom," which is "directed against particular forms of and demands of civilization or against civilization altogether" (43). At this critical moment, the subjective motivations revolt and turn against the inner workings of the collective, defying the social and moral matrix and the conventional notions of law. Generally, these motivations awaken from a realization of "what is internal—what belongs to the ego—and what is external—what emanates from the outer world" (14). That realization, Freud claims, is the basis for the repression of the individual and the origin of the discontent:

> This differentiation [between what is internal and what is external], of course, serves the practical purpose of enabling one to defend oneself against sensations of unpleasure which one actually feels or with which one is threatened. In order to fend off certain unpleasurable excitations arising from within, the ego can use no other methods than those with which it uses against unpleasure coming from without, and this is the starting-point of important pathological disturbances. (15)

The conflict between elements of discontent—from within and without—creates the dissatisfaction that leads the individual to act against his or her macrocosm. The ambiguous motivations for the discontent may then confuse an individual, creating the belief that the troubles come from without when they may originate substantially from within. It is in this ambiguous territory that Walt belongs. Consequently, the objective of this analysis is to lead a thematic investigation of the first two seasons of *Breaking Bad*, centering on the character of Walter White (but scrutinizing his relations with the most notable characters surrounding him as well) from the standpoint of *Civilization and Its Discontents*, especially when referring to the clash between the interests of the collective and those of the subjective. In order to investigate such a thematic connection, one must bear in mind that "we tend to think of character—of people, to begin with—in terms of conflict, which may be moral, social, or psychological in nature" (Hochman 1985, 51). Characters are conceived in fiction as representations of real-world issues and often existential dilemmas, and in most audiovisual drama "our experience of characters is shaped in terms of *allegiance*, that is, in moral and emotional terms, by the manner in which the narrative represents them as (for example) generous or mean, brave or cowardly, diligent or irresponsible" (Smith 2010, 234).

As regards context, Walter White lives in Albuquerque, an urban area four hours from the Mexican-American border and thus a zone of ethnic clash with conflicting cultural issues. There is a strong and stable niche of drug dealing in the city as well as covert disputes between the local dealers and manufacturers. Walt has to resort to the wilderness, a hostile environment composed of rocky barrens in a sunny region, places where such illegal activities are carried out. The series frequently frames these desolations as the common landscape around Albuquerque, and the series depicts it as an area where Walt hides to become his other persona. In the pilot of the series, the initial sequence shows Walt in a flash-forward, driving away from the scene where he has just cooked methamphetamine, establishing the landscape as a danger zone, a transition from civility to barbarism, from legality to transgression, and from conventions to criminal secrets. Sirens are heard, a sign of lawful intervention, which Walt fears and anticipates as his demise. Therefore, the deserts of New Mexico can represent a zone of transgression, paranoia, and natural hostility alike. At the start, however, Walt acts solely from the comfortable position of his own world, the city's middle-class universe of families, some of which he relates to (his relatives Hank and Marie Schrader and former associates Elliot and Gretchen Schwartz). At the beginning of the series he is turning fifty years old, and the editing of the series as well as the framing of his mannerisms seem to focus on his solemn behavior as a reflective man who starts to think about his life's objectives and the future of his family, through the lengthy shots of his reserved countenance and the close-ups of his thoughtful gazes.

Consequently, the initial episodes of the series depict the transitions of emotion in Walt's life, the fragmentation of his stability as a family man, and his own perspective on the world around him. When he is given the initial news about his cancer, he goes through a moment of anguish about the direction that his life is veering toward. Walt apparently feels that his life should have been more unconventional, and his views on what is right or wrong begin to transform. His views on life and death also intensify: He is seen giving more attention to Skyler's body, as though he were contemplating the new life as a continuity of his own and his new child as a contrast to his decaying life. He then idealizes his family as an impenetrable entity, a sacred entity that is his ultimate belief rather than real people who share their lives with him. He seems to internalize that notion and make it part of his own psyche and instincts, the driving force that makes him confront his discontents and, at the same time, lose awareness of the consequences of his actions. Moreover, as he discovers the world of drug dealing and considers his options to participate in that world, he ambiguously tries to use his family as a motivation to start his activities and to profit from them, but he also tries to keep his family away from his business and from involvement with criminal individuals. His family and his bonds to it are, paradoxically, both the starting point and the main obstacle to his second life.

Freud (1962) delineates three directions as possible sources of human suffering and anguish: "from our own body, which is doomed to decay and dissolution . . . ; from the external world, which may rage against us with overwhelming and merciless forces of destruction; and finally from our relations to other men" (24). In the case of Walter White, such directions can be associated with his illness, with his manipulation of nature through his chemical knowledge, and with the possibilities of intervention from people related to him. As regards the first direction, the lung cancer is a strong indication that his perspective on his existence has been rendered more pessimistic, as though he perceived such an existence to be more ephemeral and fragile. His body becomes a barrier to his happiness and peace of mind and sets up a countdown that dictates the urgency and continuity of his actions in order to secure his family's welfare in the future. His chemotherapy's effects on his body, such as hair loss and nausea, seem representative of the weakening of the body with age. Traces of reflexive melancholy can be noticed in his countenance (in season 1, episode 6) as he feels the strength of the treatment affecting his vitality, an anguish that calls for the urgency of his secret actions.

Freud's second direction could be derived not from the anguish caused by the destructive forces of nature, but instead from the ways that Walt finds to defy nature and manipulate its principles to create a drug that will both ensure his family's comfort and reiterate his position as a chemist. Such a manipulation is an attempt to redirect his libidinal orientations—his instinctual pleasures and accomplishments—since "another technique for fending off suffering is the employment of the displacements of libido which our mental apparatus permits. . . . One gains the most if one can sufficiently heighten the yield of pleasure from the sources of psychical and intellectual work" (Freud 1962, 26). Walt could never attain his dream of becoming a successful chemist, nor those of sharing the achievements of Gray Matter Technologies (a company that he founded with Elliot Schwartz), which adds to his failure in alluring any attention or interest from his students. He feels as though his full potential is not properly recognized and is unjustly crystallized in the bureaucratic work of a teacher, a conventional and disregarded member of the public service. For better or worse, Walt has to put his expertise to some use, and it is in doing what he does best—cooking high-quality methamphetamine—that he finds his scientific niche and his subconscious pleasure. We are introduced to Elliot Schwartz in the episode "Gray Matter" (season 1, episode 5), which also depicts Schwartz's attempt to persuade Walt into accepting a friendly donation to help him pay for his chemotherapy. Walt politely declines the offer and vaguely justifies his decision to Skyler with the promise that he will sort out the situation in the end. That, in itself, conveys the idea that his wish to manufacture drugs is due not only to financial constraints but also to his own pride and the expression of his individuality as a man who wants to demonstrate that he is capable of doing what no one else can with the knowledge that he possesses, regardless of the legal implications (because, for him, the very notion of legality is imprecise and prone to subjective judgment).

Finally, there is the third direction: his relation to other people as a source of his suffering. Despite having the family as one motivation and his will to survive the cancer as another, Walt still experiences moments of discontent, with Skyler and Walt Jr. providing constraints on his personal desires. In addition to the problems of adolescence, Walt Jr. witnesses his parents' marriage sinking into a chasm of disagreement, distrust, and chaos. In "Cat's in the Bag" (season 1, episode 2), Skyler has suspicions about Walt's strange behavior—the first indication that their marriage is in trouble. Caught in the middle, Walt Jr. is in the position of the son who has to cope with various crises of his parents and also to mediate their arguments. Their unborn baby serves as a reminder to Walt that he may not be there when the child is born, which saddens him and makes him wonder about the existence of a world without him and his dreams and passions. The child is the legacy, but so is the fear in an unknown future. She means hope, but also death; she means happiness, but also anxiety and an anticipated feeling of longing. According to Freud (1962), the modern-day aspirations and benefits of having children clash directly with the "difficult conditions for our sexual life in marriage" (35). Skyler's pregnancy was unintended, which raises problems that are often subdued by the apparent value of family and the emotional prize—the arrival of a new human life. Although treated as a blessing in disguise, it is one of the principal reasons that Walt feels the urge to make huge profits in a short time, awakening more anxiety and uncertainty as well as a fear of death. In the second season, the couple undergoes a distancing process that intensifies with the growth of Skyler's suspicions. Walt's overall feelings, however, culminate in an idealization of his family and a desire to shield it at all costs, but he relies almost completely on himself to accomplish his plans in his last months of life.

He will do anything to protect his family from the evil that stems from the criminal world with which he gets involved, and his protection fortifies his own image as a capable provider and a strong man. When discussing the traits of the primeval state of family in comparison with its development into a civilized state, Freud (1962) points out that one primitive trait lost in the contemporary world is "the arbitrary will of its head, the father" (47). Walt stops listening to advice from Skyler; instead, he makes his own decisions as he comes closer to a primitive state of violence, thus increasing his feelings of self-satisfaction and righteousness. He uses the argument of "doing it for the family" to justify his drug making, but he never backs down from crucial moments that might endanger his loved ones (for example, not getting personally involved with drug dealers who might snitch on him if caught—Badger and Skinny Pete—and not leaving evidence behind). Walt assumes that by acting in secrecy he is free from the dangers of retaliation against his relatives, but he repeatedly delves into the layers of criminality that can become points of no return.

A personal contact Walt does maintain is Jesse Pinkman. Jesse knows the intricacies of drug trading, he knows the effects caused by the drug they start manufacturing, and he knows some low-level dealers. While riding in a car with his brother-in-law Hank, a federal drug agent in Albuquerque, Walt sees Jesse jumping out of a window of a drug house while the police are searching the place, and he recognizes him as a former student. Later, Walt contacts Jesse, offering him a partnership in which Walt would be responsible for making the drug and Jesse for selling it, providing a good opportunity for both of them and a way for Walt to secure the financial future of his family. But Walt never really identifies with Jesse until later in the series. He constantly insults Jesse's intelligence, undermining his importance in their operations, but then he finds himself aiding Jesse when the latter falls into depression and resumes his drug addiction at the end of the second season. Until then, Walt's interest in him resides solely in the fact that Jesse has what he lacks: experience in the criminal world and few conventional social ties.

In fact, Jesse's main social ties are with his fellow drug users, young men familiar with methamphetamine and who know a good product from a bad one. They are Skinny Pete, Badger, and Combo, and they quickly realize that there is good profit in the blue-colored methamphetamine crystals that Jesse and Walt make. Walt is not interested in dealing directly with the distributive side of the business, because he does not want to encounter the criminal layers and expose himself. He and Jesse often argue about the division of labor, and his unwillingness to get involved with distribution makes Jesse skeptical about his commitment. In the episode ". . . And the Bag's in the River" (season 1, episode 3) Walt faces his first significant moral choice—what to do with the dealer called Krazy-8, who is a danger not only to their operations but also to their lives. Trapped in a moral dilemma and under the threat of being betrayed by Krazy-8, Walt ends up killing him and then agonizing over his action.

Soon after, Jesse and Walt begin a complex relationship: Jesse considers Walt not only a father figure but also a window through which he sees the civil and lawful side of life. By the beginning of the second season, Jesse thinks about leaving his drug dealing and starting a new life, but in the episode "Down" (season 2, episode 4) his relationship with his parents falls apart. Then, in the episode "Phoenix" (season 2, episode 12), Jane, his new girlfriend, awakens in him the desire to change his life and move to another country. She tries to separate Jesse from Walt, manipulating Jesse into doing what is in her best interests while blackmailing Walt because Walt does not intend to give Jesse his half of the drug money. Simultaneously, through his contact with Jesse, Walt learns the ways of distribution and has an opportunity to become a powerful drug kingpin. During these changes, Jesse is repeatedly dragged into dangerous operations without having any solid perspective on his future or where his values are, while Walt becomes a man of unshakable resolve.

One source of Walt's discontent is the relationship with his brother-in-law, Hank, the drug agent. Freud describes the intricacies of law functioning as the ultimate restrainer of the individual pleasure set up by civil authority; he states:

> Human life in common is only made possible when a majority comes together which is stronger than any separate individual and which remains united against all separate individuals. The power of this community is then set up as "right" in opposition to the power of the individual, which is condemned as "brute force." This replacement of the

power of the individual by the power of a community constitutes the decisive step of civilization. The essence of it lies in the fact that the members of the community restrict themselves in their possibilities of satisfaction, whereas the individual knew no such restrictions. The first requisite of civilization, therefore, is that of justice . . . the assurance that a law once made will not be broken in favor of an individual. (42)

This provides the summary of how society's notions of law and justice represent the forces that attempt to end Walt's activities after he "breaks bad." That system of law and justice is personified by Hank, whose haughty demeanor indicates his position as a narcissistic member of law enforcement. His comments about his job during family meals usually upset or disconcert Walt, for he feels the constant pressure of the law-enforcement institutions that represent the most direct form of society's protection against its own individuals. Furthermore, in a conversation with Walt during Skyler's baby shower in the episode "A No-Rough-Stuff-Type Deal" (season 1, episode 7), Hank admits that methamphetamine used to be legal, which brings to the fore the discussion of legal disparity and relativity. Hank himself smokes a Cuban cigar, illegal for US citizens at the time the episode represents. Likewise, alcohol—a socially accepted drug in the contemporary Western world—went through a period of illegality in the early twentieth-century United States, and so the series proposes a discussion on the consistency of drug prohibition and the constraint of individual liberty. On a similar note, Hank is the indirect connection between Walt and drug making, since he took Walt on a ride-along to witness a search being conducted in the house from which Jesse escaped. In sum, Hank is the connection between Walt and the drug underworld, a restraint to Walt's activities—through the investigation of his operations—and a representative of the law's inconsistencies and ambiguities.

A more ambiguous member of the justice system in the series is Saul Goodman. A clownish and loquacious character, Goodman is a skillful criminal defense attorney famous for television advertisements that conclude with the slogan "Better Call Saul" (also the name of the second-season episode in which he makes his first appearance). The slogan itself is based on the premise that, if one finds oneself in trouble with the police, one should call Saul for help. Walt and Jesse find in Goodman a willing companion and a legal counselor to aid them in their criminal enterprise. Saul can then be considered the opposite of Hank: While Hank's actions create obstacles to

Walt's success, Saul's are intimately connected to his client's interests, and he becomes an ally later in the series. As the second season concludes, Saul becomes an agent of chaos within the justice system, bending rules and finding loopholes. He is the most significant character in manipulating the law and in facilitating Walt's efforts. Through their chaotic meetings, their relationship conveys the idea that Saul is the restorer of balance whenever Walt's predicaments and discontents related to law enforcement are about to come apart.

Breaking Bad entices discussions that transcend the issues of televised media and popular culture. Its flawed characters and its morality—or lack of any moral system whatsoever—emanate discord and conflict. Walter White fits into a category of amoral characters, individuals who doubt the effectiveness of civilized conventions that demand that citizens be docile and obedient, discontented and unaccomplished. Freud (1962) argues that "a person becomes neurotic because he cannot tolerate the amount of frustration which society imposes on him in the service of its cultural ideals" (34); witnessing Jesse climbing out a window in the first episode is Walt's moment of realization, the moment that awakens him to his own potential. He sees an opportunity for success in his own desperate situation, but he also sees a chance to flirt with transgression as an adventure beyond the normativity of civil behavior. Whatever Walt is like prior to the discovery of his lung cancer—the watershed moment that triggers the main drama of the series—the facts from then on are detailed and socially subversive. Walter White turns into Heisenberg, his alter ego, the code-name chosen to initiate his freer persona, his truer and individualistic self. The viewer is left with Heisenberg, not Walter White—the family man who broke bad in order to defend his interests and avoid the frustration and displeasure that tormented his life.

References

Freud, Sigmund. 1962. *Civilization and Its Discontents*. Translated by James Stratchey. New York: W. W. Norton.

Hochman, Baruch. 1985. *Character in Literature*. New York: Cornell University Press.

Smith, Murray. 2010. "*Engaging Characters*: Further Reflections." In *Characters in Fictional Worlds: Understanding Imaginary Beings in Literature, Film, and Other Media*, edited by Jens Eder, Fotis Jannidis, and Ralf Schneider, 232–58. New York: De Gruyter.

Breaking Borders and *Breaking Bad*
Using Unconventional Choruses to Build a Narcotragedy

Maria O'Connell

Breaking Bad **ran** for an intense five seasons, chronicling the transformation of Walter White from a mild-mannered chemistry teacher and family man into a badass, very dangerous, nearly legendary methamphetamine dealer known as Heisenberg as well as his gradual fall from criminal grace. Along the way, the viewers are treated to an amazing score, as well as an outstanding selection of classic and contemporary rock, contemporary and classic Spanish-language ballads, corridos, and even an original narcocorrido called "Negro y Azul: The Ballad of Heisenberg." With an unlikely hero finding destiny and purpose in his ability to make methamphetamine and display his genius as a criminal mastermind, who is eventually caught in his own pride and destiny, the series is a modern take on a classical Greek tragedy. Playing on the gang and drug culture in the southwestern United States and on masculine values of violence, honor, and male leadership, the show makes Walter White into the classical male hero but places him in a morally ambiguous border situation. It is a new form of the old classics—*narcotragedy*. Within this structure, the music chosen in the series becomes a chorus filling gaps in the plot, predicting plot twists, and providing social commentary on the characters' actions. The varied musical styles and the choice to use music in both Spanish and English allow *Breaking Bad* to move the classic tragedy into contemporary conversations about law, morality, power, and borders.

Walter White as Tragic Hero

In 1957 William G. McCollom described a number of types of tragic heroes and their paths. Those categories still work today. Tragic heroes can be (a) fundamentally, but not completely, guilty; (b) significantly superior to the average person, but not good and bound to fall from some sort of tragic flaw; (c) guiltless but brought down by fate; or (d) guilty in some ways and yet admirable in others. The last category is perhaps most acceptable for a twenty-first-century tragedy, because "innocent or guilty, the hero must pursue his course because he is who he is. . . . Faced by terrible alternatives, he sees the evil in both" (McCollom 1957, 54). Greek theater and its themes exist in translation for us, and *Breaking Bad*, with its transgressive border crossings and multiple tensions, mirrors them while also translating the main themes into modern American anxieties and preoccupations. The series, like Greek tragedy itself, "provide[s] a metaphor for the balance between transmission and transformation" (Hardwick 2013, 322) that characterizes Walter White's dealings with the Mexican cartels. He finds his situation as a chemistry teacher with a partially disabled son and a pregnant wife almost completely untenable and feels that he has been denied greatness that should accompany his intellect and ability. He sees himself as a victim of circumstance: "My wife is seven months pregnant with a baby we didn't intend. My fifteen-year-old son has cerebral palsy. I am an extremely overqualified high school chemistry teacher. When I can work, I make $43,700 per year. I have watched all of my colleagues and friends surpass me in every way imaginable. And within eighteen months, I will be dead" (season 2, episode 3). For Walt, especially once he has money and recognition from his methamphetamine process, the violence and fear that are part of his other life are like a drug. Putting his family in danger and in the path of violence is untenable, but then so is giving up a life that gives him so much of what he wants.

McCollom (1957) writes that "the tragic hero is like all other men in that he is guilty of wrongdoing. But his guilt is difficult or impossible for him to avoid if he is to pursue the values he treasures" (55). The series makes universal guilt a strong theme, as the various people around Walter White are all more or less corrupt. His brother-in-law Hank is a Drug Enforcement Administration (DEA) agent with anger issues and contempt for the people he regulates, and Hank's wife is a kleptomaniac. Walt's wife, Skyler, discovers what Walt is doing and then proves to be quite good at managing the money-laundering end of the business. Saul Goodman, their lawyer, is a primer in corruption. Yet they are neither completely guilty nor completely innocent, and neither are most of the people with whom Walt deals in the drug business. Most have convinced themselves that their deeds are justified, and the inconsistency and moral ambiguity of the drug and border laws makes moral judgments difficult. In addition, the political situation at the border, the US history with Latin America, and the sheer amount of consumption of illegal drugs in the United States make for a critique of the US War on Drugs and our own role in the violence and mayhem of the cartels.

Walt enters the world of the cartels in much the same way as the young men that are the traditional audience of the narcocorrido. This type of corrido is used to recruit new soldiers in the drug wars, to pay homage to the work of narco leaders, and to enforce the norms and expectations of their societies:

> The lavish way drug dealers show off their wealth in the communities in which they live—and the way they are celebrated in such popular entertainments as the "narcocorrido" ballads—ignites hopes and dreams among younger, adventurous, and more ambitious members of society. Particularly if they have no education or technical skills, they soon realize that the American dream will take them a lifetime to accomplish and they are neither able, nor willing to wait to cultivate the tools necessary to accomplish these goals through legitimate means. (Meráz 2006, 200)

Walt had once achieved the American dream and then lost it. His lung cancer and his age limit the time he has available to recover his former glory, and they also add to his resentment for his now humble lot in life. He sees someone like Jesse Pinkman with contempt and assumes that the people with whom he will deal will be just like Jesse. He shares the desire to be recognized for his dreams but only later comes to see that others of intelligence and ability are also in this world.

The Chorus

Breaking Bad could not be considered a traditional Greek tragedy in any fashion, yet Walter White's hubris, his struggles, his greatness, and his downfall point to something that might be considered a translation of the tragedy. In fact, the extensive use of music in the series and the manner in which the music sometimes comments on the action support such a reading. Bryan Cranston's brilliant acting adds to this sense. As Walt he is both likeable and attractive and, at the same time, able to reveal an inner ruthlessness and coldness. He often accomplishes this simply with a shift in expression, but the shift is startling and chilling. Viewers are often privy to this shift while he is negotiating with either his wife or his associates, and it becomes more apparent as the series continues.

In addition, the series transgresses boundaries and raises issues that are bound to make its viewers uncomfortable in that they address contemporary, often unresolved issues. In her essay on translating Greek plays, Lorna Hardwick (2013) notes that in classical Greece "Sophocles was playing with and adapting stories that were already present in the cultural field of Greek myth. . . . [But] what he selects, how he adapts or adds to the myth and how he uses the theatrical conventions of tragedy to meld together the mythical and the contemporary impact of the performance triggers the ways in which the spectators related the theatrical occasion to their own sense of cultural and civic identity" (327). In the same way, Vince Gilligan connects a traditional US story of the good man turned outlaw—in order to right some injustice—to a traditional cartel culture with its own sense of morality. He uses music from both sides of the border to provide a troubling commentary about what Walt is doing and how he views and treats others, both in his own US culture and in the cartels as well. In doing so, Gilligan employs choruses that are "representatives of communities within the world of the play" (328) as well as observers from outside that world, just as Sophocles did.

Most viewers of *Breaking Bad* would acknowledge that it is intensively musical. Music is featured in every episode and runs the gamut from classic rock and country to classic corridos and contemporary Mexican pop. Although setting the mood and signaling the social milieu is part of the chorus, I am interested in times when the music comments about Walt and his development into a criminal hero. These songs are picked because they are not playing in the background or in a car when something goes on; instead, they are featured. Like a classical chorus, the music almost becomes a character of its own at these moments. The songs are "Catch Yer Own Train" in season 1, episode 6; "Negro y Azul: The Ballad of Heisenberg" in season 2, episode 7; "He Venido" in season 3, episode 6; "Black" in season 4, episode 13; and the last song in the final season, "Baby Blue." The reader will note that two of the songs are in Spanish. The language is important when considering *Breaking Bad* as a translation of a classical tragedy that engages contemporary issues. Walt's actions do not just break him across the boundary between law-abiding chemistry teacher and drug gangster; they also reveal the ways that drugs and drug activity cross the borders between Mexico and the United States.

Season 1: "Catch Yer Own Train" Heralding Transformation

The future of Walt as a gangster, including his taste for violence and danger, is forecast at the end of season 1. In episode 6, aired on March 2, 2008, Walt makes Tuco capitulate about distributing Walt's product. He blows up the office with fulminated mercury—"a little tweak of chemistry" (season 1, episode 6). Tuco acknowledges Walt's "balls" and agrees to deal with him. The song "Catch Yer Own Train," by the Silver Seas, plays as Walt walks away from the office mayhem, gets in his car, and drives away. It is a moment of exhilaration for him and puts the lie to his earlier disavowal of violence. Walt likes the violence, and he likes the risk; it makes him feel alive. The song "Catch Yer Own Train" symbolizes Walt's embracing his power as a methamphetamine cook but also his releasing of a long-suppressed anger. Walt realizes that, in reference to his family, to his former colleagues, and even to the unexpectedly decent Jesse, he has no desire to be like them. He will take what he needs and they are on their own. He has long seen himself as a victim of others and as a failure because of his own weakness, but now he is coming into a world where both his brilliance and his manhood are being acknowledged. It is also a world where revenge is appropriate when someone does not have proper respect. Walt is becoming fully enmeshed in the gangster culture.

Season 2: "Negro Y Azul" and Cartel Culture

In order to signal Walt's shift to criminality, the writers bring in more
Mexican music and scenes of border culture, especially the drug culture.
When Los Cuates de Sinaloa opened episode 7 of season 2 in 2009 with
the corrido "Negro y Azul: The Ballad of Heisenberg," it caused a great
deal of comment and controversy. The group's reputation as singers of
serreno and the narcocorrido style of the song situated Walt's Heisenberg
persona as a player in the world of the Mexican cartels. It also showcased
the narcocorrido as herald, a message to all the participants of the cartel
culture about power shifts, insults, and revenge. The repeated refrain that
predicts a violent end for Walter White / Heisenberg is a warning and a
signal of the direction the story will take. Here Gilligan's use of a group
that is steeped in cartel culture and known for its narcoballads makes them
representatives of Walt's new, drug-dealing world. Their role here is to
establish something about the cartels and their own values. As Meráz
(2006) makes clear, the people in the cartels consider themselves a cohesive
group, so "group members will base [their] social identity on favourable
comparisons that can be made between in-groups and relevant out-groups"
(201). Walt challenges this social identity because he is a gringo from the
United States who is attempting to control the market. As the song notes,
the cartels perceive his presence and his power as a lack of respect. In the
second season, Walt discovers his talent both for cooking methamphetamine and for negotiating the cartels' culture of masculinity, pride, and
revenge. His increasing unwillingness to leave the culture, his pride in his
abilities, and the name he has made for himself, not to omit his highly
charged testosterone level, start his downfall. Viewers can see Walt falling
in love with his new persona and the power of violence.

As he moves forward with this persona, his appearance changes. He
adopts the hat and the scruff, moving ever farther from the mild-mannered,
teacherly appearance at the beginning. He would have to be the man that,
in Slotkin's (1998) terms, "knows Indians," or in this case narcos, and he
must be "marked by both 'nobility' and a propensity for savage violence"
(135), dominating the savagery of the cartels with his own smart and clin-
ical use of violence. Walt adopts the nom de guerre of Heisenberg both as
a way to protect himself and also as a way to project his superiority. He
likes the inside joke from quantum physics and feels the name expresses
his own intelligence. Meráz (2006) writes that "an individual with an

Anglo Saxon background has little to no possibility of being admitted into a drug smuggling organization whose membership is mostly of Latin American descent without contacts or knowledge of their culture, customs and values" (203). Walt feels that his new, superior method of cooking methamphetamine will carry him beyond those limitations, yet the narco-corrido makes it clear that he is heading for a fall and that he should be prepared to face a war.

Season 3: "He Venido" and The Erotics of Violence

By season 3, Walt, now known as Heisenberg, leaves behind his amateur status and becomes fully immersed in the criminal culture. One of the symbols of his new status is getting rid of the RV. He undertakes this without Jesse's permission (Jesse owns the RV) because, as he tells his lawyer, Saul, "[It] is covered with my fingerprints" and "it's only a matter of time before he [Hank] tracks it down." Saul tells him, "So get rid of it!" (season 3, episode 6). After a very close confrontation with Hank, Walt's DEA agent brother-in-law, the RV is finally crushed and the song "He Venido" plays. It is an old-fashioned bolero by the Cuban close-harmony group Los Zafiros. A slow love song, it hints at both the DEA's pursuit of Walt and Walt's coming into his own as a player in the world of the cartel. But by now he and Jesse are moving apart. Jesse, who resists violence and faces down Gus for using children in his operation, not only finds that he is a decent guy but tries to hold Walt to the same standard. However, his conscience only seems like weakness to Walt. As Jesse tells people in his group meeting, "My boss is a dick," and Gus Fring—technically Walt's boss—is "a super dick" (season 3, episode 9). Like the lover in "He Venido," Walt has something to prove, and he loves what he's doing. Nothing will stop him. The title, translated as "I Have Come," has resonance with the general growth in Walt's ego. Because the song is in Spanish and because it is Cuban, it also comments on the drug problems at the borders of the United States. Those problems did not originate in Mexico, and they are part of a long and troubled relationship between the United States and all of Latin America. Like Walt, the United States is not an innocent victim but is fully implicated in the drug market and in the politics surrounding it. Walt is comfortable being top dog because he thinks he deserves it and because he feels contempt for the cartel leaders. Outsmarting them and hurting them reaffirm his contempt and strengthen his sense of justification. His violence is justified in the cause of a savage war (Slotkin 1998). The risk and the game turn him on, and he frequently has sex with Skyler after a violent or risky encounter.

At this point in the series, Walt has to negotiate a change in management. His new boss, Gus Fring, provides both a new super laboratory and a new laboratory assistant, but Walt knows his days are numbered. He begins to plot a way out of his situation, capitalizing on the fact that, for now, he is the only one who can make the pure methamphetamine that Fring needs. He uses the situation not only to prove his own worth but to demand a test of loyalty from Jesse Pinkman. Because Walt is safe only until his new laboratory assistant, Gale Boetticher, learns the process, he demands that Jesse kill the man. While Walt is under watch by Fring's soldiers, he concocts a reason to call Jesse and tells him where to find Gale. The men threaten him, but Walt says, "You might want to hold off. . . . your boss is going to need me" (season 3, episode 13). Jesse, who is coming to abhor violence and to distrust Walt, has no choice but to shoot Gale. Walt manipulates the situation and manipulates Jesse so that he (Walt) is safe. Jesse, however, is a pawn in the game and seems to be important to Walt only as someone to use.

Season 4: "Black" as Walt's Mood—Masculinity and Resentment

Season 4 begins with Walt under Gus's control, and he is afraid of losing control of the methamphetamine production. It ends with Gus's death at Walt's and Hector's hands. The plot to kill Gus and regain control of Heisenberg's *narcotraficante* empire develops over the entire season. During this time, Walt begins to take offense at any aspersions on his manhood and on his ability to manage his business. He particularly resents his wife for taking control of their money-laundering operation and for controlling his behavior. In episode 6, he makes the famous speech that ridicules Skyler's fear and her concern that he will die, culminating with "I am the one who knocks!" He is angry because Skyler does not think he's a hardened criminal. As he reminds her, "I am not in danger, Skyler. I am the danger" (season 4, episode 6). This scene sets up the movement toward the height of Walt's power and ego, but it also reveals that Walt is not a mild-mannered chemistry teacher. He is not mild at all, and he never was. Walt is highly intelligent and capable, but in his own eyes, underestimated. His feeling of being undervalued gives him a tie with Hector Salamanca, who is in a nursing home and being tormented psychologically by Fring. Because he is unable to talk or to move much, Hector is unable to respond to his tormentor or tell what he knows. Eventually Walt makes contact and finds a way to fulfill Hector's dual desires to die and to take Fring with him. After Fring threatens to kill the "crippled little rata" (season 4, episode 13), Hector rings a bell rigged to a bomb, presumably one that Walt had earlier attached to Fring's car but which never detonated. The song "Black" by Danger Mouse and Daniel Luppi begins to play as Walt calls Skyler and tells her "I won" (season 4, episode 13). The lyrics provide a chorus, once again foretelling Walt's fall and reminding the viewers that he has finally, and irreversibly, chosen to live a life in the darkness. Walt's attempts to get the admiration he considers his due lead to his destruction, but he is determined to succeed or die on his own terms.

Season 5:
"Baby Blue," Tying Up Loose Ends, and Saying Good-Bye

The most famous choral moment in *Breaking Bad* would have to be the final scene and the playing of "Baby Blue" by Badfinger. This scene is a culmination of a season that was all about tying up loose ends and preparing Walt to let go of his business. In episode 13, Walt engages in a number of confessional moments, and he finally admits to Skyler that he never did these things for the family, nor to pay the medical bills. He tells her, "I liked it. And I was good at it." It made him feel alive. This brings the viewer back full circle to the Walt Whitman reference in the pilot, "I am awake." By the time he reaches the methamphetamine laboratory where he dies, he has set up a way to take out Declan and his gang; he has killed Lydia . . . by spiking her Stevia with ricin; he has killed Jack and his gang in revenge for Hank's death; and he has allowed Jesse to kill Todd. In perhaps the only truly decent act in his criminal career, he allows Jesse Pinkman to escape (Jesse had been enslaved by Todd to make Heisenberg-quality methamphetamine). After everyone else is dead, Walt tries to provoke Jessie into killing him, but Jesse refuses, even after Walt says, "I want this." Refusing to be a pawn anymore, Jesse leaves Walt to either bleed to death or kill himself. As the police cars pull up to the laboratory, Walt wanders through the equipment. He lovingly touches the cooker, then collapses on his back and dies with a smile on his face. Although the song starts with what seems like an admission of guilt, it moves on to what is really important, which is that he feels he should have stayed with his "special love" and not let it go to others. His death is his due because Walt's baby blue is his crystal methamphetamine, and his only regret is giving it up.

Conclusion

The music used in the series, from "Dead Fingers" in the first episode to corridos and narcocorridos to "Baby Blue" in the final scene, functions as a Greek chorus. It reveals and comments upon the moral dilemmas facing Walt. Like a classic Greek tragedy, the arc of the story starts with Walt as an ordinary man who, eventually, finds his destiny. At first he is simply looking for a way to pay for his cancer treatment, but he is also looking for a thrill, a reason to feel alive. As he tells Jesse in the pilot episode, "I am awake." He is feeling the thrill of the chase and the stark contrast between the craziness of the drug-making life and the staid, stale nature—in his eyes—of his own. He justifies what he does by telling himself that what he does may be illegal, but his family will be better off. He even tells himself that he is saving for his children's future. But Walt's actions have little to do with his family. They have everything to do with his sense of self.

As he becomes more and more aware of his own intelligence and ability, he develops the hubris that so often becomes the downfall of tragic heroes. By season 4, episode 6, he angrily tells his wife, "I am not in danger, Skyler. I am the danger. A guy opens his door and gets shot and you think that of me? No. I am the one who knocks!" This is the fulfillment of the narcocorrido prophecy. He has already revealed his identity to Skyler, and as his business becomes more complex he has to be open with more people. In the end, he cannot leave the cartels because it is too risky for all concerned and because he cannot let go of a world where he feels valued. Walt dies because he wants to, not because he fears getting caught, but because he cannot face leaving the one thing that has, from his perspective, given his life meaning. Although he did not win a Nobel Prize and although he has not had the career he expected, Walt has succeeded, at least for a time. He has been recognized in this one area of life, and although he has a tragic fall, he dies with a smile on his face. The real tragedy is that he never recognized his life before as meaningful because it did not fulfill his ego. Only his baby blue could do that.

References

Badfinger. 1971. "Baby Blue." On *Straight Up*. London, UK: Apple Records.

Danger Mouse and Daniele Luppi. 2011. "Black." On *Rome*. Berlin, Germany: Parlophone.

Hardwick, Lorna. 2013. "Translating Greek Plays for the Theatre Today: Transmission, Transgression, Transformation." *Target* 25 (3): 321–42.

Los Cuates de Sinaloa. 2009. "Negro y Azul." On *Pegando con tuba*. Miami, FL: Sony Music Latin.

Los Zafiros. 2007. "He Venido." On *Locura Azul*. Miami, FL: Fuego Entertainment.

Meráz Garcia, Martin. 2006. "'Narcoballads': The Psychology and Recruitment of the Narco." *Global Crime* 7 (2): 200–13.

McCollom, William G. 1957. "The Downfall of the Tragic Hero." *College English* 19 (2): 51–56.

Silver Seas. 2007. "Catch Yer Own Train." On *High Society*. Los Angeles, CA: Cheap Lullaby.

Slotkin, Richard. 1998. *Gunfighter Nation: The Myth of the Frontier in Twentieth-Century America*. Norman: University of Oklahoma Press.

Breaking the Caper, Subverting the Heist

Matt Wanat

I guess what's left of the old rebel in me is that I like authority being conquered, so I always want my guys to succeed, and since I'm on their side, I always find good things for them to do.

—Jules Dassin, director of *Rififi*, 2001

I have done this long enough to know that there are two kinds of heists: those where the guys get away with it, and those that leave witnesses.

—Mike Ehrmantraut, *Breaking Bad*, season 5, episode 5

***Breaking Bad* has** been noted for its genre-bending characteristics, particularly for its dramatic transformation of initial protagonist Walter White from terminally ill reluctant criminal to methamphetamine kingpin. During its five-season run, the crime drama demonstrated generic characteristics ranging from gangster drama to more traditional tragedy, but individual episodes are also noteworthy for their forays into established film genres. Consider, for example, "Dead Freight" (season 5, episode 5), an episode for which writer-director George Mastras received an Emmy nomination. The bulk of the action in the episode is devoted to the robbery of methylamine from a freight train, a heist that is orchestrated through a combination of generic mainstays (e.g., a stalled truck on the tracks) and creative variations (e.g., the storage of the stolen methylamine at the crime

97

site, in a stock tank buried in the New Mexico desert). Most remarkable, however, is the episode's ending, which subverts the expectations of the caper or heist film.

In the typical caper film, either the criminal masterminds succeed or intricately laid plans are doomed to failure, but rarely are the failures in the caper of the sort with which *Breaking Bad*'s creators chose to end "Dead Freight." The present essay uses caper films *The Asphalt Jungle* (Huston 1950), *Rififi* (Dassin 1955), *The Killing* (Kubrick 1956), and *Ocean's 11* (Milestone 1960), among others, as a framework for understanding *Breaking Bad*'s "Dead Freight" and the episode's subversion of the conventions associated with the caper plot.

The Classic Caper

Ronald Schwartz (2001) calls Huston's *Asphalt Jungle* the model for *Rififi*, *The Killing*, and other subsequent capers, and indeed Huston's film embodies many key conventions of the genre. Dix, a hood with gambling debts and dreams of returning to the Kentucky horse farm of his childhood, becomes the muscle in a heist orchestrated by mastermind Doc Riedenschneider and dependent for funding upon Emmerich, a wealthy lawyer who betrays the crew in an attempt to flee his own debt with his mistress, Angela. The professional code of conduct followed by Dix, Doc, and driver Gus is juxtaposed with the pathetic treachery of Emmerich and bookie Cobby, who rats out the crew to a crooked policeman, making *The Asphalt Jungle*, like many capers, a study in the relative characters of the crew and cops.

The home lives of the criminals—which involve Dix's loyal girl, Doll; Emmerich's wife, May; the mistress; and Maria, wife of a safecracker fatally wounded during the heist—form a series of subplots that humanize the crew, inform their motives, and offer additional commentary in an ensemble structure rich with moral, psychological, and social implications. Add to these implications a conflict between the assertion of individual agency and the forces of social and cosmic determinism that are visited upon the characters—from Dix's family losing the horse farm during hard times in the past to a series of strange twists of fate, including sound waves tripping an alarm and the discharge of a dropped gun killing the safecracker, twists that disrupt the crew's meticulously planned crime.

Lawrence Russell (quoted in Schwartz 2001) notes *The Asphalt Jungle*'s indebtedness to the environmental determinism of American naturalist writers, calling environment in the film "the architect of fate" and noting that the characters "are driven by the human need for freedom rather than the psychopathic need to kill" (88). While there are examples of the "psychopathic need to kill" in later caper films—consider, for example, Mr. Blonde in Tarantino's *Reservoir Dogs* (1992) or, more figuratively, the psychopathology of racism in *Odds Against Tomorrow* (Wise 1959)— Russell's point about Huston's film applies to many variations on the heist film, which frequently explores the psychological needs of the thieves. The heist film often, as in Huston's film, connects these needs to domestic entanglements, and also as in Huston's film, the environmental determinism and gritty realism of American naturalist writing are common features of the heist film, which articulates the planning and execution of the plot with meticulous attention to the material realities of the crime and frequently indulges in a fatalism characteristic of both naturalism and film-noir style, where events conspire against the successful execution of best-laid plans.

In *The Asphalt Jungle* the fatalistic expresses itself in the aforementioned tripping of the alarm and discharge of the dropped pistol, but also in Doc's apprehension by the police, which occurs, as Doc notes, only because he has taken a few extra minutes to watch a girl dance in a local diner. And perhaps the most memorable expression of the caper's fatalistic tendency occurs when Dix, gut shot and accompanied by Doll, drives back to rural Kentucky, staggers into a pasture, and drops dead in a circle of indifferent equines— tokens of his deepest motives for participating in the heist to begin with.

I discuss Huston's film at length because it embodies many conventions of the caper, conventions exploited by the "Dead Freight" episode of *Breaking Bad*, one of these key conventions being a sense of determinism or fatalism. A classic example of film noir, *The Asphalt Jungle* combines the fatalism typical of noir style with the conventions, always as ideological as they are narrative, of prior genres like the gangster film in order to infuse the caper with a sense typical of both thirties gangster movies and forties noir that, in the end, "crime doesn't pay." But when one compares *The Asphalt Jungle* with a film like Stanley Kubrick's *The Killing*—released six years later with the protagonist again played by Sterling Hayden, but in a stiffer, colder, more Kubrickian satirical world approaching dark parody—what begins to emerge is a sense of the fifties heist as not only fated to fail by crime-doesn't-pay ideological platitudes, but also as fatalistic in a more mysterious existential sense.

In other words, the fifties heist film seems to punish the protagonists, as the Hollywood gangsters suffered before them, in an upended, negative version of the Horatio Alger myth, but also to celebrate, along with their cruel defeat, the resourcefulness and resilience of existential antiheroes in a stylish, perhaps mythic landscape of inequality and failure.

This convention of the heist is differently stylized but also further codified with the 1960 Lewis Milestone film *Ocean's 11*, in which the Rat Pack of Sinatra, Davis, Martin, Lawford, and Bishop, plus six, fail to keep the money they have stolen from Las Vegas casinos in a complex caper. In their defeat the eleven walk heroically down the Las Vegas strip in what amounts to a postmodern celebration of Rat Pack style, with the names of the aforementioned five on a marquis behind them, and Sammy Davis Jr. is the last to saunter past the camera in perhaps the coolest moment in his cinematic body of work. In other words, in the fatalistic universe of the fifties heist film, the criminal ensembles' defeat is common, and crime frequently doesn't pay, but even in defeat there is a kind of stylized, perhaps existential heroic persistence in the character of the defeated.

Of course, the heist does not always end in failure. In the Clint Eastwood vehicle *Kelly's Heroes* (Hutton 1970), a variation on the caper set during World War II, American GIs join with a German soldier they have been fighting in order to steal German gold in a film that is alternatingly a comic action film and a satire about the absurdity of war, a perfect balance for the Vietnam era. But by virtue of its sense of absurdity, *Kelly's Heroes* maintains a kind of existential heroism, along with the rebelliousness of prior examples in the genre—and it should be remembered that the criminal team in *Ocean's 11* is also made up of GIs. In addition, Eastwood's other heist film for the early seventies, the Michael Cimino movie *Thunderbolt and Lightfoot* (1974), continues to explore the genre's rebellious underdog ethos, but in this case in service of a buddy road film with the anxieties about masculinity and general malaise typical of that seventies genre.

Clearly the caper film crosses stylistic categories and genres, with examples ranging from the gangster film and the police procedural to the Western bank and train robbery, the war film, or the cat burglar film, from *To Catch a Thief* (Hitchcock 1955) to *The Pink Panther* (Edwards 1963) to *The Thomas Crown Affair* (Jewison 1968), and recently to more fantastic and speculative films like the magicians' heist in *Now You See Me* (Leterrier 2013) and the great brain robbery of *Inception* (Nolan 2010). Along similar lines, plots involving the well-guarded room, particularly in spy films and jewel heists, offer a stockpile of pleasurable clichés that by the seventies had worked their way deeply into the mainstream of action television, with jewel-heist plots like the *Charlie's Angels* episode "Diamond in the Rough" (season 2, episode 16) and, in the wake of the oft-parodied shot of Tom Cruise dangling above the floor in Brian De Palma's film version of *Mission: Impossible* (1996), with even children's television's *The Backyardigans* (season 1, episode 5) getting in on the action (Smith 2004). In addition, there is a generic affinity between the caper and another genre, the escape film, which in examples like *The Great Escape* (Sturges 1963) pits meticulous planning against deterministic external forces in much the same way that caper films pit the planning for the heist against the unlikelihood of its execution. With this in mind, it is perhaps unsurprising that one of the greatest caper films, *Rififi*, a film to which I will return later in this essay, was brought to the screen by Jules Dassin, a filmmaker who had already directed a foundational prison escape film, *Brute Force* (1947).

Breaking the Caper

Keeping in mind these generic variations, one might generalize only with caution, but what interests me most about the caper plot is that in a genre that in the middle of the twentieth century dutifully punished its protagonists, these criminals eventually, and perhaps even originally, are in their punishment often characterized as rebelliously and ingeniously heroic.

Enter *Breaking Bad*'s Walter White, a.k.a., Heisenberg—chemistry teacher, cancer victim, methamphetamine mastermind. In a series that mixes and redefines a whole host of generic conventions, including classical (e.g., the tragedy), cross-cultural (e.g., the narcocorrido), and filmic (e.g., the gangster genre), it is unsurprising that the show would also offer its own versions of the heist: for instance, with season 5's first episode, "Live Free or Die," wherein Walt and methamphetamine-business partner Jesse use a giant magnet to erase surveillance video from a computer locked in evidence inside the Albuquerque Police Department. But more important for our discussion is the episode "Dead Freight," wherein Walt, Jesse, Kuby, Mike, and Todd attempt to steal methylamine from a train, without—as Jesse, the more nonviolent member of the partnership, insists—harming the railroad engineer and conductor.

After finding surveillance devices on their usual barrels of methylamine, a key ingredient in their drug business, Walt and Jesse, along with their muscle, Mike, agree with Lydia, a crooked Madrigal executive and previous methylamine supplier, that they should rob a freight train while it passes through a dead zone in the New Mexico desert and is, therefore, out of reach of Homeland Security. As is the case with most caper plots, the robbery is preceded by a conventional planning session, in this case one in which Lydia unfurls a map in a dimly lit room and explains the caper to the three men. Jesse seeks a means of robbing the train without following Mike's suggestion of killing the drivers (in character with his idea of using the magnet in "Live Free or Die"), and the group arrives at the plan of replacing the methylamine with its equal weight in water while Kuby distracts the drivers with a stalled dump truck on the tracks and Mike works lookout. The episode plays out as a tense but mostly well-planned caper, culminating in the final moment of the episode, in which a forgotten bystander from the show's prologue interrupts Walt, Jesse, and Todd's celebration of their successful transfer of the methylamine to a tank in the desert ground: a boy on a dirt bike stumbles on the crime scene while riding in the desert and catching a tarantula, apparently.

Walt, Jesse, and Todd stare at the boy on the dirt bike. He stares back, waves. Then, almost casually, after waving at the boy, perhaps heeding the advice from Walt and Jesse earlier in the episode about the seriousness of the plan, Todd shoots, killing the boy, their only witness, as Jesse screams "no" in the desert sun.

Viewers of *Breaking Bad* are familiar with the show's prologues, which are sometimes more figurative than germane to the episode's plot and sometimes, as in the prologue to "Live Free or Die," flash-forward several episodes. This familiarity with the occasional non sequitur quality of the show's prologues makes it easy for the audience to forget the boy's existence until this last frame, and it is partly from our forgetting that the boy on the dirt bike exists at all that the episode draws the power of its final seconds, giving the audience subtle foreshadowing, particularly insofar as the prologue contains faint sounds of the train in the distance, but little explicit warning that they are about to watch Todd murder a child.

Nevertheless, the ending of "Dead Freight" is characteristic of some of the surprising and occasionally disturbing twists on the series, recalling horrific surprises in other episodes, some involving children, and perhaps even representative of an emerging moral complexity and violence on new millennia television shows, with similar twists on HBO series and others like AMC's *The Walking Dead*. On *The Walking Dead* episode "The Grove" (season 4, episode 14), for example, adult Carol's killing of the child Lizzie, who has killed her own sister Mika to prove a delusional point about the domestication of zombies, makes for an almost unbearable five minutes of television (perhaps representative of the sort of brutality Ian Jensen, in chapter 9 of this collection, attributes to some of the shows in the television renaissance of the past decade).

Certainly, in spite of the prologue and of some more subtle hints throughout the episode, surprise plays a large part in the effect of the last seconds of "Dead Freight," but it is also worth noting that, although children have died on television shows in the past—for example on *M*A*S*H* and later medical shows—*Breaking Bad*'s inclination to put children in harm's way to such an extreme is part of a small and relatively recent trend on television, and, therefore, it can be argued that much of the shock over the death of the dirt-bike boy, identified as Drew Sharp on the next episode, comes from the understandable surprise that viewers might have at seeing this happen so suddenly on television.

But the killing of Drew Sharp in "Dead Freight" is disturbing for reasons beyond the quietness of its foreshadowing and the rarity of seeing such violence against children on television. As an ending to a caper plot, I think this episode is additionally remarkable not necessarily for its negativity, since capers frequently fail, but for its turning the tragic consequences of the crime against an innocent rather than against the criminals. It is not unlikely for the criminals in caper plots to suffer for their crimes. From *The Asphalt Jungle* to *Rififi* to *The Killing*, the fifties phase of the caper film is, if fact, full of criminals suffering for their crimes, and though variations on the caper also include heists successfully pulled off, from *Kelly's Heroes* to Steven Soderbergh's popular remake of *Ocean's Eleven* (2001), the unhappy ending (unhappy for the criminals at least) remains a viable ending to the heist, especially considering that the protagonists in these plots are almost always involved in moral transgression. What is unusual about "Dead Freight," then, is not the death or the negativity at the ending, but rather that the heist's being pulled off coincides with the caper's obligatory fatalism being visited upon a completely innocent bystander. In other words, our generic expectations that the caper plot occasionally ends in success are fulfilled at almost exactly the same moment that we are reminded that the protagonists in this particular caper are a successful and, in spite of their attempts to avoid killing, *violent* drug cartel.

"Dead Freight" as Caper

Though it can be argued that "Dead Freight" is more than simply a caper—indeed, virtually every generic point of reference on *Breaking Bad* is part of a postmodern hodgepodge of multiple other generic reference points—the episode is certainly partly a caper. The heist planning in a dimly lit room, which is missing only the cigar smoke and black-and-white photography of something like *The Killing*, is just one of a number of ways in which the episode announces its relation to the heist. At least twice in the episode there are references to the train-robbery plot, common to the Western and closely related to the caper: once when Jesse (of course it would be Jesse) drops the name "Jesse James," and once again when Walt, covered with dirt from burying the tanks to prepare for the heist, answers Skyler's "Out burying bodies?" question with the comically ominous reply, "Robbing a train." And though the episode forgoes the holdup common in Westerns from *The Great Train Robbery* (Porter 1903) to *Butch Cassidy and the Sundance Kid* (Hill 1969), opting instead for a covert train robbery closer to that in *The Wild Bunch* (Peckinpah 1969), the covertness of the robbery itself only reinforces its connection to non-Western capers, which, as I have already noted, relish intricate plans quietly executed, like the heist in Dassin's *Rififi*, which occupies thirty minutes of nearly silent screen time.

In addition to the planning scene and the references to train-robbery plots, "Dead Freight" references the caper plot directly by alluding to another caper film when Hank says at one point to Walt Jr., "Hey, I picked up *Heat* on Blu-ray. Want to watch it with me later?"—an allusion to Michael Mann's 1995 crime film which, in addition to including a heist sequence, revolves, like *Breaking Bad*, around a cat-and-mouse plot involving a criminal and a police officer.

With so many references to caper plots, in an episode revolving around the execution of a caper, it is unsurprising that *Breaking Bad*'s "Dead Freight" also emphasizes conventions of the caper, which are perfectly compatible with numerous character arcs on the series. Discussing caper films as a common feature of film noir, Andrew Dickos (2002) notes not only the aforementioned "meticulous *control* of the group" in a world where "best-laid plans of such characters crumble by the end" (200, 202), but also, with reference to *The Asphalt Jungle*, how in the caper film "the price paid through folly and fate delineates the weakness of those joined in the unholy alliance" (119). This exposure of "folly and fate" is certainly true in "Dead Freight," in which not only does fate rear its head in the chance encounter with Drew Sharp during the train heist, but also, as is typical in caper plots, hubris and hamartia precipitate failure in the form of violence and death.

As in many a caper, though admittedly characteristic also of the broader gangster genre, the violence and death in "Dead Freight" is attributable not only to chance but also to the actions and attitudes of the heist's criminal crew. Walt's aforementioned answer to Skyler that he is "robbing a train" is also, in addition to being a reference to the train robbery as a generic device, chest-puffing typical of Walt in the later seasons of the series, and Walt's prideful strutting is mirrored in other elements of and characters within the episode, for example when Kuby flatters the train engineer and conductor with his feigned confidence that they might know something about engines, in order to distract them into helping him with his stalled truck while, unbeknownst to them, the methylamine is siphoned off several train cars back.

This flattery and self-flattery, specifically masculine, is common on the show, which often has Walt in particular with a chip on his shoulder best served, it seems, through practical demonstrations of his scientific ingenuity. In "Dead Freight" the heist provides an occasion for this ingenuity, though here the idea is Jesse's, which manifests itself materially in the actions of Walt, Jesse, and Todd, as the latter two climb under and atop the stopped train and engage in the old-fashioned clanking and rattling physical labor of man against metal, rushing to remove the methylamine before the drivers can help Kuby move the truck and get the train up and running again. Fittingly, and somewhat comically, a Good Samaritan ruins Kuby's flatter-the-train-guys strategy and almost trumps the men-against-metal project of the heist crew by coming along and offering to move Kuby's dump truck off the tracks with his own big pickup. Most important, though, the masculine strutting built into the episode fits not only the series as a whole but also the conventions of the heist in at least two respects. First, the history of the caper plot is replete with men-and-metal materiality, from the nitroglycerin of *The Asphalt Jungle* to the broken drill bits and safecracking tools of *Rififi* to the use of military artillery for a heist in *Thunderbolt and Lightfoot*. Second, and more important, the caper's tendency toward folly is perfectly embodied in the masculine hubris all over "Dead Freight," and one might argue that the male posturing of the heist crew is partly responsible for Drew Sharp's death.

In his essay in this collection (chapter 5), Brandon O'Neal notes that Jesse's characterization is often associated with his desire to protect children and with his sometimes childlike behavior, which corresponds to Walt's paternalistic attitude toward his younger partner, a paternalism on Walt's part that in "Dead Freight" mirrors his father-knows-best treatment of Walt Jr. when at one moment he answers his son's protest over his and Skyler's parenting by concluding, "Because we're your parents, and you're our child." In "Dead Freight," Jesse's need to be seen as one of the big guys, that is, as a grown-up and a leader in the caper, becomes part of the heist-plot hubris that, when mixed with blind chance, leads to tragedy. This can be seen in a series of interconnected moments in the episode, beginning with Mike's paternalistically warning both Jesse and Walt that they are naïve to think they can rob the train without killing the drivers. "Bottom line," Mike says with his usual world-weary confidence, "I have done this long enough to know that there are two kinds of heists: those where the guys get away with it, and those that leave witnesses," a comment followed by an argument between the two father figures Mike and Walt that Jesse defuses by coming up with his plan to replace the methylamine with water so that the drivers never know they have been robbed.

Later, perhaps emboldened by his coming up with the plan and by Walt's telling Todd that Jesse is the mastermind behind the caper, Jesse paternalistically warns Todd, "Point is, no one, other than us, can ever know that this robbery went down. Nobody. Got it?" which is affirmed, and partly paternalistically undermined, by Walt's reinforcing for Todd the importance of what Jesse has just said. This no doubt contributes to Todd's choice to kill Drew Sharp and also ironically twists Jesse's impulse to protect innocent lives by having Jesse's paternalistic advice to Todd mimic Mike's original point that "there are two kinds of heists: those where the guys get away with it, and those that leave witnesses." Fittingly, when Todd is told Jesse's plan and compliments Walt and Jesse by saying, "You guys thought of everything," Walt and Jesse smile smugly, but by the end of the episode it becomes clear that Walt and Jesse's attempts to be heist leaders and to assert their independence from Mike's cold criminal pragmatism have actually led to an innocent's death.

The folly that Dickos joins with fate in his description of the conventions in the caper plot seems, in "Dead Freight," to be drawn from masculine one-upmanship in the relationships between members of the heist crew, where Walt resents Mike's paternalism, Jesse seeks Walt's recognition of his worth, and Jesse resents Todd's intrusion as the new kid. Here, "Dead Freight" resembles features of the caper plot in general, in which the hubris of characters can indeed lead to mistakes that usher in their downfall, and in this respect "Dead Freight" works quite conventionally as a caper.

Likewise, I can think of at least one caper film, Dassin's *Rififi*, where the mistakes of the men involved in the heist seriously endanger a child. In *Rififi*, heist leader Tony and heavy Jo pull off an intricate jewel heist only to find that Jo's son, and Tony's godson, Tonio, has been kidnapped, with the jewels or fence's money demanded as ransom. Though Tony finds the boy and kills his abductors, Jo, unaware that Tony has already freed the boy, dies trying to exchange the fence's money for his son's life, and Tony himself is fatally shot, in the end of the film driving erratically through the streets of Paris as he bleeds to death while Tonio, pre–seat belts, jumps around the inside of the convertible, leaving the audience to wonder whether the fatalism of the caper film extends to include the death of children in cars. Significantly, however, the child in *Rififi* does not die, and Tony's and Jo's deaths—made frustrating by Jo's understandable lack of faith in his partner's ability to find the boy in time and by the temporal blind chance of Jo's being killed before he knows his son is safe—are nevertheless deaths typical and even partly justified within the logic of the caper.

Drew Sharp's death, on the other hand, remains shocking, and the hindsight of analysis linking his death to fate and to the mistakes of Walt, Jesse, and Todd is not enough to deaden the blow of "Dead Freight" and its final tragedy. "Dead Freight" is ultimately a heist mininarrative, a caper embedded within a longer television crime series, and as such it contains features of the caper plot in general mixed with plot trajectories, character arcs, and themes firmly established in the series. But whereas the heist typically ends with the morally innocuous success of masterminds or with the suffering of criminals foiled despite best-laid plans, "Dead Freight" ends with success sullied by moral culpability and human tragedy. The hard lesson of "Dead Freight," like the emotional power of its ending, comes not from the caper's generic cliché that "crime does not pay." More cruelly, less conventionally, the lesson in "Dead Freight" is that *crime does pay*. It pays quite generously. Unfortunately, it is the innocent, Drew Sharp, who must pick up the bill.

References

Cimino, Michael (director). 1974. *Thunderbolt and Lightfoot*. Beverly Hills, CA: United Artists.

Dassin, Jules (director). 1947. *Brute Force*. Universal City, CA: Universal Studios.

—— (director). 1955. *Rififi*. Paris: Pathé Cinéma.

——. 2001. 1980 interview special feature on *Rififi*. Criterion Collection, no. 115. DVD.

De Palma, Brian (director). 1996. *Mission: Impossible*. Hollywood, CA: Paramount.

Dickos, Andrew. 2002. *Street with No Name: A History of the Classic American Film Noir*. Lexington: University Press of Kentucky.

Edwards, Blake (director). 1963. *The Pink Panther*. Beverly Hills, CA: United Artists.

Hill, George Roy. 1969. *Butch Cassidy and the Sundance Kid*. Century City, CA: 20th Century Fox.

Hitchcock, Alfred (director). 1955. *To Catch a Thief*. Hollywood, CA: Paramount.

Huston, John (director). 1950. *The Asphalt Jungle*. Beverly Hills, CA: Metro-Goldwyn-Mayer.

Hutton, Brian (director). 1970. *Kelly's Heroes*. Beverly Hills, CA: Metro-Goldwyn-Mayer.

Jewison, Norman (director). 1968. *The Thomas Crown Affair*. Beverly Hills, CA: United Artists.

Kubrick, Stanley (director). 1956. *The Killing*. Beverly Hills, CA: United Artists.

Leterrier, Lewis (director). 2013. *Now You See Me*. Santa Monica, CA: Summit Entertainment.

Mann, Michael (director). 1995. *Heat*. Burbank, CA: Warner Brothers.

Milestone, Lewis (director). 1960. *Ocean's 11*. Burbank, CA: Warner Brothers.

Nolan, Christopher (director). 2010. *Inception*. Burbank, CA: Warner Brothers.

Peckinpah, Sam (director). 1969. *The Wild Bunch*. Burbank, CA: Warner Brothers—Seven Arts.

Porter, Edwin S. (director). 1903. "The Great Train Robbery." New York: Edison.

Schwartz, Ronald. 2001. *Noir, Now and Then: Film Noir Originals and Remakes*. Westport, CT: Greenwood Press.

Smith, McPaul. 2004. "Secret Mission." *The Backyardigans*, season 1, episode 5. Aired October 14. New York: Nickelodeon.

Soderbergh, Steven (director). 2001. *Ocean's Eleven*. Burbank, CA: Warner Brothers.

Sturges, John (director). 1963. *The Great Escape*. Beverly Hills, CA: United Artists.

Tarantino, Quentin (director). 1992. *Reservoir Dogs*. Santa Monica, CA: Miramax.

Wise, Robert (director). 1959. *Odds Against Tomorrow*. Beverly Hills, CA: United Artists.

"I Watched Jane Die"

Theorizing *Breaking Bad*'s Aesthetic of Brutality

Ian K. Jensen

Although it ended only recently, *Breaking Bad* would seem already to be in the conversation about which television series is "the best show ever." If a quick Google search of the terms *"Breaking Bad"* and "best show ever" that produces about 59,800 results is indicative of broad cultural trends—and what could be more reflective of our times and interests than a lazy Google search?—*Breaking Bad* is at the very least, in Terry Malloy's famous term, a contender. Of course, it goes without saying that discussions about the best show ever are good for little more than garnering revenue-generating clicks and giving graduate students something to argue about at pubs. In fact, this essay is not interested in whether *Breaking Bad* is the best show ever, even if the author tends to think it might well be. Instead, I want to begin with a heuristic consideration of that conversation before

I look a bit more closely at what I call the aesthetic of brutality in *Breaking Bad*: its character, its most obvious precedent, and its implications. First though, what kinds of series tend to be included in the sweepstakes of "best show ever" and why?

Despite the implicit oxymoron, we are—accurately I think—said to be in the midst of a new or Third Golden Age of television.[1] And indeed there is a persuasive argument to be made that, somewhere around the middle of the first decade after the turn of the millennium, series television surpassed both the novel and the motion picture as the dominant form of narrative fiction. This new Golden Age is partly defined by the role of auteuresque showrunners such as David Chase (*The Sopranos*), Jenji Kohan (*Weeds* and *Orange Is the New Black*), Beau Willimon (*House of Cards*), David Simon (*The Wire* and *Treme*), Dan Harmon (*Community*), Mitchell Hurwitz (*Arrested Development*), David Benioff (*Game of Thrones*), Matthew Weiner (*Mad Men*), and of course Vince Gilligan of *Breaking Bad*. Although it is important to acknowledge that the auteur theory has many problems both theoretical and practical, and that, as Michael Szalay (2013) reminds us, our present auteur showrunners like Weiner and Gilligan are "hardly the first to create, write for, and produce" (111) their own series,[2] it seems clear that the relative carte blanche given to showrunners in the post-*Sopranos* era of subscription networks like HBO and Showtime, "mature themes" (i.e., sex, violence, and profanity), and limited or no commercial interruption have something to do with this "new" Golden Age (see *Californication*, *Oz*, *Weeds*, and *Six Feet Under* to name only a few) (111). But of course simply presenting "adult themes" uninterrupted by commercials does not make for a good television series. So, what does make for a good, even great show in the eyes of viewers and critics?

Compelling plot lines, well-developed characters, strong acting, in some cases notable cinematography—all of these seem important, even if none is necessarily crucial. But these factors must be insufficient for the simple reason that they are largely formal or technical. All of them then must be in service of a story, or stories, or even ideas that keep us watching. The shows should be about something. Perhaps the most illustrative examples of this hypothesis, despite the fact that the two are very different series indeed, are *The Wire* and *Community*. While *The Wire* featured great story lines, indelible characters like Bubbles, Omar, and Snoop, and thrilling action, what makes *The Wire* a candidate for "the best show ever" is clearly its central project—an almost Dickensian social realism that both reflects and critiques US "inner city" poverty, the so-called War on Drugs, and the structural racism that fuels both. It is in these senses that one can argue for *The Wire*'s candidacy as possibly the best artistic engagement with contemporary US social problems ever produced, and thus perhaps the best television series ever.[3] Like *The Wire*, *Community*—despite not meriting mention in the "best ever" conversation—is about something. Both shows present the respective idiosyncratic visions of their creators and both are "idea" shows. One would have to stretch a bit to claim that the idea in *Community* has any social import. In fact, *Community* is about pop culture, and more particularly, like *Seinfeld*, it is about itself as a pop-culture artifact. To say the show has no depth, only surfaces, is a misrepresentation, of course. Instead, Harmon produces a heart-on-the-sleeve parallel to Certeau's (1984) consumer-actor model of culture in *The Practice of Everyday Life*. If one were unkind, one might say that *Community* is the perfect adequation of Generation X's love of postmodern irony and popular-culture fetishism with the deeply affective narcissism of so-called millennials. Regardless, because in being about itself *Community* can be said to be about something, to have the quality of aboutness at its core, so to speak, it resembles *The Wire* and other prestige television series that are similarly centered on thematic matters—*Mad Men*, *Deadwood*, and *House of Cards*, to name only a few—although few are as single-mindedly about something as *The Wire* and *Community* are. It might appear then that having a solid thematic core, an aboutness as I have put it, should be added to the provisional list of criteria for "the best show ever" that this essay has begun. There are two obvious exceptions to this criteria of aboutness though: the series that started the present Golden Age and the one that seems to have taken a common stylistic trait of the "great" shows, the antihero, to its extreme. I mean of course *The Sopranos* and *Breaking Bad*, respectively.

The shows share more than just an antihero as a protagonist. In fact, they are similar in that both could be said to be predicated on a "pitch." It's clear enough from watching the first season of *The Sopranos* what Chase's pitch was: Suburban family man / mob lieutenant and tough guy suffers from anxiety and depression due in part to his overbearing mother and starts going to a psychiatrist as a result. The show plays out the tensions and juxtapositions of contemporary American life through violence, psychoanalysis, comedy, and sex. Of course, since Francis Ford Coppola's *Godfather* films, every film about organized crime is always already about capitalism, the American dream, and family. So to say that *The Sopranos* is not about anything or that it developed entirely out of the two or three sentences of an imagined pitch is to vastly oversimplify. At the same time though, those thematic resonances are largely legitimacy-lending background material in *The Sopranos* rather than central issues. The greatness of the show comes down to its characters, its actors (especially Edie Falco as Carmella Soprano and the unfortunately deceased James Gandolfini as her husband, Tony), and its near mastery of the dramatic tension produced by alternating between the figurative quietness of family life and the deafening loudness of violence and adulterous sex.

The pitch for *Breaking Bad* seems equally clear, perhaps even clearer: Nice-guy chemistry teacher is diagnosed with terminal cancer and ends up making meth with a loser former student in order to make enough money to take care of his family. Mayhem ensues. Gilligan's earlier work seems to reflect his debt to the logic of the pitch. Prior to becoming the showrunner of *Breaking Bad*, Gilligan worked extensively as a writer on *The X-Files*, where he specialized in stand-alone episodes, often colloquially referred to as "Monster of the Week" episodes, that operated outside the series' larger conspiracy theory–burdened story arc. These stand-alone episodes generally operate more as discomfiting horror stories than do the conspiracy episodes, which often foreground paranoia and suspense instead of horrific situations. Indeed Gilligan wrote some of the standout Monster of the Week episodes of *The X-Files*—season 3's "Pusher" (episode 17, featuring future *Breaking Bad* star Bryan Cranston) and season 4's disturbing "Unruhe" (episode 4) and "Paper Hearts" (episode 10), to name a few. Gilligan's modus operandi then can be said to be that of the pitch. That is, the Monster of the Week episodes of *The X-Files* are largely exercises in horror that, almost like a Poe story, take a single conceit to sometimes-gruesome and often-unflinching extremes. That single conceit, which would be a gimmick in lesser hands, is the heart of the pitch. And on the whole, Gilligan's pitches or conceits from his *X-Files* days are not particularly interested in larger thematic issues. If such themes do appear, they are used, much as they are in *The Sopranos*, as background while the horrifying effect that really interests Gilligan is front and center. Understood a certain way then—and this is not at all a critique (precisely the opposite, in fact)—*Breaking Bad* is not really "about" anything in the way that many of the other prestige programs mentioned earlier are. In fact, if anything, the show's later attempts to embrace prestige television–appropriate themes (e.g., capitalism and its effect on the so-called nuclear family) seem tacked on and unconvincing. Thematic concerns and thematic aboutness then are ultimately window dressing in *Breaking Bad*, window dressing that rarely if ever gets in the way of the effect of show. Like the aborted story line on Marie Schrader's penchant for shoplifting, the stabs at social commentary in *Breaking Bad* amount to filigree.

At this point I should clarify what I mean when I say that *Breaking Bad* isn't "about" anything. It might help to illustrate with a contrast. Famously, the seminal 1990s sitcom *Seinfeld* is by its own admission "a show about nothing." And although that familiar saw is inaccurate in one sense— certainly *Seinfeld* is about the absurdity of sitcoms—it is accurate in another. That is, at its best *Seinfeld* reduces the tropes of the situation comedy to almost pure formalism. The laughs are produced for better or worse almost mechanically, and this fact serves to highlight the fundamental emptiness of sitcom tropes. So in *Seinfeld*, deeply cynical show that it is, we laugh at the very meaninglessness of sitcom "situations." At the same time we laugh, subconsciously perhaps, at the very absurdity of our own laughter in the face of a maw of emptiness. This last laugh, if you will, is analogous to Samuel Beckett's serio-comedy—the same laughter about which Nietzsche writes in a fragment collected in *The Will to Power*, "Perhaps I know best why man is the only animal that laughs: he alone suffers so excruciatingly that he was *compelled* to invent laughter" (1974, 74). On this reading, *Seinfeld* is at least partially about what existential philosopher Martin Heidegger (2000) called, most famously in the lectures that constitute *Introduction to Metaphysics*, "the Nothing." As he puts it, the traditionally overlooked question of the Nothing, the question of why there are "beings at all instead of nothing," is central to any philosophy of being, any ontology. In order to understand what is, Heidegger tells us, we must first start to think what isn't. As a result of the question of the Nothing, then, "all that is not Nothing comes into the question, and in the end [so does] even Nothing itself" (2000, 2). The point, ontological investigations and Heideggerian obscurity aside, is that *Seinfeld* is actually about "not nothing" precisely because it is about the Nothing(ness) of the sitcom.

Breaking Bad is not like *Seinfeld* in this way then. The latter is about nothing, while the former is not about anything even when it pretends to be. Let us take an example: the character Saul Goodman (nee James McGill) played by Bob Odenkirk. Upon first being introduced to Saul, the viewer cannot be blamed for thinking that he is meant not just as a type—the sleazy lawyer—but that perhaps he, like the inflatable Statue of Liberty proudly displayed above his office, is a none-too-subtle jab at the absurd notion that American justice is blind. Saul first appears in the series when he interrupts the police interrogation of small-time dealer and Jesse Pinkman associate Brandon "Badger" Mayhew (season 2, episode 8). Odenkirk plays Goodman as the ultimate ambulance-chasing slickster, and the scene ends predictably with a humorous discussion of pecuniary matters; Saul is catholic as far as payment goes, but he does not take American Express.[4] It is true enough that in time Saul becomes a major character and his role becomes more and more clearly defined, moving him away from his almost-allegorical flatness. But counterintuitively, Saul actually becomes less compelling as his character develops and he becomes comic relief. Despite his centrality to the show, and despite Odenkirk's excellent and against-type performance, the audience soon realizes that Saul isn't a satire of US justice, nor is he commentary on our increasingly litigious tendencies in the United States. Instead, like the conventional characters of the medieval mystery play, Saul serves a formal purpose and not a thematic one. Saul is, and this is metonymic for the logic of *Breaking Bad*, about effect—here both relief and heightening of tension—and not about meaning or content, satirical or otherwise.

Like Saul's character then, at its best *Breaking Bad* is not about nothing; rather, it is not about anything—the latter being very different indeed from the former. To not be about anything, though, means to be lacking in a central way what I have infelicitously called aboutness. But even if the show isn't about anything, it is far from pointless. In fact, its center is what Aristotle called a dynamis in the *Poetics*, a word S. H. Butcher and Lane Cooper translate with the phrase "essential quality" (Whalley 15).[5] In the *Poetics* that dynamis, that essential quality, can be understood as what Andrzej Warminski (2013) terms poetry's "power, faculty, capacity, ability, to do something" (202). *Breaking Bad* wants to do something, then, even at the very moment that it is not about anything, and it is this doing to which I will now turn. Think of the most indelible scenes in *Breaking Bad*: of Jesse and Walt attempting to dissolve the body of Emilio and of Walt strangling Domingo Molina, also known as Krazy-8, early in season 1. Think of Tuco's and Hank Schrader's respective beatings of Jesse Pinkman, of the death of Jesse's girlfriend Jane, and maybe most of all think of the season 5 murders of Hank, and of Brock's mother and Jesse's ex, Andrea Cantillo, and of relative newcomer Todd Alquist's heartless execution of a little boy on a dirt bike.

These scenes and others like them indicate the core of *Breaking Bad*: watching it is, at the show's best, almost unbearably intense. This is because, very much like the second scene in Leone's (1968) *Once Upon a Time in the West* in which another child is killed, rather than supplying relief to the viewer by resolving tense or possibly disastrous situations, *Breaking Bad* more often than not takes the audience to—and sometimes even just past—the limits of bearability. No doubt many viewers of *Breaking Bad* have had the same reactions that we had in my household—that of taking a temporary viewing hiatus to gain respite from the intensity or of vowing not to watch *Breaking Bad* before bed because of the dreams it caused! And in fact in the wake of the series' success, *New Yorker* television critic Emily Nussbaum (2013) goes so far as to suggest that "good television" has, with its focus on intensity and violence, become like, quoting a tweet from *Time*'s James Poniewozik, "a chili-pepper-eating contest." This characterization points to the show's great strength and its essential quality or dynamis: intensity, or more properly its ability to produce an experience of intensity in the audience. As I have argued, it is incorrect to say that the show is about intensity, of course. At the same time, it does exist primarily to produce an experience of emotional, even visceral, intensity in its audience—a goal at which it succeeds almost too well sometimes. In what follows, then, I am interested in that experience of intensity, in its character, how it works, and in what an analysis of it might have to say on theories of experience per se.

The word I have used so far to describe this essential quality, *intensity*, is insufficient, though, because it fails to fully account for the experience in question. The quality of intensity can be ascribed to any number of perceptions and qualities, from sweetness and ecstasy to pain and smell. Since my present goal is to be precise about the essential quality of Gilligan's show, we have need of another word. I propose then that the essential quality, the dynamis, of *Breaking Bad* can be said to be the show's ability to produce the experience of an aesthetic response I will call brutality. Indeed, the essential quality of *Breaking Bad* is the production of the experience of brutality in the same way that Aristotle famously argues that the dynamis of Attic tragedy is the production of catharsis. And in fact we should be precise when we refer to catharsis in tragedy. It would be incoherent to say simply that the essential quality of tragedy is catharsis, because catharsis is not inherent to the tragic play itself. Rather, catharsis comes about in the affective reaction a given tragic play produces in an audience. It is in this sense that we would be advised to speak of an experience of catharsis when we speak of the dynamis of tragedy, rather than simply catharsis. In a similar manner, when we speak of the dynamis of *Breaking Bad*, we must also speak of an experience of brutality, not simply of brutality. And this in turn means that the essential quality of the show, as is the case with tragedy, is aesthetic all the way down. This is for the simple reason that its production of experience necessitates an audience. And when we speak of an audience, as opposed to spectators, for example, we imply just this kind of dialectical relation between the aesthetic object and the aesthetically attuned, receptive viewer. So while the term *aesthetic* is conventionally understood to involve sensuous perception or matters of taste, I mean it here in a broader, but simultaneously more restricted, sense. The aesthetic object by definition requires an audience precisely because it cannot perform its dynamis without one. So we can refer to an object as aesthetic in the present sense if it is composed and produced in order to achieve some effect or experience in an audience.[6] We can in turn refer to an experience as aesthetic if it (a) takes an aesthetic object as its focus and (b) through interpretation or reaction from an aesthetically attuned audience produces an affective or intellectual response.

I have already argued the rather uncontroversial point that *Breaking Bad* operates on a logic of intensity, and I have just noted that this logic is in an essential way an aesthetic one. But our task here is to bring matters to a finer point, to the point of brutality. In order to do so, it will benefit us to look more closely at this logic. One of *Breaking Bad*'s greatest tricks is its ability to top itself by relentlessly intensifying scenes and situations that were already cringe-inducing. Some of this aptitude results from the show's willingness to portray intense and sudden acts of violence, of course. Those acts are sometimes so gruesome in their depiction, consequences, or execution (suggested or otherwise) that they produce in the audience a very literally visceral response. But it is not violence that makes the show. As we know, overreliance on violence, even sudden and gruesome violence, will have a numbing effect on the audience over time, a fatigue that *Breaking Bad* deftly avoids. And in fact some of the most intense scenarios in *Breaking Bad* are not at all gruesome: The murder of Andrea is not; in fact, it is almost clinically clean. And who can forget the tableside guacamole scene from the episode "Confessions" (season 5, episode 11)? Intense, yes; violent, no. More important, perhaps the most discomfiting aspect of the entire series is Walt's sociopathic manipulation of the emotionally broken

Jesse Pinkman, a manipulation that is psychically but not usually physically violent. In fact, the "relationship" between Walt and Jesse serves as an illustrative analogy of how the show's intensity operates in that their relationship is a series-long red herring. Because Walt comes off at times as, if not sympathetic, at least masterful, and because unlike Walt, Jesse seems to have some kind of a moral compass, the audience persists in hoping that Walt has some true affection for Jesse. Until the very last, we hope against all hope that Walt will, if not feel regret for his horrific actions, at least gain some perspective on his mistreatment of Jesse.

The closing scene of the series finale puts that entirely foolish hope to bed once and for all. Because it seems to offer Walt self-justification as he smiles as on his deathbed, the finale essentially forces the audience into the uncomfortable position of being what Nussbaum has called the "bad fan."[7] Like the generation of fans who see the title character of Brian De Palma's (1983) *Scarface* as a hero, a reading that the film does somewhat ambiguously sanction, if the viewer of *Breaking Bad* has been even partly in Walt's corner she must confront her own status as a bad fan, or at least a fan who is in bad faith. Animating this effect is a complex mix of generic expectations and canny defiance of genre. Because the show, especially early on, stresses Walt's family life, and because we expect against all evidence that the Walt-Jesse relationship will blossom into a standard television ersatz father-son relationship for the simple reason that that always happens in television series, we are able to largely suspend our moral judgments of Walt. The show's depiction of the Whites' white (no coincidence that), suburban, middle-class family life operates in the same manner; it lures us into thinking that perhaps everyone will live happily ever after. After all, families always live happily ever after on television, unless there is social critique (*The Wire*), unrelenting miserablism (*House of Cards*), or nihilism (*House of Cards* again) in a given show's DNA. This same effect is achieved by *Breaking Bad*'s tendency to flirt with outright, if never truly lighthearted, comedy. In fact, paradoxically, the show's erratic mood swings between the comedic—think of Saul Goodman again—and the awful do not serve so much to lighten the mood as to provide a form of contrast that makes the show's darkness all the darker.

But, and this is a crucial distinction, even as the comedic aspects of the show highlight the intensity of its darkness, *Breaking Bad* never completely alienates its audience with that darkness. Part of the reason is that *Breaking Bad* self-consciously rejects the kind of realism found in *The Wire*. With its evil fried-chicken drug kingpin, its twin assassins, and its often-surreal cinematography, the world of *Breaking Bad* is very self-consciously that of a television program. And that world is only tangentially related to the audience's experienced reality—at least outside the show's portrayal of the domestic sphere. And while much of the show's drama springs from that sphere, it is the precisely because the show does such a persuasive job of bracketing the rest of its world from "real life" that the audience accepts its grotesque extremes. The audience then is a willing, even active, partner to the show's grueling intensity. We are energized in a strange way by our anticipation of the next and likely even more horrific moment precisely because we are at a safe distance from our experienced reality, a fact that the show marks in its stylistic bombast.

I have already noted that one way that *Breaking Bad* is able to produce this experience of brutality is that it self-consciously distances its world from the real world through comedy, caricature, and a self-awareness about the tropes of US television and their audience effects. In short, because of this self-conscious distancing or bracketing—this aestheticizing—of the lived world, the audience is less likely to perceive the horrific moments of the show as purely sadistic cruelty. So the horrific moments in *Breaking Bad* retain their power to shock and even titillate, never becoming tiresome or, more important, unwatchable. And in fact they also become de rigueur precisely that which keeps the audience watching. We know what it is coming, or we think we do, after watching a season or so of *Breaking Bad*: inevitably it is something terrible. Of course, when that something terrible doesn't come in a given episode, we can feel relieved. But whether or not we are willing to admit it, we are disappointed as well. We wanted that awfulness, perhaps even desperately. Indeed, we crave it. We look forward to the next shock; indeed this is why we watch. We know nothing good will happen and we are perversely reassured by this knowledge. We have broken bad along with Walter White. Because of this fact, whether or not we cheer for Walter—whether or not we become "bad fans"—is not important. By simply watching the show, we are fully complicit in its gleeful nihilism.

The experience of watching *Breaking Bad* can be summed up then as looking forward to the ever-upping ante of awfulness, an experience that only intensifies as we become further accustomed to the show's brutal logic. In short, to the extent that we buy into *Breaking Bad*, we become connoisseurs of the horrific, the brutal. And ultimately it is this ambivalent enjoyment of the horrific that defines the experience of brutality. Of course that experience is one of intensity, even almost-unbearable intensity, but that intensity is predicated on a special—if not unique, as I shall argue in a moment—pair of factors. The first is the almost-unbearable awfulness, but the second is the position of safety occupied by the viewer in regard to that awfulness. It is aesthetic distance that allows for such safety, of course. We are, as Kant famously said, interested but simultaneously disinterested. We are safe from moral claims because, after all, it's just a television show. This point should come as no surprise. Visceral entertainment like roller coasters and horror films often allow us to experience something that under other circumstances would be traumatic. The psychological safety of the experience of brutality is not, then, a defining point. What is a defining point of this experience is that, in addition to giving the audience a thrill by presenting horrific acts and scenes in a safe manner, it trains us, in an important way, to savor those horrific moments—the very ones from which we initially turned away, literally or figuratively. Unlike a roller-coaster ride though, in the experience of brutality the audience member is not simply excited by a thrilling or even terrifying experience. Instead she derives pleasure from her complicity, willing or otherwise, in utterly morally reprehensible figured acts of cruelty and murder. That pleasure is no doubt in part produced by the viewer's own repressed cruelty. At the same time though, and more important, it is animated by a feeling of consequence-free moral transgression that results from the viewer's awareness of her complicity in the show's brutality.

Breaking Bad is unique in prestige television not only because of its relentless focus on the experience of brutality, a focus I have argued is its essential quality, but because it was incredibly successful critically and commercially by dint of that focus. If it is correct to say its dynamis is the production of that experience, *Breaking Bad*'s popular and critical success must be understood as a widespread initiation into the phenomenon of this experience. And this is unprecedented in mainstream entertainment. Certainly Gilligan's work on *The X-Files* intermittently revels in its brutality, as do certain episodes of new Golden Age series, for example *Six Feet Under*'s infamous "That's My Dog" (season 4, episode 5) and "Kennedy and Heidi" (season 6, episode 18) in the final season of *The Sopranos*. These are isolated episodes though, and precisely because they are isolated they cannot be said to represent a wider engagement with an ethos of brutality. But is the focus on brutality in *Breaking Bad* completely sui generis? I argue no. In fact, prior to the success of *Breaking Bad*, this experience of brutality can be found in another, significantly less mainstream, genre: death metal.

Death metal of course is a kind of rock music, and more specifically it is a species of the genre of rock music called heavy metal. Heavy metal is a relatively recent genre, having come into its own only in the mid-1970s. The term *heavy metal*, despite its somewhat mysterious origin, is particularly apt for this genre because of the so-called heaviness of the music itself, heaviness that manifests particularly in the use of distorted, sometimes detuned, guitars playing so-called power chords, chords that are often dissonant or unsettling. Thundering drums and screaming or guttural vocals contribute to this atmosphere of heaviness. The roots of heavy metal can be found largely in British Invasion blues-rock and psychedelia turned up, as it were, to eleven. Commonly cited progenitors are the Jimi Hendrix Experience, the Jeff Beck Group, Blue Cheer, Vanilla Fudge, Iron Butterfly, Deep Purple, Led Zeppelin, and most important Birmingham, England's, Black Sabbath. While heavy, riff-based rock music existed well before Black Sabbath's 1970s eponymous debut album, that record—packed with tritones, piercing vocals, lumbering tempos, evocations of the occult, and a truly Manichean world view—codified heavy metal's darker aspect. The influence of Black Sabbath on heavy metal cannot be overstated. Indeed, many of the seemingly inexhaustible subgenres of heavy metal derive either direct or indirect inspiration from Black Sabbath. The most obvious example would be what is called "doom metal," a subgenre that takes the slow, heavy, mournful aspects of Black Sabbath's early work to the extreme. Doom metal is typically considered to be a kind of "extreme metal," a grouping of subgenres of heavy metal that encompasses its less mainstream, and less accessible, permutations. Sociologist Keith Kahn-Harris (2007) argues that the main genres of extreme metal can be understood to be doom metal, thrash metal, grindcore, black metal, and, of course, death metal (4–5).[8] As Kahn-Harris argues it, death metal springs from thrash metal in the mid 1980s.[9] This darkness, in lyrical content, in album art, and of course in the music itself, is Black Sabbath's most obvious legacy to death metal. That is, just as doom metal took Black Sabbath's sound to the extreme, death metal takes the band's fascination with evil and darkness to the extreme by simultaneously distancing the music itself from its roots in the blues and by introducing a very 1980s interest in "body horror," serial killers, and so-called slasher films. But because, as Kahn-Harris also notes, in death metal the vocals become almost indecipherable, the genre's fascination with all things horrific is conveyed not through lyrics as a medium of understanding but rather through song titles, album art, and the distorted "death grunt" (or growl) style of singing pioneered by Jeff Becerra of Possessed, Kam Lee and Chuck Schuldiner of Mantas/Death, and Tom G. Warrior of Hellhammer and later Celtic Frost. I note these identifying characteristics because one result of what appears to be the endless subcategorization of heavy-metal genres is that question of how to place a given group, which becomes a topic of much debate. And this question in turn comes down to the question of what makes something death metal. Certainly when a listener with some experience hears bands like Cannibal Corpse, Suffocation, Death, Morbid Angel, Nile, Cryptopsy, early Opeth, Entombed, and Carcass, or even sees their album covers, she can fairly easily identify them as death metal from their heaviness and detuned guitars, their subject matter, and their vocals. But ultimately the essential quality of death metal, its dynamis, is the same of as that of *Breaking Bad*—the production of the experience of brutality.

We should then be able to map this experience of brutality in death metal onto *Breaking Bad* and, in fact, we can. In death metal, brutality is not simply about violent imagery in lyrics or on album covers, just as *Breaking Bad* does not derive its aesthetic effect through graphic violence alone. In fact, both lyrics and album art are paratextual in death metal, which means that although they can certainly contribute to brutality they are not essential to it. By way of illustration, an Amy Grant record with a Cannibal Corpse cover is not brutal, nor is the melody to "When I'm Sixty Four" (Beatles 1967) paired with the lyrics to Morbid Angel's (1989) "Immortal Rites." Brutality resides in the music itself. But it is not reducible to a certain formula of chords, notes, time signatures, instruments, a style of singing, or distorted amplification, even if it relies on each of those to a greater or lesser degree. For example, of the so-called Big Four of thrash metal, Metallica, Megadeth, Anthrax, Slayer, all of which use essentially the same sonic palette, only Slayer is brutal. So if brutality isn't about imagery, or even about a specific sound, what is it about?

Brutality in death metal refers to an experience the initiate or fan has when listening. That experience is oppressive, gut wrenching, and exhausting. One is happy in a strange way when the album, or even the song, is over. The listener has been through a difficult journey, she has been sonically abused, and there is palpable relief when it stops. So far this should sound familiar to us from our discussion of the experience of brutality in

Breaking Bad. But if these things were sufficient to explain brutality in death metal, the genre would be little more than an exercise in masochism. While that may be partly the case, it would be difficult to imagine that a musical genre would prosper for roughly thirty years if all it had to offer were aural self-flagellation. The question then would be whether death metal, like *Breaking Bad*, offers the excitement of anticipation of the awfulness to come, a peculiar savoring of the horrifying, and a satisfaction, even pleasure, that results from depictions that would normally be considered nihilistic and immoral at best and truly repugnant and evil at worst.

The short answer is yes, and this is in fact what indicates to us that death metal shares its essential quality with *Breaking Bad*. Indeed, the defining factor of death metal, the one thing death metal must have, is brutality. And in fact when I use the term *brutality* to talk about *Breaking Bad*, I am borrowing the term, which serves both a descriptive and normative purpose, from fan characterization of death metal. Death metal is by definition brutal in the ways that I have outlined so far. That brutality, which is a shorthand way of talking about the genre's central goal of producing the experience of brutality in the listener, results from a concatenation of themes, song titles, album art, and the music itself, but it cannot be reduced to these for the simple reason that they must be understood to be in service of the two goals I have already gestured at: first, the inaccessibility for the uninitiated and, second, the peculiar blend of pain and pleasure that is the experience of brutality. To the experienced listener, to the fan, the best death metal is the most brutal death metal. And as we saw above with *Breaking Bad*, that brutality is fundamentally pleasurable for the show's fan.

But this is true only for the initiate, and here is where we can see a central difference between death metal and *Breaking Bad*. That is, for the uninitiated listener death metal played at loud enough volumes may produce physical pain and even disorientation. It will certainly not produce pleasure. A death-metal aficionado though will have a much richer experience. She won't experience just the painful aspects, although she will experience them.[10] For the fan, the negativity and brutality in death metal is tempered with a strange kind of enjoyment. That enjoyment stems in part from familiarity, of course. A person who has never really listened to death metal is likely to be taken aback by it, while a familiarized listener will know what to expect by and large. But familiarity is not the only factor, and it is certainly the case that one can become familiar with death metal without ever coming to enjoy it. The unpleasantness may diminish over time, of course, but the nonfan will never have the full experience of brutality because he or she will miss out on this pleasure. Indeed, many partners of death-metal fans have firsthand knowledge of this phenomenon.

One must be fully initiated in order to truly experience death metal's aesthetic of brutality, and to be initiated is to overcome or bracket what we generally find pleasurable in popular music: melody, harmony, depictions of interpersonal relationships. And indeed, death metal prides itself on being inaccessible to the casual listener. And in fact the stylistic markers I have noted—manic blast-beat drumming, guttural and indecipherable vocals, oppressive heaviness, a fixation on violence and death—are in service of this inaccessibility. But as stylistic gatekeepers, they articulate an inclusivity that draws the line between initiate and noninitiate. More important, they also provide the grist for the pleasure, the deliciousness, of the experience of brutality in death metal. Once she has learned the ins and outs of the genre, as it were, she becomes increasingly able to see past its alienating qualities while still feeling their negative effects, and she becomes aware that those qualities themselves are constitutive of the pleasure generated by the music. That pleasure is a pleasure in ugliness, to be sure, a suffocating, discomfiting pleasure that can only be described at the same time as delicious. That deliciousness, so central to the experience of brutality, is derived less from the depiction of an individual's repressed tendencies toward violence and cruelty than from her ability to navigate depictions of cruelty and violence safely and pleasurably through generic tropes. This kind of navigation can be illustrated with a quick glance at Jonathan Demme's acclaimed 1991 thriller *The Silence of the Lambs*. We are likely to be horrified watching the serial killer Buffalo Bill torment his victim, the abject Catherine Martin. As depictions of sheer sadism, these scenes will be deeply troubling to most viewers. On the other hand, we are fascinated by Hannibal Lecter, who is also, of course, a serial killer. Lecter is different though because we do not perceive him as a true sadist. Lecter is instead a connoisseur of experience, a player of games, a person with what can only be called, despite the pun, taste. In fact, this kind of taste, this finely tuned "aesthetic," would appear to mirror one of the essential aspects of the experience of brutality: the ability to take aesthetic pleasure in what appears at first to be entirely horrific.

Breaking Bad then brings to the masses an experience previously found in the marginal or underground genre of rock music called death metal.

I won't go as far as to say that Gilligan's series takes inspiration directly from death metal, but I do want to argue that the best way to understand the essence of *Breaking Bad* and the irrelevance of questions about the show's aboutness is to see them in terms of the experience that death metal provides to its fans. There are of course some crucial differences between the two, the most of important of which is the very ability of *Breaking Bad* to appeal to a wide public, something death metal prides itself in not doing. Precisely because *Breaking Bad* craftily uses and repurposes all-too-familiar tropes derived from decades of US television rather than organizes itself against the familiar as death metal does—because *Breaking Bad* appears to play by the rules, that is—it attracts a wider audience rather than winnowing it down. *Breaking Bad*'s true uniqueness then can be understood as its ability to produce the experience of brutality found in death metal but to a general audience. *Breaking Bad* has no use for death metal's rigorous disciplinary policing, demonstrating instead that, first, such policing is not an inherent part of the experience of brutality, and second, that an aesthetic experience assumed to have only limited appeal, perhaps only to certain subcultural "sickos," is perfectly capable of enthralling the water-cooler crowd.

If what I have claimed so far about *Breaking Bad* is true, a fair response might be that even if at its center *Breaking Bad* seeks to reproduce the essential quality of death metal, that is the experience of brutality, isn't this just counting angels on the head of a pin? While I think it is useful to understand the three main related points I have addressed thus far—that *Breaking Bad* isn't about anything, that its dynamis is the production of the aesthetic experience of brutality, and that this dynamis can also be found in death metal in a more limited form—if only so that we may most accurately characterize the show, I want to push the matter just a bit further by addressing two final questions. Those questions are as follows: What does it mean to have an experience in the sense I have been discussing here? And what, if anything, can the experience of brutality tell us about experience as such?

Allow me then to close by looking at the other key term, *experience*—a task I undertake with the help of two major figures of twentieth-century continental philosophy: the thinker, essayist, and cultural critic Walter Benjamin and the hermeneutic philosopher Hans-Georg Gadamer. Although both German and born only eight years apart, Benjamin and Gadamer have roots in very different intellectual traditions. Benjamin's thought draws from many schools, including both philosophical and cultural Marxism, sociology, literary theory, mystical Judaism, and psychoanalysis, among others. Benjamin was a powerfully original thinker who had a complicated relation to Marxism, but it is not incorrect to note that his project lines up fairly well with the cornerstones of Frankfurt School Critical Theory—a dialectical and skeptical examination of culture and society that is defined by, as Martin Jay ([1973] 1996) puts it, its "aversion to closed philosophical systems" (41). Gadamer, on the other hand, although equally and essentially interested in culture and its interpretation, was a student of Heidegger's—a thinker whom the Frankfurt School's de facto leader Theodor Adorno despised. Gadamer draws from the phenomenological tradition, from German *Existenz* philosophy, from Aristotle, and particularly from Hegel. Despite their many differences, differences that are far too numerous and complex to discuss here, both attend to what might glibly be called the uses and abuses of culture. In doing so, both discuss experience as it relates to culture, which is to say aesthetic experience. The lens they use is provided by the nineteenth-century German philosopher Wilhelm Dilthey (1985), one that results from the distinction implied in the two different German words for experience: *Erfahrung* and *Erlebnis*.[11] Prior to Dilthey's work, the standard German word for experience was Erfahrung. Under the influence of the Kantian distinction between the world as such and our perception of the world as well as the romantic tendency to focus on experience, Dilthey argued, we ought to understand the phenomenon of lived experience as Erlebnis, with its etymological derivation from the German *leben*, to live, rather than Erfahrung, which he argued had to do with perception and cognitive judgment and not with what we might call the actuality of lived experience. Put too simply, for Dilthey, Erlebnis is a comprehensive understanding of experience that takes into account what later thinkers influenced by him would call the *Lebenswelt* or "lifeworld."[12] Broadly speaking then, for Dilthey experience as Erlebnis takes into account the lifeworld of a person, cultural and even individual, in a way that an empirical and perhaps even mechanistic Erfahrung does not.

This distinction between the attenuated notion of experience as Erfahrung and experience that exists within social and psychological context, that is, Erlebnis, becomes an important one for both Benjamin and Gadamer. Benjamin discusses Erfahrung and Erlebnis most directly in the long essay called "On Some Motifs in Baudelaire" ([1968] 2007a), originally published in 1939). In that essay he questions the relevance of lyric poetry in modernity by writing that "if conditions for a positive reception of lyric poetry have become less favorable, it is reasonable to assume that only in rare instances is lyric poetry in rapport with the experience of its readers. This may be due to a change in the structure of their experience" (156).[13] If a long excerpt can be excused, Benjamin addresses the difference between Erlebnis and Erfahrung in *Les Fleur du mal* in section 4 of that essay as follows:

> The greater the shock factor [*Anteil des Chockmoments*] in particular impressions, the more vigilant consciousness has to be in screening stimuli; the more efficiently it does so, the less these impressions enter long experience (*Erfahrung*) and the more they correspond to the concept of isolated experience (*Erlebnis*). Perhaps the special achievement of shock defense is the way it assigns an incident a precise point in time in consciousness, at the cost of the integrity of the incident's contents. This would be a peak achievement of the intellect; it would turn the incident into an isolated experience. Without reflection, there would be nothing but the sudden start. (163; emphasis added)

Here we can see that the usefulness of the distinction between Erfahrung and Erlebnis is that for Benjamin, Erfahrung (long experience) is the premodern, preurban understanding of experience. In this way, Benjamin's view of Erfahrung differs from Dilthey's, even though they agree that the two are distinct types of experiences. For Benjamin, Erfahrung contains within it historicity and a certain kind of "content," a meaning that is, if not objective, at least not privatively subjective. Benjamin's Erlebnis, on the other hand, is exactly this—privatively subjective. A useful comparison might be Benjamin's ([1968] 2007c) well-known conception of the aura from "The Work of Art in the Age of Mechanical Reproduction." The argument made in that essay is that prior to modernity, the unique art object had an aura that inhered in it: a locus of history and tradition.[14] In the age of mechanical reproduction, Benjamin argues, aura is lost and replaced by what he calls in the excerpt above "shock" (*Chock*). Shock is an ahistorical, privative, and purely subjective kind of experience. Ultimately, Benjamin ([1968] 2007a) argues that in *Les Fleurs du mal* Baudelaire "give[s] the weight of an experience (*Erfahrung*)" to "something lived through (*Erlebnis*)" (194). Like the aura of the work of art, Benjamin implies, in capitalist, urban modernity experience as Erfahrung has been replaced by experience understood as

Erlebnis, as subjective, psychic, and ahistorical: experience (Erlebnis) as shock (*Chock*).

Gadamer ([1975] 2004) too is concerned with Dilthey's distinction. In his magnum opus, *Truth and Method*, originally published in 1960 in the German, Gadamer in essence concurs with Benjamin on Erfahrung and Erlebnis. But while for Benjamin the loss of experience understood as Erfahrung in modernity has ambiguous normative repercussions, for Gadamer it is a symptom of a highly problematic subjectivism—a subjectivism that Gadamer, like his teacher Heidegger, vigorously critiques. Gadamer illustrates this in part I of *Truth and Method*, called in English "The Question of Truth as It Emerges in the Experience of Art," and which contains a careful examination of art and its reception in modernity. In fact, a portion of this first part of *Truth and Method* is called "The Aesthetics of Genius and the Concept of Experience (*Erlebnis*)." Here Gadamer attacks neo-Kantian aesthetics, writing that "Kant's doctrine of the 'heightening of the feeling of life' (*Lebensgefühl*) in aesthetic pleasure helped the idea of 'genius' to develop into a comprehensive concept of life (*Leben*). . . . Hence, by trying to derive all objective validity from transcendental subjectivity, neo-Kantianism declared the concept of Erlebnis to be the very stuff of consciousness" (52). For Gadamer then, who proceeds to offer a philosophic etymology of the word Erlebnis, experience as Erlebnis can be said to be the experience of art that stems from modern post-Kantian subjectivity. It is therefore a degraded notion of experience; one that understands personal experience as "material to be shaped," as "immediacy, which precedes all interpretation, reworking, and communication" (53). This understanding in turn produces an artificial "alienation" from "history," just as we saw in Benjamin (56), and in doing so also alienates us from tradition as well as what Gadamer calls "prejudice" (*Vorurteil*).[15] All of this is of course in contrast to the premodern understanding of "historically effected consciousness," which has "the structure of *experience (Erfahrung)*" (341) and in which "the spiritual creations of the past, art and history" (56) were clearly articulated with history, tradition, and prejudice.

So in the distinction between modern Erlebnis and premodern Erfahrung borrowed in part from Dilthey, Benjamin, and Gadamer, Erlebnis is conceptualized as fundamentally alienated from, even at odds with, tradition and history. A useful illustration of the difference might be found in a gloss of Gadamer's ([1975] 2004) take on Hegel's (1975) famous pronouncement from his lectures on aesthetics: "art, considered in its highest vocation, is and remains for us a thing of the past" (11). For Hegel, art has ended in the romantic (i.e., Christian) era precisely because in that era art becomes entirely the province of experience as Erlebnis. The experience of art under the regime of Erlebnis becomes aesthetic in the contemporary sense in that it loses what Benjamin called its content—content that was available to us in the regime of Erfahrung—and replaces it with entirely personal, subjective, ahistorical, private, and essentially incommunicable "experience." According to Hegel—for whom art was merely a step along with religion to the supreme knowledge granted Absolute Idealist philosophy—and to Gadamer, it is this subjectivist understanding of art upon which we operate today. It is in contrast to what Hegel calls classical art, the art of the Greeks, which he considers to be the highest form of art because it retains "content," therefore allowing for Erfahrung. That is, the experience of art enjoyed, supposedly, by the Greeks was one in which art was not cleaved off from spirit, society, tradition, and history.[16] One did not go to a museum, look at an artwork, and have an experience (Erlebnis). Instead, the experience of art was always already communal and, following Charles Taylor (1989), we might say embedded in society, history, religion: in culture. So, although Benjamin and Gadamer draw very different conclusions from the distinction between Erlebnis and Erfahrung they inherit from Dilthey, they fundamentally agree both on the nature of the difference and on its relevance to the analysis of art and culture.[17]

I contend that the experience of brutality found in *Breaking Bad*, an experience that I consider to be singularly analogous to the initiate's experience of death metal, demonstrates that the distinctions Gadamer and Benjamin see between Erfahrung and Erlebnis can be deceptive. What Benjamin calls the shock that disintegrates the aura of the artwork, and which is illustrative of the general character of the individual's experience of modernity, can be understood to be the shock of the new.[18] In his analysis, and to a certain degree in Gadamer's, that shock of the new isolates the individual's experience (Erlebnis) from its previous historical and traditional cultural context (Erfahrung). What is fascinating about the experience of brutality is that it is one of "shock," as I have already noted, but in a different way from the shock of the new. That is, the brutality of *Breaking Bad* is—like that of death metal—shocking in a disruptive way, but only at first. As the viewer is initiated into the logic of the program, and that happens quickly for the reasons we have seen, as she attunes herself to the show's tangential relation to the real world, as she becomes aware that nothing good will or even can come about in this particular fictional world, she comes to expect and even perversely anticipate the next terrible event or outcome. The viewer is not shocked by the new, but she is "shocked"—and the scare quotes are vital here—by how events play out. She is likely to mutter to herself something to the effect of, "My god, I can't believe he/she/they/the show did that!" but she does so in full awareness that although the specific resolution is not necessarily predictable except in its awfulness—say Jesse's murder of the hapless Gale in "Full Measure" (season 3, episode 13) or Hank's death in "Ozymandias" (season 5, episode 14)—she does know that things will end poorly. And it is this fact that allows her to savor the deliciousness of the horrific even as the dread of it all oppresses her.

As I have argued, the complex interweaving of comforting dread and anticipated "shock" that simultaneously produces a strange connoisseurship of the dreadful anticipation itself and of the terrible event is the defining factor of the experience of brutality. That experience is at the heart of *Breaking Bad*, and it is possible only through the viewer's familiarity with its inexorably brutal logic. But as we have seen, she first must be familiar with the generic conventions of prestige television, and of US television more broadly speaking. She has to know what to expect and how to process what comes. This generic knowledge, both of television in general and specifically of *Breaking Bad*, is nothing other than Erfahrung. That is, it is not a private, isolated moment of experience. Instead, it is a shared awareness of the history and tradition, if you will, of US television and of *Breaking Bad*'s own internal logic of brutality. Without both, the essential quality of the show, its dynamis—the experience of brutality—cannot be produced.

In fact, it is only with this situated Erfahrung that the experience of Erlebnis, the shock that the show relies on, even becomes possible. The point then is that the depth of that aesthetic experience of shock simply cannot be exhausted by calling it Erlebnis, for it is simultaneously private and communally situated. It is private in the sense that the experience of brutality is fundamentally an aesthetic, and thus subjective, one very much in the neo-Kantian sense that Gadamer critiques. It is also crucially communal, though, in the sense that in order to have this experience at all, the viewer must take part in a particular aspect of the project of human culture whether she is aware of it or not. The apparent Erlebnis of viewer shock in *Breaking Bad* then is at the same time ahistorical and deeply historical. As Erlebnis, it is momentary, a passing inner state that gives us no real knowledge and that is unsituated, if not untimely. At the same time, this shock is historical for the simple reason that it requires of the viewer an attunement to generic precedent, to the duration of genre if you will. In the case of the experience of brutality found in *Breaking Bad*, then, communal Erfahrung serves as the ground for subjective Erlebnis. This is true of death metal as well, but because of death metal's intentional marginality it remains essentially untheorized. By taking this centrally aesthetic experience of brutality and making it accessible while at the same time maintaining its disruptive power, *Breaking Bad* allows us to think the aesthetic differently, to think the character of brutality in the present sense differently, and to think both death metal and Gilligan's series more rigorously.

The experience of brutality as we have seen it would appear, in a Gadamerian analysis, at first blush to be the worst kind of subjective aestheticism. This is because it relies on personal sensation, the sensation of delicious shock. To Benjamin ([1968] 2007b), perhaps, this shock can be a disruptive and destructive break from tradition, something like the messianic power of his angel of history. But the experience of brutality shows that at least in some cases defining experience in terms of discrete Erfahrung or Erlebnis is problematic. While we can certainly experience the pure, private Erlebnis of Benjamin's shock, and while the communal hermeneutic tradition of Erfahrung persists in religion, law, and humanistic study, what Gadamer fails to see and what Benjamin ([1968] 2007a) says occurs only in Baudelaire's *Les Fleurs du mal*—nothing less than a transubstantiation of Erlebnis into Erfahrung—is itself the dynamis of the experience of brutality. Thus to the extent that *Breaking Bad* is synonymous with the experience of brutality, it has demonstrated that the circle of Erlebnis and Erfahrung can be squared, in both theory and practice. As the death metal of television, far more so than *Metalocalypse*, *Breaking Bad* instantiates the fairly radical notion that the subjectivist structure of modern aesthetic experience sometimes called Erlebnis in the Continental tradition is rooted—perhaps paradoxically—in what is understood as its precursor and opposite, communal Erfahrung. When we look closely at the experience of brutality then, something that the present analysis of *Breaking Bad* has allowed us to do, we find that it has important things to teach us about what literary critic Paul de Man (1996) considered the paradigmatic ideological construction, the aesthetic.

Acknowledgments

I am grateful to the following people for their assistance with various versions of this essay. Without the initial guidance of John H. Smith and a stimulating exchange with Philip Walsh, it would not exist at all. Without the careful eyes and thoughtful suggestions of Beverly Andrews, Shane Billings, and Beverly Tjerngren, whatever clarity it now has would not have come to be.

Notes

1. In fact, an article at the influential popular arts and culture website *The A.V. Club*, "The Golden Age of TV Is Dead; Long Live the Golden Age of TV" (VanDerWerff 2014) features as its lead-in image a still of *Breaking Bad*'s Walter White.
2. Szalay (2013) advises us to remember "Norman Lear, Aaron Spelling, Steven Bochco, Chris Carter, Aaron Sorkin, and many others" (111).
3. I have reservations about this position based in part on the tendency *The Wire* has to rely on realist tropes that serve to obscure the artifice of the series.
4. The scene also includes a veiled reference to a modern master of horror-suspense, and a clear influence on Gilligan, John Carpenter (*Assault on Precinct 13*, *Halloween*). Saul's shell corporation, to which Badger's payment is to be made, is called Ice Station Zebra. The name comes from the title of a 1968 film by Fritz Lang starring Rock Hudson that Carpenter is an avowed fan of, and which plays a small role in Carpenter's made-for-television biopic *Elvis* (Williams 2004, 121).
5. See "The Future Past of Literary Theory" in Warminski (2013) for an in-depth discussion of dynamis in Aristotle's theory of tragedy.
6. Although in the present analysis we are concerned with Gilligan's intent for the aesthetic experience the series produces, we do not actually need an account of intent that goes beyond that of creating art for the present definition of *aesthetic* to function. The question of intent in art is a tricky one, of course, but I think in this case we are on solid ground when we note the intentionality in the specific case of *Breaking Bad*.
7. Nussbaum (2013) writes that "if you ignore the dead kids, son, you are watching '*Breaking Bad*' wrong." This is an untenable position in light of the series finale.
8. As even the most cursory glance shows, heavy metal—like its relative, hardcore punk—is an almost absurdly variegated genre. The list of "extreme" subgenres provided here represents only a very small number of subgenres.

And even death metal itself is subdivided into types by style (melodic death metal [aka melodo-death], technical death metal, brutal death metal) and by location of origin (Swedish death metal, Florida death metal, etc.). The reasons for this almost pathological subcategorization within heavy metal are too complex to address at present, but the phenomenon is fascinating indeed.

9. "Thrash engendered a variety of ever more radical extreme metal genres. . . . Bands such as Death and Possessed created death metal out of thrash metal. Vocals became less and less intelligible, songwriting became more complex and guitar 'riffs' . . . sounded increasingly . . . dark" (Kahn-Harris 2007, 3).

10. If our hypothetical fan experienced none of the oppressive and grueling aspects of death metal, she would have no reason to listen to it.

11. Philosopher David Vessey (2007) offers a useful discussion of the two words and their respective associations:

> *Erlebnis* is constructed from *leben*, to live, and refers to subjective, first-hand experiences. (In English we have a way of talking that parallels the German; consider the sentence "To understand something you need to live it.") It is this subset of experiences that Husserl and Wilhelm Dilthey saw as a possible source for philosophical foundations. *Erfahrung* refers to that subset of experience that connects directly to judgment; it is often inferred, need not be first-person, and emphasizes cognitive insights. *Erfahrung* is constructed from *fahren*, to travel, as the realizations in the experiences move and transform one. It is the correlate for the English word empirical, as in the empirical sciences (*Erfahrungswissenschaft*) and being experienced (*erfahrend*). (3–4)

12. Dilthey's primary intellectual project was a theoretical account of the human sciences, and perhaps his greatest contribution to such an account was arguably the notion that human life, that is, lived experience, exists in a way that Heidegger would later call "always-already" within interpretive cultural and historical contexts.

13. *"Das könnte sein, weil sich deren Erfahrung in ihrer Struktur verändert hat."*

14. In that seminal essay, Benjamin writes,

> Even the most perfect reproduction of a work of art is lacking in one element: its presence in time and space, its unique existence at the place where it happens to be. This unique existence of the work of art determined the history to which it was subject throughout the time of its existence. This includes the changes which it may have suffered in physical condition over the years as well as the various changes in its ownership. . . . The situations into which the product of mechanical

reproduction can be brought may not touch the actual work of art, yet the quality of its presence is always depreciated. This holds not only for the art work but also, for instance, for a landscape which passes in review before the spectator in a movie. In the case of the art object, a most sensitive nucleus—namely, its authenticity—is interfered with whereas no natural object is vulnerable on that score. The authenticity of a thing is the essence of all that is transmissible from its beginning, ranging from its substantive duration to its testimony to the history which it has experienced. Since the historical testimony rests on the authenticity, the former, too, is jeopardized by reproduction when substantive duration ceases to matter. And what is really jeopardized when the historical testimony is affected is the authority of the object.

One might subsume the eliminated element in the term "aura" and go on to say: that which withers in the age of mechanical reproduction is the aura of the work of art. This is a symptomatic process whose significance points beyond the realm of art. One might generalize by saying: the technique of reproduction detaches the reproduced object from the domain of tradition. (220–21)

15. It is crucial to note that for Gadamer "prejudice" cannot and should not be avoided. In terms of what we have seen of Dilthey, we might say that Gadamer's prejudice is a central part of the lifeworld.
16. Although Heidegger does not notably engage with the Erlebnis and Erfahrung distinction, his well-known discussion ([1977] 1993) of the Greek temple in "The Origin of the Work of Art" is an excellent example of an analogous analysis.
17. Benjamin ([1968] 2007a) sees a certain radical, perhaps even violently disruptive, potential for liberation here when he writes of "the disintegration of the aura in the experience of shock" (194). In contrast, Gadamer ([1975] 2004) advocates for a rejection of what can be called the ideology of Erlebnis in favor of an acknowledgement of the crucial meaning-making of a hermeneutic approach that acknowledges tradition, history, and positive prejudice; in other words, Erfahrung.
18. Benjamin's (2002) analyses in *The Arcades Project*, and in various essays available elsewhere, of the collector, the *flamer*, the experience of the Parisian Arcades, the storyteller, and others echo this diagnosis if in a distinct way.

References

The Beatles. 1967. "When I'm Sixty-Four." On *Sgt. Pepper's Lonely Hearts Club Band*. Parlophone CDP 7 46442 2, compact disc.

Benjamin, Walter. 2002. *The Arcades Project*. Edited by Rolf Tiedemann. Translated by Howard Eiland and Kevin McLaughlin. Cambridge, MA: Belknap Press.

———. [1968] 2007a. "On Some Motifs in Baudelaire." In *Illuminations: Essays and Reflections*, edited by Hannah Arendt, translated by Harry Zohn, 155–200. New York: Random House–Schocken.

———. [1968] 2007b. "Theses on the Philosophy of History." In *Illuminations: Essays and Reflections*, edited by Hannah Arendt, translated by Harry Zohn, 253–64. New York: Random House–Schocken.

———. [1968] 2007c. "The Work of Art in the Age of Mechanical Reproduction." In Benjamin [1968] 2007, 217–51.

Certeau, Michel de. 1984. *The Practice of Everyday Life*. Translated by Steven F. Rendall. Berkeley: University of California Press.

Demme, Jonathan (director). 1991. *The Silence of the Lambs*. Los Angeles, CA: Orion.

DePalma, Brian (director). 1983. *Scarface*. Universal City, CA: Universal Studios.

Dilthey, Wilhelm. 1985. *Poetry and Experience (Das Erlebnis und die Dichtung)*. Edited by Rudolf A. Makkreel and Frithjof Rodi. Princeton, NJ: Princeton University Press.

Gadamer, Hans-George. [1975] 2004. *Truth and Method*. 2nd rev. ed. Translated by Joel Weinsheimer and Donald G. Marshall. New York: Continuum.

Hegel, Georg Wilhelm Friedrich. 1975. *Hegel's Aesthetics: Lectures on Fine Art*. Vol. 1. Translated by T. M. Knox. New York: Clarendon.

Heidegger, Martin. [1977] 1993. "The Origin of the Work of Art." In *Basic Writings*, rev. and exp. ed., edited by David Farrell Krell, 139–212. New York: HarperCollins.

———. 2000. *Introduction to Metaphysics*. Translated by Gregory Fried and Richard Polt. New Haven, CT: Yale University Press.

Jay, Martin. [1973] 1996. *The Dialectical Imagination: A History of the Frankfurt School and the Institute of Social Research 1923–1950*. Berkeley: University of California Press.

Kahn-Harris, Keith. 2007. *Extreme Metal: Music and Culture on the Edge*. Oxford, UK: Berg.

Leone, Sergio (director). 1968. *Once Upon a Time in the West*. Hollywood, CA: Paramount.

Man, Paul de. 1996. *Aesthetic Ideology*. Edited by Andrzej Warminski. Minneapolis: University of Minnesota Press.

Metalocalypse. 2006–. Created by Brendan Small and Tommy Blacha. Aired August 6. Atlanta, GA: Adult Swim.

Morbid Angel. 1989. "Immortal Rites." On *Altars of Madness*. Combat/Earache 88561-2022-2, compact disc.

Nietzsche, Friedrich. 1974. *The Will to Power: An Attempted Transvaluation of All Values*. Vol. 14 of *The Complete Works of Friedrich Nietzsche*. Edited by Oscar Levy. Translated by Anthony M. Ludovici. New York: Gordon Press.

Nussbaum, Emily. 2013. "That Mind-Bending Phone Call on Last Night's '*Breaking Bad*.'" *New Yorker*, September 16. http://www.newyorker.com/culture/culture-desk/that-mind-bending-phone-call-on-last-nights-breaking-bad.

———. 2014. "Snowbound: The Minnesota Noir of *Fargo*." *New Yorker*, June 23. http://www.newyorker.com/magazine/2014/06/23/snowbound-2.

Sturges, John (director). 1968. *Ice Station Zebra*. Beverly Hills, CA: Metro-Goldwyn-Mayer.

Szalay, Michael. 2013. "The Writer as Producer; or, The Hip Figure after HBO." In *Mad Men, Mad World: Sex, Politics, Style, and the 1960s*, edited by Laura M. E. Goodlad, Lilya Kaganovsky, and Robert A. Rushing, 111–31. Durham, NC: Duke University Press.

Taylor, Charles. 1989. *Sources of the Self: The Making of Modern Identity*. Cambridge: Cambridge University Press.

VanDerWerff, Todd. 2014. "The Golden Age of TV Is Dead; Long Live the Golden Age of TV." *A.V. Club*, September 10. http://www.avclub.com/article/the-golden-age-of-tv-is-dead-long-live-the-golden--103129.

Vessey, David. 2007. "Gadamer's Hermeneutic Contribution to a Theory of Time-Consciousness." *Indo-Pacific Journal of Phenomenology* 7 (2): 1–7.

Warminski, Andrzej J. 2013. *Material Inscriptions: Rhetorical Readings in Theory and Practice*. Edinburgh, UK: Edinburgh University Press.

Whalley, George. 1997. "On Translating Aristotle's *Poetics*." In *Aristotle's Poetics: Translated and with a Commentary by George Whalley*, 3–32. Montreal, Canada: McGill-Queen's University Press.

Williams, Tony. 2004. "From Elvis to L.A.: Reflections on the Carpenter-Russell Films." In *The Cinema of John Carpenter: The Technique of Terror*, edited by Ian Conrich and David Wood, 118–27. London: Wallflower Press.

Breaking Bad and Django Unchained
Strange Bedfellows

Glenda Pritchett

Post-9/11 movie and television audiences have, to a degree, moved away from traditional American film depictions of good and evil, right and wrong, and have gravitated toward the more complex and morally ambiguous narrative, as reception of the series *Dexter* and the film *There Will Be Blood* makes clear. As one cultural critic puts it, "Earnest melodramas with clear distinctions between good and evil are simply not commercially viable in contemporary American culture industry when compared with narratives that blur them" (Pine 2011, 346). Unlike the squeaky clean Superman of the mid-twentieth century, even the popular superhero genre has now elevated the antihero. Spider-Man, whose early alter identity was the rejected, lonely teen Peter Parker, by 2010 joins the Avengers as an adult but is dogged by insecurity. More notably, Batman's troubled youth leads

Christian Bale, the most recent star of *The Dark Knight Rises*, in 2012 to lament, "He's not a healthy individual, this is somebody that is doing good, but he's right on the verge of doing bad. . . . He's got that killer within him that he's desperately not trying to let off his leash" (quoted in Sacks 2012).[1] So it comes as no surprise that Vince Gilligan's AMC cable series *Breaking Bad* has been extraordinarily successful precisely because it depicts an anti-hero, Walter White, in a world in which stability is shaken, morality is questioned, and the most unlikely candidate is susceptible to breaking bad.

Almost as unique in its sharp turn away from earlier film tradition, in this case depictions of slavery in the United States, is Quentin Tarantino's controversial *Django Unchained*. This brash, over-the-top slave-revenge narrative pairs two most unlikely characters, the captured slave Django, who is on a mission to rescue his wife Broomhilda, and Dr. King Schultz, a German dentist-turned-bounty-hunter, who needs Django to identify several key criminals. *New Yorker* critic David Denby (2013) notes, "The audience is definitely alive to it, reveling in its incongruities, enjoying what's lusciously and profanely over the top."

Audiences have been "alive" to both these works because of what might be termed a shared "historical field" (Berlant 2008, 846). Indeed, James Bowman (2013) has identified what he calls the "big secret" of Walt's audience appeal, and one might argue that of the series:

> Walter has found the way into viewers' sympathies, pioneered by
> cowboys and gangsters in the American entertainment industry of
> past generations, by exempting himself (in his case with the help of
> his diagnosis) from enlightened ideas of Good and Bad and returning
> to that frontier state of nature where the only thing that matters is the
> skill to survive. Or that and a sense of honor. (166)

In these terms both *Breaking Bad* and *Django Unchained* qualify as twenty-first-century Westerns of a sort. *Breaking Bad* is set in modern-day Albuquerque but, as Bowman points out, the raw frontier into which Walt ventures is the alternative world of drug cartels and crystal methamphetamine. *Django Unchained* is set primarily in pre–Civil War Texas and Mississippi, and the frontier challenge for Django—once he is literally unchained by Dr. Schultz at the film's opening and ideologically unchained at the end—is not the rugged nineteenth-century frontier but the institution of slavery itself. Both Walt and Django begin with clearly identified goals—Walt, to make just enough money selling methamphetamine to leave his family financially secure upon his death from lung cancer, and Django, to rescue his wife from slavery and lead them both to a life of freedom—but neither is at all clear about how he will accomplish his goal. That is, until serendipity places in each man's path just the right person.

What these two widely diverse narratives share is a partnership of male characters in which neither can be successful without the other. One element of appeal in this narrative construct is the seeming relationship to the buddy film in which two male characters, often from different backgrounds or races and with every reason to distrust one another, are paired and grow to become friends, overcoming whatever sociocultural obstacles seem to be looming. So Walter White / Jesse Pinkman and Django / Dr. Schultz, inhabitants of entirely different worlds, find themselves paired both by choice and necessity. Django and Schultz develop a uniquely harmonious relationship best captured by the astute if harsh observation by Schultz that their respective enterprises—slavery and bounty hunting—are basically "flesh for cash" businesses. But *Breaking Bad* is no *Butch Cassidy and the Sundance Kid* remake. Despite numerous scenes of growing reciprocal understanding and even tenderness between Walt and Jesse, theirs is to be, in the end, no buddy relationship.

Referring to films principally from the past two decades such as *Brokeback Mountain* and *The Departed*, and citing buddy films and Westerns as antecedents, David Greven (2009) has coined the term "double-protagonist film" in which "*two* protagonists, each played by a star . . . lay legitimate claim to narrative dominance" (22). He argues that recent double-protagonist films suggest "that manhood's center cannot hold, that manhood is split, that the warring elements of manhood spill out beyond the individual subjectivity of the star-protagonist, and that the burden of male representation must be carried by two stars rather than one" (23). While neither *Breaking Bad* nor *Django Unchained* closely fits this analysis, Greven's discussion of Hollywood's treatment of American masculinity bears scrutiny. Focusing on classic Hollywood male protagonists, he observes, "Of the core identity of American manhood, D. H. Lawrence's description remains exact: 'The essential American soul is hard, isolate, stoic, and a killer.' And this is the crucial next line: 'It has never yet melted'" (24). This line is crucial, according to Greven, precisely because the double-protagonist film uncovers a softening, a melting of this image of the solitary male protagonist "whose center cannot hold." Similarly, David Pierson's (2013) description of Walt as "a tired, unhappy, overworked, and emasculated middle-aged man" (20) can be seen to represent, for Gilligan's audience, the American male on the heels of the recession of 2007–2009, when *Breaking Bad* debuted, a time when "only the ruthless capitalist entrepreneurs, whether legitimate or illegitimate, are handsomely rewarded and the timid often find themselves marginalized or even victimized in a winner-take-all modern society" (11). It is not hard then to imagine that Walt might embrace his terminal diagnosis as somehow freeing, allowing him to envision himself and what remains of his life in a whole new light, a new man, as it were, "hard, isolate, stoic, and a killer."

What is fascinating about a study of these partnerships in two such wildly different works is that it affords a glimpse into the current appeal of the antihero—the rebel hero who violates established norms of behavior and defies societal institutions, yet thereby achieves certain ends, either wholly or in part, and in the two works under discussion here, directly through a relationship with another male. This paper examines four features of the principal male relationships: (1) one of the pair is ostensibly in a position to teach the other, though both learn from one another; (2) one of the pair is educated and highly articulate, while the other is inarticulate but not unintelligent; (3) the goal of both main characters is rooted in love of family; and (4) both main characters are motivated by a grudge against / hate for a society that is unfair and are frustrated by their inability to make things right. In the end, both Walt and Django find themselves moving inexorably down a devious, violent, and vengeful path that they could not have foreseen nor traversed without the aid of their partner. As a result, both discover within themselves untapped depths of rage and cunning that are exploited to the fullest.

The highly original teaser of the *Breaking Bad* pilot, trousers billowing against the clear New Mexico sky, and shortly after, the owner, unceremoniously arrayed in dress shirt and tighty-whity briefs, introduces Walter White, meek family man and high school chemistry teacher whose promising early brilliance was somehow cut short and whose diagnosis of terminal cancer leads to the consequential invitation (a threat, really): "But you know the business and I know the chemistry. I'm thinking maybe you and I could partner up. . . . Either that or I turn you in" (season 1, episode 1). This proposition to Jesse Pinkman, former unpromising chemistry student and now "Cap'n Cook" in the local Albuquerque drug scene, initiates the relationship that to an extent defines the series. It is clear from the outset that Walt considers himself intellectually and morally superior to Jesse, and indeed by all practical measures, at this time he is. Jesse refers to his own method of cooking methamphetamine, with his signature additive of chili powder, as art, but even with his derisive critiques of Walt's purist chemical techniques, with the first batch he declares Walt's product to be "pure glass," "art." What Walt needs from Jesse are street smarts, but while Jesse prides himself on being able to demonstrate expertise to his former teacher and now demonstrably superior methamphetamine cook, Jesse's gangsta street credentials prove to be less than stellar. The schooling for both has just begun.

As mature, educated professionals, both Walt and Schultz are in a position to mentor and teach Jesse and Django, even as both plainly recognize that the young men have invaluable experience and information to impart. Of course, there is no comparing Schultz's superior status, education, and even 1858 street smarts to those of the slave Django. But just as Walt is paralyzed without the ability to get his product to market, Django has knowledge that Schultz cannot attain elsewhere—the ability to identify the three criminal Brittle brothers next on Schultz's to-kill list. Schultz has been tracking two slavers with their half dozen shackled slaves and happens upon them in a forest at night. Having dispensed with the slavers in self-defense and speaking to Django man to man, not man to slave, Schultz offers Django a business partnership that benefits them both, including ultimately granting Django his freedom. He is a patient mentor, carefully explaining verbally or motioning to a wide-eyed and largely mute Django how he should conduct himself in the initial encounters with white townspeople and lawmen, encounters that Schultz orchestrates precisely to incense the gathered audience as well as, one suspects, to impress. More than once, he marvels at his apprentice's abilities, such as Django's presumably first experience with a firearm, which elicits the pronouncement to no one in particular, "The kid's a natural." As the relationship grows, so does the potential payoff. Moved by Django's single-minded quest to locate and rescue Broomhilda, Schultz agrees to add this enterprise to the end of the winter bounty-hunting list if Django agrees to stay on.

Unlike Schultz and Django, Walt's mentoring of Jesse bears a decidedly condescending tone, though in truth these two have history and the latent teacher-student roles are at the ready. Jesse is stupefied that "Mr. White" has suddenly appeared and wants to partner with him to cook methamphetamine: "Man, some straight like you, giant stick up his ass, all of a sudden at age what? Sixty? He's just going to break bad?" (season 1, episode 1). Later, when Jesse presses him for a reason, Walt answers simply, "I am awake." Newly awake, yes, but utterly unprepared for the dark and sordid world in which his guide Jesse is an amateur at best.

Their first botched encounter with hardened drug dealers Krazy-8 and Emilio, who try to kill Jesse and Walt, results in Emilio's death and the question finally of how to kill Krazy-8. It is surprising that gangsta Jesse is unwilling to commit murder, preferring to dispose of Emilio's body (another amateurish fiasco resulting from his failure to heed Walt's precise instructions). Instead, Walt summons reason, logic, and what's left of his conscience in his approach to the demise of Krazy-8. From this confrontation in which Krazy-8 almost convinces Walt of his humanity at the same moment that he attempts to kill his captor, Walt gets a glimpse of the ruthless killers that inhabit this world. Almost from this moment, his first kill, Walt begins his psychological and emotional metamorphosis into Heisenberg, though not until he is avenging Jesse's brutal beating at the direction of the murderous drug lord Tuco does he adopt the outward identity—dark clothes, shaved head, porkpie hat—that will come to define him. As the series progresses, Walt serves as father figure to Jesse, whose own family has abandoned all hope of his sobriety, while at the same time he manipulates Jesse into killing another chemist, and even go so far as to watch—without assisting—as Jesse's beloved girlfriend chokes on her own vomit and dies. Dustin Freeley (2013) argues that "Jane's presence [as his lover and role model for sobriety] threatened to remove Jesse from the picture, thereby removing Walt's partner" (47), but by this time Jane and Jesse have both relapsed into drug use. Freeley also, however, suggests that "Jesse is . . . an empty vessel into which Walt-as-Heisenberg can impart knowledge that he's unable to pass to his biological son—not on account of intelligence, but because of its illicit nature" (47). Just as Walt chooses a lucrative drug deal over being present at the birth of his daughter, he effectively murders Jane to ensure that his emotional and professional needs are met above all. Walt has perhaps learned his lessons too well.

Jesse goes through several stages in his tutelage under Walt—enthusiasm to be aligned with the methamphetamine cook par excellence, then alternating bursts of confidence as his skills and earnings increase and skepticism as he experiences a cascade of dangers attendant on this particular partnership. One morning, as Jesse shares his teen sketchbook of imaginary superheroes with Jane, he points out one named Rewindo, who "makes everything go in reverse." Jane immediately asks, "You mean like time? Time travel?" Though Jesse says no, she wonders aloud what a psychiatrist might make of it. With their fragile new love and even more fragile sobriety, little wonder that these two might dream of starting over, making different choices in their lives. Finally, throughout all Walt's lies and manipulations, one thing is clear—Jesse is not a cold-blooded killer. He has a heart, Walt has used him mercilessly, and he finally turns on Walt. To say that Jesse is a slow learner is an understatement.

Clearly, Walt and Schultz are the more articulate and highly educated, and each is keenly aware of his respective position. Schultz, an avid abolitionist, is also a cold-blooded killer, though he clarifies to Django that he kills only "bad people." He is careful in his schooling of Django never to patronize or talk down to him but to give sufficient detail for understanding in his directions and explanations, often far more than necessary. As critics have noted, Schultz is the film's embodiment of Tarantino's obsession with language and dialogue: "What the film is really about is his [Tarantino's] chronic and inspired need to talk" (Thomson 2013). Early on, perhaps having learned through experience the consequences of speaking freely to a white man, Django cautiously answers Schultz's questions in clipped phrases and monosyllables. Incredulous at the righteous delight that Schultz takes in dispatching the two slavers and then unshackling—in effect, freeing—the remaining slaves, Django expresses amazement with Shultz's conscientious explanation of his current profession: "You mean you kill white people for money?" This exchange represents the dominant mode of communication between Schultz and Django, the latter tentatively translating Schultz's often long-winded orations and Schultz confirming.

Two related scenes most clearly indicate both Django's increasing command of language and, more important, his growing understanding of his new position with Schultz and his underlying sense of right and wrong. Poised on a ridge overlooking a man and his son plowing a field, Schultz and Django assess the next target for bounty. When Django hesitates to shoot the criminal with the son standing by, Schultz matter-of-factly explains, "This is my world, and in my world you've got to get dirty." Django then shoots to kill. Later, when the two are implementing their scheme to outwit plantation owner Calvin Candie and thereby win Broomhilda, Django flawlessly performing the part of a black slaver who trains Mandingo fighters, Schultz uncharacteristically shows sympathy for a captured runaway slave about to be torn apart by dogs. Django, with just a look, reminds Schultz of his earlier admonition and proceeds to further denigrate the poor slave as a worthless "pickaninny." Django has learned and understands all too well what is at stake in the current endeavor.

Very unlike Schultz, Walt in the beginning seems restrained and at a loss for words, even in the simplest of interactions with his own family, yet evidence of his formidable intellect hangs unobtrusively on the living-room wall in the form of a plaque commemorating his work at Los Alamos: "Walter H. White, Crystallography Project Leader for Proton Radiography, 1985, Contributor to Research Awarded the Nobel Prize." His opening comments to a high school chemistry class, lost on the apathetic students, reveal a world-weary teacher and a scientist without a research laboratory or novel experiment in the works. Soon his relationship with Jesse will lead to a series of "laboratories," however, and the grand experiment of his life.

Walt is at his finest expounding to Jesse on the basic principles of chemistry and the vital importance of proper equipment and safety precautions, yet the mismatch of these two in the early episodes is as evident in Jesse's telling facial expressions as in his floundering street-lingo responses to Walt's derisive critiques of his sloppy technique:

JESSE: Now let me tell you something else. This ain't chemistry, this is art. Cooking is art. And the shit I cook is the bomb, so don't be telling me.
WALT: The shit you cook is shit. I saw your set-up. Ridiculous. You and I will not make garbage. We will produce a chemically pure and stable product that performs as advertised. . . .
JESSE: What the hell is this?
WALT: Lab safety equipment. We're also gonna have an emergency eyewash station. These chemicals and their fumes are toxic, in case you didn't know that.
JESSE: Well, you can dress up like a faggot if you want. Not me.
(season 1, episode 1)

Jesse is portrayed as an average middle-class kid who has fallen into the clutches of the drug world of methamphetamine, and his linguistic bravado is the mark of the low-level dealer-addict, always one drug bust away from jail and financial and personal catastrophe. He delights in enlightening Walt to the ways and the language of the street:

WALT: How much meth did you sell?

JESSE: Nearly an ounce.

WALT: Last time I checked, there were 16 ounces to a pound. What'd you do with the rest? Smoke it?

JESSE: Yo, I been out there all night slinging crystal. You think it's cake moving a pound of meth one-tenth at a time?

WALT: Why are you selling it in such small quantities? Why don't you just sell the whole pound at once?

JESSE: To who? What do I look like, Scarface?

WALT: This is unacceptable. I am breaking the law here . . .

JESSE: You may know a lot about chemistry, but you don't know jack about slinging dope.

(season 1, episode 6)

Ironically, Jesse's final move to part company with Walt and the methamphetamine world reveals a more resolute Jesse, still spare in his language but clear about Walt's increasingly dire tactics: "Whatever, man. You don't want to pay me? I don't care. It's on you. I'm done" (season 5, episode 7).

Both Walt and Django espouse love of family as the basis for the series of decisions and actions that lead to their full-blown metamorphosis into antiheroes. Walt pleads financial security for Skyler, Walter Jr., and Holly after his death; Django is desperate to rescue Broomhilda from the despicable Calvin Candie. Noting that the lead character in Sergio Corbucci's 1966 spaghetti Western *Django* is Caucasian, Stephen Grasso (2013) argues that "the collision of western cinema tropes and a black slavery narrative" is not, as has been suggested, "crass and exploitative," but rather a progression from late 1960s Jamaican reggae music and later Jamaican crime films featuring antihero types glorifying gun violence. Another link between the two *Django* films, however, may be the American male's understanding of home and family on the frontier, which leads to a telling insight into *Breaking Bad*.

Noting that buddy movies are "more interesting than is generally recognized," Robin Wood (1986) maintains that these films are grounded not primarily in "the presence of the male relationship but the absence of home," which Wood argues is "to be understood not merely as a physical location but as both a state of mind and an ideological construct, above all as ideological *security*" (227–28).[2] From the opening scenes of Tarantino's film, as Django trudges barefoot in chains across the rugged desert Southwest, he sees visions of the wife he dreams of rescuing one day. On the evening after

Schultz demonstrated his considerable skill for intricate planning in ridding Daughtry, Texas, of its criminal sheriff, Django confides in Schultz that he and Broomhilda were captured trying to escape, were branded as runaway slaves, and were sold off to different plantations. Powerless to have prevented these calamities, he is on a mission to locate his wife and gain her freedom. As a slave, Django is property, chattel attached to whatever physical home shelters the holder of his bill of sale. But in terms of his state of mind, even before he partners with Schultz, his quest to free Broomhilda is a desperate attempt to achieve, through whatever means, the only home that could ever satisfy the deep need for "ideological security," namely their freedom.

In the original 1966 film, the character Django is a loner, a former Union soldier on a mission to kill the racist Klansmen leader Major Jackson, who murdered his wife. This Django is also spare with words, expressing regret that he was "far away, too far away," presumably in the Civil War, to have saved his wife. And though the prostitute he saves from brutal execution by two rival gangs clearly loves him and offers him a new life, he rejects any notion of reclaiming a sense of home and family, his only ideological security being the ultimate murder of a murderer.

Both Django characters function in terms of the value they ascribe to home and family, the one as a memory never to be forgotten or replaced, the other as a dream for the future to be fought for at all costs. So how do these characters' motivations in two thoroughly Western films relate to *Breaking Bad*?

Though he does not at first divulge his cancer diagnosis or his rationale of leaving his family financially secure, from the initial invitation to Jesse the audience realizes exactly what Walt is up to, but not how far his journey will eventually take him. Throughout the series, Walt repeatedly pleads home and family as the justification for his actions. Yet his actions belie a man who is obsessed with the newfound power of his position as formidable drug lord Heisenberg. Whereas Walt may have chosen this moniker both to link himself to the Nobel-winning physicist and to symbolize his presumed unpredictability to his foes by virtue of his singular intellect, the uncertainty principle "provides an interpretive frame for Walter White's actions" (Brodesco 2013, 59), as at every turn Walt's very presence and actions affect the outcome in unpredictable ways. Gradually, those closest to Walt—Skyler and Jesse—come to realize what he refuses to see and cannot admit to himself, until the very end. He is, in fact, addicted to something as deadly as his Blue Magic—the high of ultimately accomplishing everything that had eluded him previously, namely immense wealth and power, and the deep pride that he feels in these accomplishments. Never mind that he systematically abandons virtually every shred of morality and conscience in the process, as evidenced by the fact that despite his repeated and delusional protestations to the contrary, he long ago abandoned his home and family. Even in the final brutal clash with Skyler and Flynn (Walter Jr.), Walt rages, "What is wrong with you? We're a family!" (season5, episode 14). Walt is not yet able to acknowledge that his "absence of home" is the result of conscious, deliberate choices that he has made.

Finally, no one doubts that a slave, former or not, would harbor extreme hatred toward slavers, slavery sympathizers, and a social order that condones and promotes such inhumanity. But Django not only has lived the experience of the unimaginable cruelty of slavery, as part of the elaborate scheme to trick Candie into selling Broomhilda he has lived the role of slaver, as Schultz's supposed trainer of Mandingo fighters and participant in this unholy institution. Getting dirty, indeed. As Django gradually senses that he is coming close to realizing his dream, he transforms from the role-playing initiate into a full-blown agent of vengeance and retributive justice. Tarantino concludes the film with two spectacularly hyperbolic shootouts, the first of which results in Schultz's death as he kills the malevolent Candie. Django disposes of a number of Candie's henchmen and is captured, only to outwit his captors with the same articulate, flawless English and ingenious subterfuge that he learned from his mentor, Schultz. He returns to Candieland and from the opulent second-floor landing proceeds to slaughter in a hail of bullets every white person left at the plantation. But this "surreal sort of bloodletting," as in a graphic novel or comic book, according to T. A. Wardrope (2013), "signal[s] the essential unreality of his [Tarantino's] story." Django is an antihero in an antislavery phantasmagoria, and he has one last villain to confront.

Critics agree that the most exquisitely outrageous character in *Django Unchained* is Stephen, the head house slave: "He is an Uncle Tom whose servility has mutated into monstrosity and who represents the symbolic self Django must destroy to assert and maintain his freedom" (Scott 2012). Django shoots Stephen in both knees and leaves him to perish in the fiery conflagration that destroys Candieland. Only with this final act can Django in any sense be said to have made things right or hope to achieve the ideological security that will allow him finally to discover home.

Flashbacks in the pilot episode of *Breaking Bad* reveal Walt's ineffectual position in virtually every aspect of his life, including evidence of his early promise never being realized. From the disrespect of his students to his having to work a second job at a car wash to his brother-in-law Hank's mocking his unfamiliarity with firearms, Walt's days are filled with reminders that "people see [him] as a mild-mannered man and a loser" (Faucette 2013, 76). But after the diagnosis of terminal cancer, a first glimpse of the "new" Walt is seen in the clothing store with Skyler and Walter Jr., who has cerebral palsy. Skyler typically plays the role of her son's protector, but to the stunned surprise of his family looking on, Walt springs into action, physically taking on the boorish teenage thug who is mocking Walter Jr. Later, in a delightfully devilish scene, he blows up the fancy sports car of an equally boorish and self-absorbed businessman whose typical behavior both in the bank and on the road reeks of entitlement and self-importance. Walt in these acts of reprisal is getting his first taste of fighting back at a society that crushes the weak and those who, as he views himself, have played by the rules yet not achieved the promised success. But *Breaking Bad* is no Saturday-morning superhero saga. As he moves from cooking methamphetamine into the dark and ruthless business world of drug cartels, and more important, as he comes to wield more power than he could ever have imagined and experiences the resulting high, Walt is asserting, according to Faucette, "more traditional models of American masculinity" (75) that allow him to "reclaim his masculine authority both in society and at home through brutality, intimidation, and stubborn will power" (84). In fact, Walt's cancer remission in season 2 comes as a stunning disappointment because it means that he no longer has a reason to cook and sell methamphetamine and thus can return to his previous unremarkable life, clearly not an option for this Walter White. There is to be no remission for Heisenberg.

Walt eventually commands the purest methamphetamine-production operation in the Southwest, but his frontier skill to survive proves inadequate in the end against the truly soulless neo-Nazi cartel. Just as Schultz justifies his bounty-hunting tactics to Django as killing "bad people," in the end Walt—with perhaps a remnant of his sense of honor—orchestrates an apocalyptic rampage against the neo-Nazis with a hidden M60 machine gun that frees Jesse, being held prisoner in the super laboratory, but results in a mortal wound to Walt.

It is interesting that the original *Django* film presents a similar scene that may serve as a lens through which to interpret the *Breaking Bad* finale.

In the first scene, Django is walking in the desert Southwest, dragging at the end of a rope a wooden coffin bearing a cross. When asked who is in the coffin, he replies, "Django." Later, when questioned how he can possibly hope to prevail against the overwhelming odds of Major Jackson's heavily armed men, Django answers simply, "I have all the help I need." Django's help is in the coffin, a Gatling gun that mows down most of Jackson's militia. Unlike Django (and Tarantino's Django), Walt does not survive his surprise shock-and-awe attack on his enemy, nor does he intend to. This final showdown, if not some measure of redemption or atonement, reveals a man who has come to fully know himself. Previously in this finale episode, Walt admits to Skyler what he could never say even to himself: "I did it for me. . . . I was alive." Heisenberg is immanent in Walt from the beginning. He has always had this capacity for good and evil, or put another way, all the help he needs.

Like Django's Dr. Schultz, Jesse appears in a deus ex machina move that launches his unique relationship with Walt based on mutual need. But as raw and tough as gangsta Jesse tries to appear, to the very end the audience is aware that he could never be a Heisenberg. All along, he naïvely believes that his business partner Walt and his blue methamphetamine will provide "all the help" he needs. Yet gradually and very painfully he comes to realize that he—unlike Walt—is just a drug-dealing street addict, not a cold-blooded murderer addicted to power. Whereas his several attempts at sobriety always failed when the pain of personal loss (Walt's causal shadow always looming) became unbearable, Jesse finally realizes that the only ideological security, the only home, that means anything now is to be alive *and* free—free of Walt and the drug world. As he speeds away in his final scene, his primal scream through laughter and tears is testimony that although he has lost all that was precious to him several times over, he is the one who is alive. Like one of the superheroes in his sketches, he has escaped death, and no drug high even comes close.

In a 2011 interview, Gilligan was asked about the point of his *Breaking Bad* experiment—"transforming a hero into a villain"—and he replied, "To see where we can go, to see where it takes us" (Romano 2013). Walt's grand experiment is to test whether he can make good on the American dream using his intellect and what Bowman describes as "the frontier state of nature, the skill to survive." Referring to "Walter White unleashed," Romano suggests that the final message of Gilligan's experiment is "that America encourages and almost mandates precisely the sort of ravenous striving for individual success and self-actualization that Heisenberg so desperately pursued." In the end, Walt is a tragic antihero whose initial disaffected ordinariness resonates with viewers who may also be wondering about their own survival skills in twenty-first-century America.

Notes

1. I express my thanks to Russ Ketchum for his insight on the rise of the print-comic antihero. Marvel Comics (now owned by Disney) led the shift to grittier characters and the darker antihero (Spider-Man, the Avengers, X-Men, etc.) ten to twenty years before television and movies. DC Comics (now owned by Warner Brothers) aroused debate recently with *Man of Steel* (2013) as a conflicted Superman kills General Zod dramatically, with no clever cinematic device to obscure the action, rather than returning him to prison.
2. David Greven (2009) also cites Robin Wood in his discussion of 1970s buddy films as antecedents to the double-protagonist film, asserting that the absent home is post-Vietnam and -Watergate America (28).

References

Allum, Felia, and Stan Gilmour, eds. *Routledge Handbook of Transnational Organized Crime*. London: Routledge.

Berlant, Lauren. 2008. "Intuitionists: History and the Affective Event." *American Literary History* 20 (4): 845–60.

Bowman, James. 2013. "Criminal Elements." *New Atlantis* 38: 163–73.

Brodesco, Alberto. 2013. "Heisenberg: Epistemological Implications of a Criminal Pseudonym." In *Breaking Bad: Critical Essays on the Contexts, Politics, Style, and Reception of the Television Series*, edited by David P. Pierson, 53–69. Lanham, MD: Lexington.

Corbucci, Sergio (director). [1966] 2004. *Django*. N.p.: Blue Underground, 2004.

Denby, David. 2013. Review of *Django Unchained. New Yorker*, January 22.

Faucette, Brian. 2013. "Taking Control: Male Angst and the Re-emergence of Hegemonic Masculinity in *Breaking Bad*." In *Breaking Bad: Critical Essays on the Contexts, Politics, Style, and Reception of the Television Series*, edited by David P. Pierson, 73–86. Lanham, MD: Lexington.

Freeley, Dustin. 2013. "The Economy of Time and Multiple Existences in *Breaking Bad*." In *Breaking Bad: Critical Essays on the Contexts, Politics, Style, and Reception of the Television Series*, edited by David P. Pierson, 33–52. Lanham, MD: Lexington.

Grasso, Stephen. 2013. Review of *Django Unchained*. *Quietus*, February 1.

Greven, David. 2009. "Contemporary Hollywood Masculinity and the Double-Protagonist Film." *Cinema Journal* 48 (4): 22–43.

Pierson, David P., ed. 2013. *Breaking Bad: Critical Essays on the Contexts, Politics, Style, and Reception of the Television Series*. Lanham, MD: Lexington.

Pine, Jason. 2011. "Transnational Organized Crime and Alternative Culture Industry." In *Routledge Handbook of Transnational Organized Crime*, edited by Felia Allum and Stan Gilmour, 335–49. London: Routledge.

Romano, Andrew. 2013. Review of *Breaking Bad*. *Daily Beast*, September 30.

Sacks, Ethan. 2012. "Christian Bale Says Goodbye to Batman with *The Dark Knight Rises*, and He's Okay with That." *New York Daily News*, January 23.

Scott, A. O. 2012. Review of *Django Unchained*. *New York Times*, December 24.

Tarantino, Quentin (director). 2013. *Django Unchained*. Culver City, CA: Columbia Pictures.

Thomson, David. 2013. Review of *Django Unchained*. *New Republic*, January 5.

Wardrope, T. A. 2013. Review of *Django Unchained*. *Twin Cities Daily Planet*, March 6.

Wood, Robin. 1986. *Hollywood from Vietnam to Reagan*. New York: Columbia University Press.

11

"It Wasn't Whole Foods, Was It?"

Identity Management, Duplicity,
and the False Consciousness of Suburbia

Brad Klypchak

As illustrated by this collection, *Breaking Bad* offers a great many manners in which the series might be thematically explored. For this chapter, I am choosing to focus on the prevalent and important theme of identity management and the performed representation of normalcy in everyday life. Across the whole of the series, characters routinely practice several forms of duplicity as a means of presenting a publicly acceptable persona regardless of its degree of genuineness. Most readily apparent, chemistry teacher Walter White obscures his illicit side as meth lord Heisenberg, and the arc of the series foregrounds this conscious manipulation of persona in the viewer's awareness. Beyond the deceptions hiding his illicit, criminal enterprise, Walt obscures a variety of truths within this overarching aim: insecurities or lies devised to save face, emotional upheavals and fears brought on from his cancer diagnosis, pride and his resistance toward charity (most explicitly, denying financial help from Elliot and Gretchen Schwartz), and manipulative ploys to fulfill his own agendas, to name a few. The plan to hide in plain sight (a strategy Walt shares with Gustavo Fring) weakens when role expectations shift situationally: Walt shifts his roles of father, teacher, husband, in-law, and criminal and in doing so routinely and readily employs duplicity as a primary tactic for obscuring stigmatizing realities.

Less immediately apparent are supporting characters, who, while less prominent in the story arc, are still telling in their own right. One such character is Marie. Sister of Skyler, in-law of Walt, and wife of drug enforcement agent Hank, Marie represents a variety of identity-manipulative personas.[1] Whether obscuring her kleptomania (the primary focus of this chapter), denying her husband's self-doubt, or ignoring the multitude of dysfunctions tied to being part of the extended White family, Marie inevitably represents herself through a persona of idealistic suburban security. The false consciousness of such a pursuit is conveyed throughout the narrative, leaving the audience with a sense of the failures embedded within this myth of modernist suburbia. To forge this argument, I rely upon two key theoretical foundations, Dan Blazer's framing of postmodernity as fostering an "age of melancholy" and Erving Goffman's canonical work on identity management and stigma.

Suburbia, Modernist Myths, and the
Postmodern Age of Melancholy

In their canonical *Popular Culture: An Introductory Text*, Nachbar and Lause (1992) establish ten grand narrative myths commonly reflected and referenced within primarily North American popular-culture outlets. Of these ten, arguably eight are readily evidenced within suburban middle-class stereotypes, more often than not as indicating suburban qualities as modernistically desirable—the "American dream" of progress; material abundance; secure, safe, and loving families; and the unfettered ability to pursue liberty and happiness that comes to routinely inform the world views of postwar Baby Boomers and succeeding generations. Davison (2013) summarizes the notion as follows: "Both the intellectual creators of the suburb and its critics shared a conviction that a particular urban form—low density, detached house and garden, in a semirural setting, remote from the city—would create, or at least facilitate, a desirable way of life: quiet, secluded, law-abiding, family-centered, perhaps conservative" (841). Despite the utopic vision, there is also, as Davison notes, the gradual fissure between the initial ideology and the outcome in which suburban settings, homogeneous and conformist as they are, still experience "as much domestic misery, ill health, ugliness, and class conflict" as found in the city (842). Nonetheless, the popular-culture tendency to regenerate this myth remains, as evidenced by Coon's (2013) admission that "although it may be a far cry from reality, the idea of a perfect suburban life still exists in the collective imagination of millions of Americans" (6).

Blazer (2005) argues that the postmodern dissolve of modernist myths like that of a perfect suburban life has fostered a contemporary proclivity toward depression. To Blazer, anxiety arises as a result of the inability to connect and find meaning within "the sacred canopy of modern progress" (136), resulting in anomie, a condition of loss of identity highlighted by disconnection from a meaningful social belonging or sense of community. Viewing urbanization as breaking up of the local community, Blazer proposes that people could no longer rely on face-to-face relationships to build connections to civic loyalty and, as a result, exchanged personal responsibility for personal entitlements.

All told, Blazer suggests that the modern self has lost its reference points for establishing security and hope. Contextually situated in postmodern uncertainties, severe depression becomes understandably predictable, a condition that signals a sense of not being secure in one's self through having lost "orientation, meaning, and hope" (150). Amid the many conditions Blazer cites as reflecting loss of hope, I offer two, loss of story and loss of self, as being directly applicable for use as an analytical lens for deconstructing the character and behaviors of Marie.

Blazer situates loss of story as personal narrative no longer in connection with a larger societal whole: "narrative is embodied in the community and specifically in the stories that shape the community; that is metanarratives. These embodied narratives ground the world view of a given community" (152). Where generating a personal narrative could previously have connected into a collective metanarrative (or set of metanarratives recalling those of Nachbar and Lause, Davison, and Coon), the postmodern condition of anomie and the dissolved faith in grand narratives diminish the restorative power in telling one's story. Lacking communally recognized references to ground one's story in a purposeful or meaningful

158   Brad Klypchak

way, symptomatic states of anxieties—"meaninglessness, hopelessness, self-denigration, nihilism, fragmentation, alienation, disorientation, suspiciousness, and loneliness" (151)—are likely occurrences.

Clearly connected to a sense of story is one's sense of self. Within modernity, the stability of grand narratives afforded confidence in self-identifications. Postmodernity problematizes the process as previous securities are complicated into shifting, fleeting continua of instability and distrust. The self then drifts further from trustworthy sources of comparison and, as a result, becomes more dubiously performed in the face of the loss of meaning and faith in the roles, traditions, and societal world views previously embraced.

Story, Self, Stigma, and Identity Management

Difficulties in rectifying story and self in effective ways bring about furtive attempts to (mal)adapt as a coping mechanism. The anxieties brought about from failing to find satisfaction in connecting or emulating an objective grand narrative's claim drives acts of desperation seeking to at least temporarily stem the tide: "Hints of catastrophe haunt our times. People busy themselves with survival strategies. People have withdrawn from societal concerns to personal preoccupations. We therefore live for the moment as we lose confidence in the future" (Blazer 2005, 151). I offer manipulations of the self and one's story as being reflective of such postmodern anxieties and the short-term survival strategies that come about accordingly.

Erving Goffman's works are rife with prejudice, patriarchy, heteronormativity, and other oppressive hegemonies. Nonetheless, his conceptualizations of the presentation of self in everyday life are useful, and Goffman remains a key figure in contemporary sociological thought. Befitting modernist grand narratives, Goffman (1956) ultimately acknowledges the role of morality ever present in the process of identity management: "In his mind the individual says: 'I am using these impressions of you as a way of checking up on you and your activity, and you ought not to lead me astray'" (161). Yet often duplicity does emerge within impression-management maneuvers. One common instance where duplicity occurs is related to behaviors, conditions, and attributes deemed stigmatizing.

Goffman describes stigma as occurring when a person is "reduced in our minds from a whole and usual person to a tainted, discounted one" (3). To carry the label of stigma is to threaten social standing, and this threat extends beyond the stigmatized individual. Goffman proposes that being deemed "with" someone can result in an extension of the stigmatizing social meaning: "a person wanted for arrest can legally contaminate anyone he is seen with, subjecting them to arrest on suspicion" (47). If one can evade detection or does not fall subject to being discredited, the stigmatized person can "pass" as being one of what Goffman terms the "normals" (5).

Role expectancies fuel the system of evaluation embedded within the dramaturgical systems of performances and perceptions. Goffman illustrates this using a conceptualization of "wife": "of the category 'wife,' for example that she will look after the house, entertain our friends, and be able to bear children. She will be a good or bad wife, and be this relative to standard expectations, ones that other husbands in our group have about their wives too" (53). Because of the tendency to personalize roles and maintain a conscious awareness of performing in those roles, it is not all that long a conceptual step to extend Goffman's notions of stigma into the realms of Foucault's (1991) panopticism and the system of self-awareness and self-policing it entails. As one is constantly subject to scrutiny and observation, the threat of visibility (and by extension, the potential for the discreditable to become publicly known) immerses the individual in an ongoing state of self-awareness. Fear of being categorized as anything but "normal" invites comparisons back to those normative role expectations. Living up to these roles becomes of paramount importance.

It is from this comparative positioning that I examine Marie's duplicities in both story and self. Her intertwined roles as wife, aunt, X-ray laboratory technician, and, perhaps most prominently, member of the suburban bourgeoisie routinely correspond to the grand narrative myths of suburban materialism and an all-consuming need to retain membership amid the "normals" she presumes surround her.

Baby Tiaras and the False Hope of Material Abundance

Marie's kleptomania marks the most immediate instance of stigma. Underlying Marie's transgression is a declaration of what Goffman (1963) calls "blemishes of individual character" (4). Theft itself violates both legal and moral expectations, and Marie's inability to maintain self-control violates the presumed normalcy of societal obedience to legal and moral standards. In season 1, episode 3, Marie's theft of a pair of shoes from a boutique affords enough uncertainty to allow audiences to ascribe any of a number of interpretative judgments to Marie's actions. If anything, the delivery of the sequence itself positions potential audience complicity.

A pig-tailed, pierced-nose salesclerk preoccupied with a personal phone call is demonstratively annoyed when Marie asks for her assistance. As Marie tries on the shoes, a stylish pair of spike-heeled pumps, the salesclerk, still clutching the phone, castigates Marie for her failure to use a disposable sock. (Marie retorts, "I'm extremely clean.") The superficial exaggeration of customer service "politeness" by the salesclerk prescribing store policy patronizes Marie all the more, and the cynicism within the exchange becomes palpable. The clerk leaves the sales floor to check on stock for her friend on the phone, leaving Marie alone. A small smirk crosses Marie's face, and she wears the heels out of the store, leaving her own shoes behind in the very spot where the heels were displayed.

To the viewer, the passive aggression of the "trade" reads as potentially justifiable in consideration of the shoddy customer service and one's iden-tification with Marie in experiencing social disregard. By leaving the shoes behind, the act of shoplifting seems to be mitigated symbolically as an exchange of goods rather than an outright theft. Having had no previous experience with Marie's kleptomaniac behavior, the viewer, while privy to witnessing the theft, does not know whether this is truly a stigmatized act or some aberration of an otherwise normal character.

The opening to the episode itself, however, features Marie's rigid con-demnation of the very shoes she leaves behind. Telling within the specific details of Marie's dialogue are the apparent markers of stereotyped expec-tations and an implied desire to distance herself from such categorizations. An establishing shot shows Marie's vividly blue Volkswagen Beetle outside the White residence. A cut to the shoes themselves, pristinely white train-ers perfectly laced, pans up to reveal Marie dressed for work in an appro-priate knee-length-while-sitting-down burgundy dress, white laboratory coat, and subtle gold jewelry as accessories. During the pan, Marie's dec-laration, "I hate these shoes," begins a series of perceived significations she ascribes to the shoes: "they make me look like I should be changing bed-pans"; "squeaking around bringing soup to some disgusting old person"; "take the bus home to my sixteen cats." Yet, when Walter Jr. questions the shoes themselves, Marie justifies their functionality: "I like the support. My arches happen to be severely arch-y."

This brief interlude conveys the sheer importance Marie ascribes to the material object. Likewise, she evidences her investment in status hierarchies and the desire to eschew presumably negative associations to lower positions (curiously, Marie later is shown both changing Hank's bedpan and bringing him soup during his convalescence in season 3). Trivializations of riding the bus (implying not having the material means to have a trendy new Bug), having sixteen cats (implying loneliness and the failure to have secured an appropriate husband), and contact with abjection (bedpans; old people presumed disgusting through inability to resist aging and retain bodily control; her own hygienic claim of being extremely clean carrying a corollary of some other whose stigma necessitates the precaution of a disposable sock) hearken back to myths of material abundance and nuclear families. Yet, through the pragmatism of the trainers, she engages the medicalized rationality for herself and her arches, a rationality that is completely dismissed by the theft of the arch-demanding spike heels. Use value is exchanged for commodity value and the symbolic discretionary wealth such an impractical shoe conveys. The immediate satisfaction of consumption and ownership stemming from Marie's theft invites framing Marie's connection to materialism as both a significant component to her world view and a coping device to reclaim the security of bourgeois normalcy.

Marie's kleptomania recurs within a story arc presented in the finale episode of season 1. A baby shower held in the White home is depicted through a home video camera. Marie is the first person to provide testimony to "Esmeralda," the exotic name Marie deems worthy for the child-to-be. Marie's testimonial primarily focuses on Marie herself, projecting that in twenty years "Esmeralda" will be unable to notice any sort of difference in her aunt because of Marie's remarkable ability to retain the appearance of youth. She then introduces the camera operator, Walter Jr., and directs him to follow suit in speaking to his sister while on camera. As he does so, Marie admonishes Walter Jr. ("not up the nose") for his unflattering lack of cinematographic awareness. Further snippets of Skyler and Hank reflect unease at being filmed, particularly when contrasted to Marie's zealous commitment to the documentation transpiring.

Perspective changes once gift opening ensues as traditional cinematography resumes. A wide-angle shot captures a circle of nine women in the living room surrounding Skyler, fully performing to the expectations of a baby-shower ritual. Hank also is seen, but he exists outside the performance both in space (sitting outside the circle at the far end of the room) and action (attention is directed to his cell phone rather than toward Skyler). Marie proudly hands Skyler a small present "from me. . . . oh, and Hank."

Marie proudly accepts and restates Skyler's compliment of "always finding the best wrapping paper" and happily prepares pen and notepad to continue to record each respective gift and giver. Skyler unwraps the box and is perplexed by the object revealed, a baby tiara that Marie explains as being made of "white gold and several carats worth of zircons." Skyler's hesitancy in praising the gift is cloaked in a face-saving maneuver ("You spent too much on this. You really shouldn't have . . . but it's really . . . sparkly!") with Marie gladly accepting the performed enthusiasm. Witnessing the event, Hank suggests to Walt that they escape the feminized ritual completely in favor of a more masculinized one of their own, drinking top-shelf hard liquor and smoking contraband Cuban cigars outside by the pool.

Marie's enthusiasm in gifting a gold-and-gemstone tiara for a baby is rife with preposterous qualities yet fully speaks to her blinded investment in material goods. The little princess her niece represents is to be adorned with an utterly valueless item from the standpoint of use, itself extravagantly flaunting material abundance in both its composition and inadaptability for any age aside from the newborn. As Skyler and Walt later discuss, the sheer impracticality of the tiara (and the $500–$600 price tag Skyler estimates for its cost) could readily be exchanged for a far more pragmatic diaper pail. For Marie, however, functionality matters little in comparison with the allure of showy materialistic presentation and performative value of wealthy appearances.

When Skyler attempts to return the tiara to the store she believes it has come from, an upscale jewelry boutique, the stigma is unveiled, but in this instance, Skyler is presumed to be the thief. When the store manager declares her as such, two witnesses in the background can be seen emanating schadenfreude, delighting in the spectacle of the stigmatized being publicly exposed. The scene cuts to a back room where the manager and a security guard bookend Skyler. Upon declaring her lasting innocence and the truthful receipt of the tiara as a gift, the store manager engages duplicity by claiming a recollection of seeing one of his employees showing the tiara to "a tall blond woman . . . who walked right out the door." Skyler immediately returns that lie with one just as fictitious, yet laden with considerable damning discreditability: "I can talk to the Channel Three News . . . tell them how you people, without a shred, a modicum of evidence, illegally detained an innocent, pregnant woman in a dank storeroom. . . . I'm not getting enough air back here. I don't think I can breathe. . . . Oh no. I think

I'm going into labor." The sequence ends depicting Skyler exiting the jewelry store and immediately calling Marie to confront her indiscretion.

Curiously, while her presumption of truth initiates Skyler's attempt at returning the tiara (Skyler at that point never remotely considers the prospect of Marie as thief), the immediate stigmatizing judgment overrides any presumption of truth thereafter. The manager's demonstrative public accusation and vigilant pursuit of punishment seemingly indicates a commitment to morality and honest pursuit of justice, yet he tarnishes that pursuit through his own fabricated tale of a tall blond woman, a testimony designed to close the presumptive gap of categorizing Skyler as the actual criminal. But Skyler does not choose to refute his lie, but contrives her own with enough detail to prove plausibly threatening enough (regardless of its veracity) to free herself from the scenario. Faith in the justice system and the pursuit of fact are circumvented. Rather, it seems the ability to convey the more sensational narrative with just enough markers of credibility (such as Skyler's ability to employ fitting erudite vocabulary and the social-class role presumptions that performance reflects) is what truly counts.

Skyler's initial confrontation with Marie takes place in yet another boutique. The sequence opens with Marie taking an interest in a pair of earrings, her smirk recurring as she examines them in the mirror. At this moment, Skyler arrives and expositionally declares a series of Marie's avoidances, to which Marie attempts to reflect an impropriety of social graces back upon Skyler. ("I did not sneak. I was going to lunch. . . . Geez, what are you, the paranoia police?") A second attempt at displacement happens when Marie expresses offense and hurt feelings upon hearing of Skyler's choice to return her gift. From that juncture, the more direct that each of Skyler's attempts become at garnering an explanation, the more resistant the denials from Marie become (a shrug, a discrediting denial of knowledge, a more forceful statement of distancing denial). Skyler gives up and leaves the store in befuddled frustration after hearing Marie's final denial: "I can't really admit to something when I have no knowledge to what it is that I'm admitting."

A few points of attention merit discussion here. Once again, we encounter Marie in a store, with shopping and consumerism as a leisure pursuit of choice. This time, however, as an audience member, any previous ambiguity ascribed to Marie's shoe caper has now vanished with the tiara as evidence of her repeated shoplifting behavior. Her contemplation of the earrings reads as transgressive; she is now fully discredited in the audience's mind. During this sequence, each time Skyler uses the term "shoplifting" she does so in hushed voice as if the sheer use of the term would associate her with Marie's stigma. Rather than admit her kleptomania, Marie's incredulity about the attempted return both denies the immediacy of the confrontation itself and temporarily subjects Skyler to the blemish on her own character, the impropriety of not accepting gifts graciously. Though Skyler begins to respond ashamedly, she cuts that reaction short after a moment's recall of the reason for confronting Marie. Through denial and duplicity, Marie furtively attempts to retain her normalcy despite all indications otherwise.

Season 2 opens with no formal resolution of Marie and Skyler's impasse. The normalcy of Marie's suburbia is, however, reestablished through a brief scene in episode 1 that places Marie in her contemporarily accessorized kitchen. Using a voice-activated, hands-free telephone system, Marie leaves a message for Skyler mundanely inviting her and the rest of the White family out for Chinese food. The scene opens with a close-up of a row of five Splenda packets laid one after another on a dark granite countertop. The shot pans up to a kitschy purple mug emblazoned with "Kleinman Radiology Center," a tagline of "we see right through you" and a dancing skeleton with top hat and cane. A coffeemaker of the exact shade of purple is later revealed along with a full array of color-coordinated accessories and upscale appliances. Marie concludes her message by declaring herself as "hip" and positing a possibility that "people in China might feel like American . . . get little take-out boxes with mashed potatoes and meat loaf and try to figure out how to use the knives and forks."

The variety of material items, once again, communicates the performance of suburban myths. Synthetic sweetener saves problematic calories while the conscious attention to décor conforms to a proscribed aesthetic expectation. Her patronizing exoticization of Chinese culture becomes interwoven with a myopic universalization of Western practices as normative. When performed by Marie, we infer her genuine embrace of their modernist significations of progress, status, and desirable hierarchies, but the kitschy, empty qualities they actually connote cause a sense of the postmodern resistance to such narratives to prevail for the viewer.

A second layer of duplicity becomes evident when Hank attempts to intervene and rectify Marie and Skyler's conflict. Hank pleads with Skyler to reopen the lines of communication, to which Skyler confesses the core cause, Marie's refusal to acknowledge her shoplifting and the carry-over shame brought upon Skyler herself. Hank dejectedly accepts this information, thereby indicating his own complicity. Relying on rhetoric of addiction and recovery, Hank acknowledges Marie's problem, but he also attempts to diminish its severity through the mention of therapy and commitment pledges: "We gotta support the shit out of her," a claim Skyler finds ludicrous in light of her own circumstances:

> The almost forty-year-old pregnant woman with the surprise baby on the way, and the husband with lung cancer who disappears for hours on end and I don't know where he goes and he barely even speaks to me anymore, with the moody son who does the same thing, and the overdrawn checking account, and the lukewarm water heater that leaks rusty-looking crap and is rotting out the floor of the utility closet and we can't even afford to fix it. But oh, I see, now I'm supposed to go, "Hank, please, what can I possibly do to further benefit my spoiled, kleptomaniac, bitch sister who somehow always manages to be the center of attention 'cause God knows she's the one with the really important problems."

Skyler's monologue not only attacks Marie's superficiality while resisting the nuclear family myth about her "bitch sister" but also acknowledges the failures of the nuclear family mythos within the White household. No faith is shown in therapeutic intervention, and the impending financial crisis manifests itself in the failings of one of suburbia's entitlements, a dependably functioning water heater. Hank's attempt to invoke therapeutic rhetoric marks him as what Goffman (1963) labels the "wise," a normal whose special circumstances make them "privy to the secret life of the stigmatized individual" (28), though Marie's backsliding invalidates the therapeutic promise of recovery and subsequent normalcy.

Ultimately, Skyler does demand and receive Marie's confession. In season 2, episode 5, a barbecue at the Schraders sees the families come together. Opening as Marie complains of Hank's promotional transfer to El Paso ("an armpit") and expresses her preference for Washington ("I could see us in a cute little condo in Georgetown in a couple of years"), she continues her mundane monologue until Skyler silences her: "I will not listen to another word until you apologize". Marie attempts deflective tactics like those of season 1, episode 7, including, once again, bringing up "if you hadn't decided to return it" and then asking the accusatory "why are you punishing me?" This provokes Skyler's last and most incisive offensive yet, sisterhood and the sanctity of family, which finally breaks Marie's stonewalling denials. Where maintaining a duplicitous front of innocence has previously helped Marie avoid admitting to her stigma, the threat of forgoing family and its connection to Marie's world view proves too much for her to risk.

Stigma and the Escape of the Self through Story

Marie's kleptomania returns as a plot point in season 4, episode 3. In this instance, Marie is shown attending open houses in well-to-do homes. Contrasting the impersonal exchanges seen before in the shoe store, Marie openly welcomes conversation with the real-estate agents, but in doing so she creates a new fictive persona that she performs for the unknowing realtor. By engaging in such role playing, Marie essentially achieves two pragmatic objectives. First and foremost, she obscures her true identity and, as a result, generates a buffering distance between reality and the fictional role she adopts. Second, she connects herself with the roles and statuses she would genuinely desire to represent, to enact those expectations and receive the societal reception attributed to whatever particular status those identifiers entail.

Abigail De Kosnik (2010) applies Michel Foucault's notion of gymnasia in her analytic readings of various television series and the ways in which characters consciously perform false identities:

> *Mad Men*'s Don and Betty and *Glee*'s Artie know who they are on the inside, but they generally refuse, or have no opportunity, to show their inner selves in public. Performing allows these characters to reveal the repressed aspects (which are the most authentic, core aspects) of their personalities. The artificiality, the constructedness, of theatrical situations somehow works as gymnasia and allows these characters to expose their hidden, authentic selves. (378)

Adopting such a tactic for considering Marie, I propose that the richness of details by which she builds and conveys her fictive characters reflects her ongoing investment in material consumerism.

At the first house, Marie presents herself as Tory Costner, a divorced mother of a four-year-old high-achieving son, Eli ("a Gemini . . . he tests very highly, ninety-sixth percentile"), whom she intends to homeschool ("not for religious reasons") when she is not practicing her pottery artwork. The object she steals from this house is a small knickknack, a Hummel-esque figure of a boy carrying a ladder while riding a pig.

At the second house, Marie becomes Charlotte Blatner. The biography performed this time includes having a brother in the Peace Corps and a husband who worked for NASA (but who catered to Charlotte's call for him to quit his "too stressful" job), a career as a hand model, and a resistance to having children (despite her husband's seeming desire to have them). Here, Marie steals a small souvenir spoon from Puerto Rico.

Finally, at the last residence, Marie's story comes about by speaking with the homeowners hosting the open house. This time, Marie is Mimi, wife to an illustrator who has traveled extensively across Europe and lived in London "for years." Traveling was cut back when daughter Lucy contracted endocarditis, but her prosthetic valve brought about her recovery and Lucy can now pursue leisure pursuits of running, jumping, and riding horses. To Marie/Mimi's chagrin, the same realtor she met when portraying Charlotte enters the room and confronts the fleeing Marie about both her deceptions and of her theft of the spoon. A scuffle ensues wherein Marie's purse gets spilled, revealing a framed picture of the homeowners. The scene cuts to Hank receiving a phone call from Marie. Though Marie is never heard in the exchange, Hank's initial admonishment ("Are you seriously doing this to me again?") softens to caregiving ("Would you stop crying? I'll make a phone call. Just sit tight.").

In all the examples, significations of upper-middle-class suburbia prevail. Associations with educational attainment, having refinement of leisure pursuits requiring considerable discretionary income, and vocations of prestige are routinely made. Worldly, artistic, and exotically connected to exclusive populations, Marie crafts the grounding points to the fictive personas she performs in a deliberate reflection of her suburban utopic aspirations. In the three thefts, the objects themselves hold no use or value but are decorative and symbolic extensions of the class privilege that wealth allows.

Beyond the material markers, I find Marie's fictive biographies interesting in terms of the variety of family roles she authors. Childless, in two of Marie's alternative personas (Tory and Mimi) she adopts a motherhood role wherein each child carries exceptional qualities. In the third instance, the childless Charlotte admits her hesitancy toward having children despite her husband's apparent contrary wishes. A study by Kristin Park (2002) explores voluntary childlessness as being representative of stigmatization. One explanation Park offers for this is that "stigmatization of the intentionally childless also may stem from the association of their lifestyle with growing individualism, family breakdown, and the predominance of impersonal, rationalized roles and relationships in society" (25). Read through a lens of Blazer's postmodern critique of contemporary society, a connection to the fracturing of modernist security in self and societal-role stability can be made.

A second consideration stems from her portrayals of husbands. Where Tory is divorced (thereby marking her as independent), Charlotte seemingly has a controlling power over her husband, prompting him to leave his stressful yet prestigious job at NASA at her request. There is a slightly more subtle inference of power shown through her resistance to having children, a choice that seemingly resists her husband's expressed desires. Contrast this with Marie's genuine identity. At this point in the story line, Hank is recovering from his injuries sustained in the shootout with the Mexican cartel assassins. Surly and dismissive, Hank is portrayed as resentful of any effort Marie puts forth in encouraging his recovery. Yet upon Marie's discovery and subsequent arrest, the bedridden, convalescing Hank shifts from his frustration and anger toward Marie to a placating, supportive husband who seeks to resolve her dilemma, both legally and emotionally. To do so, he employs his privilege within law enforcement to rescue Marie from becoming publicly and permanently documented as a thief, itself an act of duplicity in the eyes of the law.

"It Wasn't Whole Foods, Was It?"
Stigma, Shame, and the Frailties of Suburban Myths

Early in season 2, Walt concocts and carries out a narrative of having experienced a fugue state to cover up his kidnapping by Tuco that leads to a prolonged absence from his family. The resultant frantic search by Skyler, Walter Jr., and Marie for the missing Walt reunites the sisters (the tiara scandal yet unresolved at this point), bonded by the common greater cause. Walt's eventual "discovery," standing naked within a Hi-Lo Market grocery store, alleviates the prevailing issue of his disappearance, but given its duplicitous origin it offers little in terms of rational explanation for anyone beyond Walt himself.

Season 2, episode 3, explores the aftereffects of Walt's disappearance and return. The sequence of shots suggests that the phone call between Skyler and Marie happens immediately after the first meeting between the hospitalized Walt and his immediate family. In her usual manner, Marie quickly shifts the scope and significance from the seemingly crucial issue of Walt's well-being to that of something far more socially evaluative:

SKYLER: They're going to run a whole series of tests.
MARIE: What could it be? I mean . . . did they give you a worst-case scenario?
SKYLER: Well, you know . . . (exasperated sigh). There's no point in really getting ahead of ourselves.
MARIE: Which supermarket? Was it like a big one, like a chain?
SKYLER: (antagonized) Marie.
MARIE: Don't get me wrong. I mean, I think it's great that he's back and he's feeling better. I just, I mean, he was naked. He was naked, naked in a supermarket. It wasn't Whole Foods, was it?
(season 2, episode 3)

Beyond the lack of tact in her inquiries on Walt's health, Marie's point of focus clearly lies in the stigmatizing transgression of Walt's behavior. The impropriety of being naked is shaming, but to occur at such a communally public venue seems the far greater cause for worry. Goffman (1963) notes, "If there is something discreditable about an individual's past or present, it would seem that the precariousness of his position will vary directly with the number of persons who are in on the secret; the more who know about his shady side the more treacherous the situation" (77). Marie fears most the public nature of Walt's behavior and its potential reflection upon her well-cultivated public image. Consequently, it is as if she is calculating the degree of damage done in proportion to the range of locations. Between visibility, the prestige the store represents, and the liability of becoming discredited, the internal calculation seemingly results with a truly worst-case stigmatizing scenario: Whole Foods. The threat of scorn and shame from the yuppie-targeted store and the clientele with whom Marie so fervently identifies materially would be devastating.

Rita Felski (2000) examines the notion of shame in connection with social class. For Felski, "Shame, then, is fundamentally connected to everyday sociability. This emotion comprises a painful experience of self-consciousness, resulting from a sudden recognition of a discrepancy between one's behavior and that of one's peers" (39). Working through Bourdieu's notion of cultural capital, Felski notes that the prospects of social mobility (upward or downward) and the liabilities of shaming events produces an "acute anxiety about status . . . hypersensitive to the most minute signs of class distinction" (40). In Marie's circumstance, the stigmatizing inability to favorably compare with the Whole Foods consumers (and the cultural-capital significations of social class the store represents) threatens her with ostracism, to be removed in status to that of the other—in this instance, to be subjected to the stereotypical negative perceptions judgmentally cast upon the working class.

For the viewer, I offer that there is a telling point of identification that may well arise in this regard. Recalling David Coon (2013), the proliferation of suburban stories within popular-culture mediums in the last twenty years reflects a point for common reference: "Suburbia is a concrete spatial arrangement that shapes the everyday lives of the majority of Americans and expresses many of the hopes and fears embedded within American society" (4). Yet the diminished faith in these suburban-utopia narratives still offers the post-Boomer a potential outlet: Reading such tales through irony or cynicism can provide temporary satisfaction through a fleeting yet stabilizing moment. Robert McLaughlin (2004), employing a lens of David Foster Wallace, offers this observation: "The effect of this on the average TV viewer, the one whose loneliness and isolation are masked by the false communities TV offers, is that she both adopts TV's world view of weary cynicism so as to be part of the TV 'community' and avoids at all costs becoming the target of others' cynicism" (63). Shame, be it Marie's or something identifiable to the postmodern viewer all too familiar with disillusionment of self, story, and the security of hope, further fuels the anxieties that the consumerism of suburban utopia no longer placates or resolves. "Keeping up with the Joneses" as a comparative marker of "normal," however genuinely or dubiously pursued, no longer retains identity reassurance. Rather, as seen through Marie, the practice proves fleetingly empty, as useful as a gold-and-zircon baby tiara.

Note

1. Although I am focusing on Marie, other characters would be equally fitting for similar analysis: Hank's hiding of his panic attacks, Skyler's business and adulterous relationship with Ted Beneke (or less sensational, her smoking), Jesse's prompting of Badger and Skinny Pete to sell methamphetamine in a twelve-step program, pretty much the whole of Saul Goodman's law practice, and so on.

References

Blazer, Dan. 2005. *The Age of Melancholy: Major Depression and Its Social Origins.* New York Routledge.

Coon, David. 2013. *Look Closer: Suburban Narratives and American Values in Film and Television.* Piscataway, NJ: Rutgers University Press.

Davidson, Graeme. 2013. "The Suburban Idea and Its Enemies." *Journal of Urban History* 39 (5): 829–47.

De Kosnik, Abigail. 2010. "Drama Is the Cure for Gossip: Television's Turn to Theatricality in a Time of Media Transition." *Modern Drama* 53 (3): 370–89.

Felski, Rita. 2000. "Nothing to Declare: Identity, Shame, and the Lower Middle Class." *PMLA* 115 (1): 33–45.

Foucault, Michel. 1991. *Discipline and Punish: The Birth of the Prison.* New York: Vintage Books.

Goffman, Erving. 1956. *The Presentation of Self in Everyday Life.* Edinburgh, UK: University of Edinburgh Press.

———. 1963. *Stigma: Notes on the Management of Spoiled Identity.* New York: Simon and Schuster.

McLaughlin, Robert. 2004. "Post-Postmodern Discontent: Contemporary Fiction and the Social World." *symploke* 12 (1–2): 53–68.

Nachbar, Jack, and Kevin Lause. 1992. *Popular Culture: An Introductory Text.* Bowling Green, OH: Popular Press.

Park, Kristen. 2002. "Stigma Management among the Voluntarily Childless." *Sociological Perspectives* 45 (1): 21–45.

The Arc of W. W.

Imperial Selfhood and Metastatic Poetry in *Breaking Bad*

Timothy Dansdill

Does Walter White's antiheroic arc surpass those of his most memorable brethren in other highly regarded series of television's "Third Golden Age"? This essay argues that the identity arc of Walter White manifests a persistently US thematic destiny. Walt goes from "A to Z" (Vince Gilligan's words). But what if he is aspiring to zeitgeist, moving and transforming across that singular arc of US identity that continues to bind and bedevil us as a nation: the arc of "the imperial self"?[1] The framing question, then, asks, What are the historical roots, the creative causes of our fascination with Walter White's antiheroic character as one that is always in motion, whose momentum is so unpredictably hybrid and round in spite of his soul?

Next, this essay looks at the integration, under the sign of "W. W.," of Walt Whitman's imperial presence as an ultimate act of referential discourse.

As an actual, historical embodiment of imperial selfhood, Whitman's entire life as a writer—not just as a poet—exemplifies a truly metastatic struggle between "inward and outward empires" (Harrison 2004, 5), especially in his lifelong insistence that the soul must not go missing from American manifest destiny as a spiritual renewal, even as the nation, as a body, was moving outward as a matter of geographic and financial empire. When Whitman's identity under the dedication "to my other favorite W. W." becomes part of the arc of Walter White's metastatic roundness (where metastasis refers to the spread of White's cancer, to his changes in character, to moments of stasis on the verge of these changes, and to Whitman's poetics), the greatness of *Breaking Bad*—and why that matters—expands because it aspires to our American zeitgeist.

This chapter then considers this question: In examining the wide-open experimentation with interconnected arcs of character that Gilligan set for himself—"a character going from A to Z" (Gilligan 2011)[2]—and once set free to run as deeply and wildly as it might, can we plausibly entertain an arc that runs from Walt Whitman through Walter White and outward to Whitman's imperialist contemporary, William Walker, a far more famous imperialist in his time, and one vastly more influential on literary and film history as the ultimate antihero and US "agent of empire"?

Finally, I will briefly reflect on Whitman's poem "When I Heard the Learn'd Astronomer." Considering the power and pervasive influence of imperial selfhood as promulgated by Whitman in "Song of Myself," "When I Heard the Learn'd Astronomer" would seem the wrong choice upon which to pivot the spiritual action or moral-of-the-story moment of the series. The poem is, however, remarkably "metastatic," right down to that word's clashing roots—a tangled blending of stagnation, change, quest, and equilibrium, moving outward into a scientific versus poetic embrace of the self and cosmos. It also reminds us of Whitman's poetic method as metastatic, moving from what Ken Egan (1987), writing on Whitman's poetic method, calls his "periodic structure," to what Henry Nash Smith (1947) reminds us about Whitman's own trajectory of imperial selfhood: "an enthusiastic nationalist and believer in the confused but exciting doctrines of Manifest Destiny" (xx).

If there is a larger, overarching question left to ask readers in this chapter's conclusion, then it is a synthesis of the three questions already posed: How might we dare to root for the "arc of W. W." as simultaneously antiheroic and heroic, as both abjectly criminal and ambivalently imperial, as poetically moving, yet morally metastatic; and if we do dare, are we more or less likely to agree with critic Allen St. John's (2013) claim in the title of his review, "Why *Breaking Bad* Is the Best Show Ever and Why That Matters"?

Allen St. John, writing on *Breaking Bad* at the end of its run, recapitulates Gilligan's early aspiration to do something different with *Breaking Bad* and its antihero.

> Show runner Vince Gilligan set his protagonist in *motion*. Television has always been about a kind of *inertia*. . . . And as that first generation of shows from television's post-millennial Golden Era threw off so many of the shackles of convention inherent in the medium, they kept this one. . . . Vince Gilligan started *Breaking Bad* with no such constraints. (4)

The critical consensus surrounding Walter White's character is all about his transformative, metastatic arc. Brett Martin (2014) has concluded that Walter White is "a radical extension of the anti-hero trend." This claim ties into Thomas Doherty's (2012) thesis of "story arc in television" as interconnected actions of characters that create a unique momentum. Chuck Klosterman (2014) touches on this pervasive sense of transformative arcs of action and momentum. He states that Walter White was "consciously designed . . . to evolve from hero to villain as the show's trajectory progressed" (48). If these critics agree on similar lines of creative and historical development, then we have a television character whose arc, set free from the inertia of the First and Second Golden Ages of television, is radically antiheroic, who not only never "resets to zero," but is, according to an *Atlantic Monthly* roundtable on *Breaking Bad* (Heller 2013), "perhaps the most villainous character a television show has ever dared us to root for."

So where in recent television history does Walter White's antiheroic hybridity, his unpredictable villainy, come from? Although it is useful to educate ourselves on the historical roots of Walter's character as an unpredictable hybrid of criminal types, it is his metastatic roundness that is most interesting for understanding his ultimate arc as a character. Judith Mayerle's analysis of 1980s television argues that character "roundness" underwent an evolutionary advance within a single series, *Cagney and Lacey*, in which "protagonists who are open-ended and often unpredictable *grow and change* as they interact with their personal and professional environment" (137; emphasis added). She demonstrates how Cagney and Lacey speak about their lives and conflicts in detail—"sometimes even supersed-ing the criminal conflict in an episode . . . making the characters round and the entire series work" (137). She claims that "such referential discourse contributes to a fuller dimension of character. . . . These discourse patterns take the narrative beyond the time and place dramatized in the episode" (141). Mayerle's sense of a new "arc" within 1980s television anticipates the critical reception of *Breaking Bad* and its radically round character as a work of "story arc in television." So where and how do we break into the arc of Walter's character?

The opening minutes of ". . . And the Bag's in the River" (season 1, episode 3) confirms our sense that Gilligan is adept at using the discourse patterns Mayerle identified in the 1980s. The episode opens with Walter and Jesse cleaning up Walt's botched acid bath attempt to chemically ren-der and "disappear" the body of one of two drug dealers on whom Walt has "turned the periodic table": they meant to force Walter and Jesse into cooking methamphetamine for them at gunpoint, which resulted in their own murders. Walter creates a chemical reaction that, meant only to sub-due them, kills one, and the other is now their captive.

The opening frames are shot from beneath the floor of Jesse's house. Walt is wiping up blood, sweeping guts, bones, and even the victim's gun from a hydrochloric-acid bath whose tub has fallen through the floor above. We are rushed into his mind as he flashes back to his early thirties as a promising chemist, in graduate school, flirting romantically with his teaching assistant.[3] They are talking shop about the periodic table of ele-ments and how it accounts for the total chemical composition of a human being—from the largest chemical concentrations down finally to the bar-est trace percentages that together produce a 99-plus-percent result. This three-minute scene, one of the most dramatic of the entire series, inter-cuts rapidly between Walt's killing-floor cleanup and this obviously pain-ful flashback. We hear the last lines spoken from his remembrance of a professional and romantic destiny now mired in a murdered body's chem-ical remains. As the two scenes intersect, Walter is sloshing bloody slurry in a toilet and coughing up blood from his lung cancer as he flushes it all down.

WALT: So the whole thing adds up to . . . we are 0.111958% shy.
GRETCHEN: Supposedly that's everything.

WALT: I don't know . . . I just . . . I just . . . just seems like something's missing, doesn't it? *There's got to be more to a human being than that.*
(season 1, episode 3; emphasis added)

The rest of the episode is an exercise in Walt's moral and strategic crisis over whether to kill the second drug dealer, held captive in the basement. That crisis runs for forty-two minutes when, with three minutes remaining, having killed the drug dealer on the discovery that he fully intended to kill Walt if set free, Walt is shown dumping the body of his murderous, amoral adversary into the river. As the body splashes, we are flashed back again to Walt's aspirational past as a young chemist in love. The remaining edge to that scene closes in a perfect helix of Walt's past and present, his memory of early promise crossed with his new nightmarish, criminal reality.

WALT: Just . . . doesn't it seem like something's missing? [He walks from blackboard showing their calculations of a human body's total chemical percentages back toward his lover sitting before him and leans close to her.]
GRETCHEN: What about the soul? [She asks with a wooing earnestness.]
WALT: [Smiling indulgently at her naiveté.] The soul . . . There's nothing but chemistry here.
(season 1, episode 3)

". . . And the Bag's in the River" is significant for a number of reasons, but for our purposes, its visual interplay is an important opening demonstration of "Metastatic Poetry."[4] His question, which closes the episode—"Doesn't it seem like something's missing?"—reverberates as we find ourselves, so early in the series, riding the fast-moving arc of a character tied to a purely material, chemical world view. This question near the beginning of the series sets up the ingenious clue that would graft his arc as "W. W." onto that of Walt Whitman's—the Poet of the American soul, who reminds us,

I am the poet of the Body and I am the poet of the Soul,
The pleasures of heaven are with me and the pains of hell are with me,
The first I graft and increase upon myself, the latter I translate into a *new tongue.*
(Whitman 2005, stanza 21; emphasis added)

Whitman's "new tongue" is the metastatic discourse between Walt's grisly business of melting a body back into its chemistry and his flashback toward what's missing in a human *being*. This rapidly hellish-to-heavenly alternation—between Walt's moral meltdown, the pained, emotional inertia on his face as he mops up the body, and his once-upon-a-time blissful unity of intellectual and romantic purpose with Gretchen, the young woman who would later marry his college science partner, Elliot Schwartz—is metastatic on many levels, from the psychological to the spiritual. That she mentions the soul and that Walt's reply is that it is nothing but chemistry are themselves essential clues to *Breaking Bad*'s momentum as interconnected arcs of "metastatic poetry." More than the sum of his references, more than a mutant intermingling of gangster and psychopath (though he surely is both), Walter White's transformational arc of identity can be said to be "missing the soul." Or, it can be argued that Gilligan's ambition was to keep his antihero moving from gangster to psychopath to a "meta" breed of the imperial self, a self that moves us, as Mayerle originally noted, "beyond the time and place dramatized in the episode" to his "guest" (more toward *geist*) star of the series: Walt Whitman, and thus into the referential discourse of manifest destiny, the zeitgeist "gliding over all" of American history.

Gilligan and his writers take "the soul" and throw it into a bag and into the river. We now sense that the question of, and quest for, soul is "missing" from Walter White's chemistry—physical, to moral, to spiritual. As a psycho-(Greek: "soul")-pathic criminal, in the fully metastatic roundness of his antiheroic trajectory, we see also that he aspires to a very different "spirit of the age": a zeitgeist where the purest individual, the imperial self, "glides over all." Moreover, Walter White's roundness is metastatic; it contains and covers the term's full semantic field, from biochemical to pathological transformation. This all-controlling, metastatic arc of the series is revealed from his most earnest teaching to his students, long before he is "breaking bad," to his aggressive advice to a fellow chemotherapy patient, upon learning that his cancer has returned. "Chemistry," as Walt laboriously tells his less-than-rapt students, "is a cycle of 'growth, decay, then transformation'" (Bowman 2013, 164). As the series itself "cycles," three seasons later, Walter intimidates his fellow, and soon frightened, cancer patient.

"Never give up control; live life on your own terms." As the patient points out, this is something of an illusion: "cancer is cancer," after all.

"To hell with your cancer," Walt snaps. "Right from the start it's a death sentence. That's what they keep telling me. Well, guess what? Every life comes with a death sentence . . . but until then, who's in charge? Me! That's how I live my life!" (Bowman 2013, 166)

We can see that Walt's character moves from his premetastatic self as a benign teacher of chemistry to his postmetastatic self as a psychopathic criminal of chemistry. In his metastatic inflection the soul is missing completely in "his glorification of autonomy—an ideal that . . . devolves into raw power" (Bowman 2013, 166). For our purposes, this glorified ideal of autonomy as raw power can be summed up as "imperial selfhood." And as Bowman reminds us, because "Walt remains at heart a man of science" (169), we can't but think of his imperial selfhood as also strangely poetic, since, under the sign of W. W., his identity is metastatic, made to interact with another self—Walt Whitman, whose imperial quest for selfhood follows the arc of the soul.

But before we can look closely into the arc of W. W., let us remind ourselves of all five key scenes that feature the name, the poetry, or the presence of Walt Whitman within the dramatic and thematic operations of *Breaking Bad*. The first two scenes occur in the episode "Sunset" (season 3, episode 6). Together they introduce and set into metastatic motion the image of Whitman. (Previously, there has been only one allusion to Whitman, the elusive source of a missing soul arc in ". . . And the Bag's in the River.") The third major moment happens in "Bullet Points" (season 4, episode 4). This is the suspense-charged yet highly comical moment in which Hank Schrader asks Walter about the identity of W. W. The last two scenes that define the arc of W. W. occur in season 5. The fourth, in "Hazard Pay" (season 5, episode 3), is a brief but potent moment when Walter finds the copy of *Leaves of Grass* that his now murdered understudy, Gale Boettinger, had given to him as a gift with a special inscription: "To My Other Favorite W. W." The fifth and final reference climaxes the season 5 midseason finale in the episode "Gliding over All" (season 5, episode 8; title from Whitman 1900, no. 271). This is the scene in which Hank Schrader, our "hero," discovers the identity of W. W. These five, explicitly interconnected references to Whitman and his poetry create a visible arc of momentum that is essential to the poetic, perhaps metastatic, greatness of *Breaking Bad*.

Whitman's premier appearance rests entirely on, but then moves murderously away from, Walter White's fellow criminal-chemist, his earnestly libertarian, highly cultivated understudy, Gale Boettinger. The scene from "Sunset" treats us to a familiar moment for all workers: two coworkers celebrate a job well done and then one of them tries to cross the work/life boundary. The diabolical difference here is that these workers are highly paid semiprisoners under close surveillance; they work for Gus Fring in his secure underground facility; and, comically, they are clad in the hazmat suits and respiration gear essential to the production of Walter White's (not Gus Fring's) wealth- and death-producing product: Blue Sky crystal methamphetamine. Walter and Gale's apparently collegial exchange, leading up to Gale's recitation of one of Whitman's most complex poems, is important for our understanding of how the "arc of W. W." first comes into awkward, comic play. The overarching importance of scene to the series is thus easily overlooked. They are drinking wine next to a batch of this pure blue sky when Gale offers a bit of his own history to Walt.

GALE: I was on my way. Jumping through hoops—kissing the proper behinds, attending to all the non-chemistry that one finds oneself occupied by. . . . That is not what I signed on for. I love the lab. Because it's all still magic, you know? Chemistry? I mean, once you lose that . . .
WALT: (Very quiet.) It is, it is still magic. It still is. (Gale smiles faintly, seeing Walt is touched by the same thing he is.)
GALE: And all the while, I kept thinking about that great old Whitman poem, "When I Heard the Learn'd Astronomer."
WALT: I don't know it.
GALE: Ah. Anyway . . .
WALT: Well, can you recite it?
GALE: (Embarrassed.) Pathetically enough, I could.
WALT: All right, well. Come on. Come on.
GALE: Sure you wanna hear it? (Walt shrugs. Gale snorts.)
GALE: What the hell, right? (Walt nods appreciatively. Gale finally recites the poem.)
GALE: Yes, I am a nerd.
WALT: Bravo!
GALE: Thank you. (Walt just smiles faintly.)
(season 3, episode 6)

The scene and their exchange parallels strangely and deeply with Walt's almost psychotic flashback in ". . . And the Bag's in the River." We sense the same love of chemistry—its magic—between two like-minded souls, except we see that they aren't. The awkwardness is palpable: Gale is reticent and Walt, though supportive, is, as always in all of his intimate, tender opportunities, withdrawn, not quite absent, but present only in his words. And his words, those echoes of "something is missing," return, perversely, in Gale's yearning phrase, actually an ironic, metastatic reversal: "Chemistry, once you lose that." (In light of the young Walter and his lover, this doubles the previous line, "The soul, once you lose that.") Yet Walt doubles down on his affirmation that chemistry is "still magic. It still is." Walt's assertion points to an apparent moment of stasis for him, or within him, but not in the sense of the word's connotation of "stagnation." *Stasis* also carries a *meta-* or spiritual sense of "motionless equilibrium." The ending direction note, indicating that he "just smiles faintly" is essentially the same "indulgent" smile he shares with his lover when he told her there is no soul, only chemistry. Walter White's equilibrium is always unpredictable. Even when he is not in actual motion, his motionless moments are restless, reserving themselves for the next move across his arc of imperial selfhood.

What Gale Boettinger has set in motion within Walter is a grim, haunted turn back to who this Walt Whitman is, really; what's he made of? Walter White neither knows the poem nor Whitman. His self-trajectory, made of disabled former selves (an earnest, open-minded, curious former teacher who has tried to repress his rage against his own decision to sell his shares in a chemical startup company, for example), is now that of a paranoid psychopathic murderer who nevertheless remains open and curious to new knowledge, or at least, to new motives. Thus, we see Walter, a few scenes later, sitting alone in his condominium, estranged from his wife and family, relaxing with a library copy of Whitman's *Leaves of Grass* after his poetic encounter with Gale. The edition is instantly recognizable to readers of Whitman. It is a copy of the 150th anniversary edition of the original 1855 edition. In the script for this scene, the director's notes read: "Home from work for the day, Walt lounges in his new living room, reading. His bare feet are propped atop the coffee table. He's feeling pretty good as he reads *Leaves of Grass* by Whitman. His expression tells us he's sorta into it. Good stuff" (Shiban n.d.). Instantly into the positive stasis of this moment he receives a telephone call from his brother-in-law, Hank Schrader, asking about Walt's former student, Jesse Pinkman, and his connection to cooking methamphetamine.

We see that Walt is only a few pages into Whitman's optimistic "Preface to a Young Nation on the Move," a nation expanding its territory while intoning the manifest destiny of its democracy. Suppose the first few pages of the preface allow Walt to join his sense of chemistry as magic (as all that matters) with what Whitman is arguing in uncanny parallel, that poetry is magic—is all that matters. What if Walter is reading Walt for some justification of his outlaw chemistry? Never mind the poetry, what if, in reading Whitman's rather imperialistic preface, Walt comes across the passage about chemists and astronomers as the poet's "lawgivers"? Is it only coincidence that one will find this passage from Whitman in the early pages Walt appears to be studying?

> The chemist, astronomer . . . are not poets, but they are the lawgivers of poets and their construction underlies the structure of every perfect poem. . . . *No matter what rises or is uttered they sent the seed of the conception of it . . . of them and by them stand the visible proofs of souls . . . always their fatherstuff must be begotten the sinewy races of bards.* (Whitman 2005, ix; emphasis added)

Whitman, ever the poet of "the soul," consigns its "visible proof" to astronomers and to chemists, such as Walter, who, as we know, has "proven" that whatever is missing from the being of a human being, the soul is an absurd substitute for it. Whitman's grand synthesis of poets and chemists read by Walter White in this scene lends credence to the notion that Gilligan and his writing team attended to the idea of story arcs in television as a sophisticated discourse reference machine,[5] one whose momentum feeds upon and glides over fantasies of "imperial selfhood."

We turn now to an important scene that many have noted, but that no one has yet argued is the outstanding arc of *Breaking Bad*. That is, if lung cancer made Walter White "break bad," then the identity of "W. W." in "Bullet Points" (season 4, episode 4) breaks open the series into a tragicomic fetish, an arch obsession with Whitman as "the imperial self" for a nation Whitman himself had imagined would be (re)born under his sign(ature)—as in 1860, from "Broadway Pageant": "I chant the new empire, grander than any before—As in a / vision it comes to me; / I chant America, the Mistress—I chant a greater supremacy" (Whitman 2005, xx).

In "Bullet Points" the tragicomic interplay between Walt and Hank, brothers-in-law on opposite sides of the law, is climbing an arc of rising tension that is best summed up by Chuck Klosterman (2014): "If a villain is the person who knows the most and cares the least, then a hero is the person who cares too much without knowing anything" (19). The scene shows heroic and antiheroic counterparts joined *together* (italicized to emphasize one of the central meanings of *meta-*:"to express notions of sharing, action in common, pursuit" [*OED*]). Hank is attempting to run down the list of possible identities that would best line up with the now-murdered Gale Boettinger. He has recovered Boettinger's private journal and laboratory book from his apartment and has asked Walter who he thinks this "W. W." might be. Hank reads, laughingly, Gale's hand-written and soul-inscribed dedication. Here is the original script.

HANK: It says, uh, "To W. W. My star, my perfect silence." Huh . . . W. W. . . .
  I mean, who do you figure that is, huh? Woodrow Wilson? Willy Wonka?
  Walter White?
WALT: *You got me* . . . Hey, man, let me see this for a second because I
  think I remembered . . . Ah. Here. Yes. Yeah . . . "When I heard the
  learn'd astronomer . . . And from time to time . . . looked up in perfect
  silence at the stars." It's a poem by Walt Whitman . . . your W. W.
HANK: You frickin' braniac. Ha. You frickin' braniac. Ha ha ha! I must
  have skipped that day in school or something.
WALT: I don't know.
HANK: Hee hee! I've been chasing my tail about that one, you know? I bet
  you're right.
WALT: Well, I'm glad I could be of help.
HANK: Yeah. Walt Whitman, huh.
(season 4, episode 4; emphasis added)

The giveaway of Walt's criminal culpability and identity is in plain sight in his highly loaded, four-sided, and, let's face it, absurdly obvious "boxed in" response. And yet, when predicated on Klosterman's formula, Walter's "You got me" works comically (and tragically) as a step within the largely invisible but always-operative US arc of imperial selfhood.

First side: Hank (as clueless hero) enables Walt (all-knowing antihero) to play clueless too. Second side: Hank has caught Walt, and Hank knows he has (unconsciously), as does Walter. But in his hero's conscience, and in fulfillment of Klosterman's formula, Hank cannot "go there" because he "cares the most and knows the least." Walt, in fulfillment of this formula, is betting that his brother-in-law cannot face the horrible truth that "Heisen-berg," the psychopathic gangster he is seeking, is staring into his eyes and stating, "You got me." Even as all the clues point away from Gale Boettinger, that enormously "pathetic" (in the original and best sense) and poetic road-kill Walter White leaves behind on his way to "empire," Hank, who cares the most, gratefully accedes to Walt's newly—murderously—absorbed knowl-edge of Walt Whitman as "W. W." Third side: thanks to Gale Boettinger's "gift" of Whitman's poetry, Walt now knows that W. W. is a moveable feast, moving fast, and as all-knowing "antihero," having exploited his heroic brother-in-law's "careful" ignorance to the fullest, he, and thus we, are free to forget about "the arc of W. W." for *an entire season*. Thus, the withheld momentum and arc behind his admission, "You got me," comes hurtling back at us in the finale of "Gliding over All" (season 5, episode 8) with all the force of Whitman's late, virtually posthumous, metastatic fragment—a kind of metaphysical meteorite—that the episode's title references.

Gliding o'er all, through all
Through Nature, Time, and Space,
As a ship on the waters advancing,
The voyage of the soul—not life alone,
Death, many deaths I'll sing.
(Whitman 1900).

The fourth, and a final, highly speculative side: Walter White's "You got me" is pure metonymy.[6] Before, and yet behind, and then yet "beyond" the name of Walter White is the "arc of W. W." with the name of "Walt Whit-man" foregrounded, but behind his initials hides the much vaster claim and name of "imperial selfhood"—*William Walker* (please see note 8). As to the "obvious" (as in plain sight) and "ingenious" (as hiding in plain sight) metonymy of plot twist (call it *plotonymy*) in "Gliding over All": yes, the scene they create to resolve and "reveal all" to our hero and to us is truly climactic—at once comedic and dramatic. It is Walt Whitman's "metastatic meteorite" come crashing into Hank Schrader's consciousness and into our own—or those of us who root for and love this fully "round" hero who is nevertheless deliberately designed to be "flat" because, in Klosterman's for-mula, he cares more than he knows.

But as we watch Hank, stricken with diarrhea, sit on Walter White's toilet and discover the true identity of W. W. while browsing Gale Boettinger's gift copy of *Leaves of Grass* that Walter, far outside his compulsively organized character as a criminal, has left in plain sight, we can't help but think: *Here is a moment we can leave alone for what it is; for some avid viewers it is a nasty dope slap; for others a tasty piece of visual slapstick.* For the purposes of this essay, Gale Boettinger's inscribed dedication to the man who would be his friend and mentor—not his murderer—simply speaks for itself as evidence of *Breaking Bad*'s artistic, perhaps sadistic, but always ironic, stake in such exotic extracurricular questions of imperial selfhood and metastatic poetry. Hank reads: "To my other favorite W. W. It's an honour working with you. Fondly, G. B." And his face transforms into a tragicomic mask of embarrassed shock.

The arc of Walt Whitman's "imperial selfhood" is now before us as we turn to *Breaking Bad*'s integration of his presence and poetry into Walter White's own antiheroic trajectory toward the inescapable zeitgeist of the United States. Walt Whitman is commonly characterized as a poet, essayist, and journalist. His *Wikipedia* entry describes him as a humanist who was a part of "the transition between transcendentalism and realism, incorporating both views in his works." In this section we remember that Whitman was also an imperialist. Within and without him, across the long arc of his life and career, what imperialist meant to him and to US history has always mixed—and mixed up—both transcendentalist and realist meanings. The former category is generally tied to his poetry, to his prefaces, to his lifelong series, *Leaves of Grass*, and to his at-large essay series, "Democratic Vistas." His realism can be tied to his equally vigorous career as a journalist and editor in his twenties and thirties.

Few students of Whitman's poetry realize that the young, aspiring man was a highly ambitious "realist-journalist-editorialist" during the 1840s—the high-blood period of US manifest destiny. By the age of 23, as a fiery editorialist for the New York City paper the *Aurora*, Whitman can be genuinely characterized not only as an imperialist but as a spokesman "dangerously close to the Native American Party" (Kreig n.d., 30). Witness his 1842 diatribes against the hordes of Irish immigrants flooding New York City, whom he described as "'foreigners,' 'filthy wretches,' 'blear-eyed, bloated off-scourings from the stews, blind alleys and rear lanes,' who broke up the meeting with 'howlings in their hideous native tongue'" (Kreig n.d., 32). If one could identify a phase in which Whitman could be said to be "breaking bad," it is during his twenties as the fever of manifest destiny swept the nation.

Whitman transformed himself, however—enough to modify his views of the Irish race. His lifelong quest for a greater, "transcendental" communion helped him to win an editorial position at the *Brooklyn Eagle* when he was twenty-seven. During the height of the troubles with Mexico, and the James Polk presidency's increasing drumbeat to go to war over US claims to its "western territories," Whitman wrote in an 1846 editorial:

> We love to indulge in thoughts of the future extent and power of this republic—because all its increase is the increase of human happiness and liberty. Therefore hope we that the U.S. will keep a fast grip on California. What has miserable, inefficient Mexico—with her burlesque upon freedom, her actual tyranny—what has she to do with the great mission of peopling the world with a noble race? Be it ours to achieve that mission! (Whitman 1846a)

Like most Americans of the time, Whitman had not modified, nor would he ever alter, his imperialist views on the reasons for or outcomes of the Mexican-American War. In this mainstream view, he was quite at odds with the views of his prophet and future advocate, Ralph Waldo Emerson. Walt Whitman was, in fact, an unrepentant, but always evolving, imperialist with nativist, rather than supremacist, tendencies. He learned from his experience as a nurse in the Civil War, as a lifelong correspondent with the wounded soldiers he had cared for, and through his humanistic study to imagine and reinvent a different kind of imperial self as he aged. Henry Nash Smith (1947) accounts broadly, and always positively, for this transformation in Whitman's imperial self from 1842 to 1860. He traces three phases of "Whitman's Utopianism, in which his nationalism has expanded almost to the point where it ceases to be nationalism" (383). But if Whitman is no longer a nationalist, and his sense of his own and his nation's manifest destiny is somehow more spiritual or metaphysical, he never abandons his imperialism as the force, the abiding arc, of his utopianism.

"Democratic Vistas," published in the early 1870s, invokes the words *imperial* and *empire* to punctuate his grandiose appeals for US domination in all fields. To be fair, he is distressed by, even as he is "certain" of, the "triumphant future of our business, geographic and productive departments, on [whose] larger scales . . . the republic must soon outstrip all . . . and dominate the world" (Whitman 1871, 71). His concern is "that our New World democracy . . . is so far, an almost complete failure in its social aspects, and in really grand religious, moral, literary, and esthetic results." For Whitman, *his* American Empire had lost its "soul." In a poignant, but also disturbingly ambiguous, declaration that the soul of the United States is, to reinvoke Walter White's word, "missing," Whitman (1871) leaves open the sense that the expansionism of his twenties is still an active remnant of his more spiritual imperialism: "In vain have we annex'd Texas, California, Alaska, and reach north for Canada and south for Cuba. It is as if we were somehow being endow'd with a vast and more and more thoroughly-appointed body, and then left with little or no soul" (58). The arrogant, illegal seizure of Mexico's territories twenty-five years in the past remains justifiable for the middle-aged Whitman, (essentially the age of Walter White as he begins his arc of "breaking bad"). But in 1870 the United States is "breaking bad" because it is obsessed with "the empire Business" (Walter White's language, to be picked up farther on). The most fair-minded interpretation of Whitman's arc of opinion on the United States would paraphrase him as saying, "Yes, become empire! But business becomes it not! In poetry we become empire!"

As to uncanny kinds of vistas, a further fascinating parallel prevails. Recall that for Walter and Gale "chemistry is magic"—a magic making them wildly wealthy in monetary terms. In "Democratic Vistas" Whitman invokes the fable of "the magician's serpent [who] ate up all of the other serpents; and money-making is our magician's serpent, remaining to-day sole master of the field" (6). He mourns the loss of the US soul as an imperial nation gobbled up by this most magic of serpents (though nowhere does he mourn the force of arms required to make this ever-expanding field safe for this serpent). And yet, as always with Whitman's imperial contradictions, with his own imperial selfhood as a soul intermingled with that of his nation's, he warns that if the United States does not heed his vision of an American Empire, it should not be surprised by the cost of its antipoetic, land-grabbing alternative.

> You said in your soul, I will be empire of empires, overshadowing all else, past and present . . . making a new history. . . . I alone inaugurating largeness, culminating time. If these, O lands of America, are indeed the prizes, the determinations of your soul, be it so. But behold the cost, and already specimens of the cost. (Whitman 1871, 89)

To read him here, as Walter White might read him, searching for some justification that this poet could make for his own sense of imperial selfhood, how can we resist this sardonic riposte as might be spoken by Walter White?

> *Oh sure . . . Walt! If only we could continue to colonize, to expand, to justify our American Empire (into Canada, into Cuba, into—ha!—my own New Mexico!) with the magic serpents of religion, literature, esthetics! Then as a nation we could be "breaking good" and begin to undo the "breaking bad" momentum of our manifest destiny!*

Whitman's highly imperiled but staunchly imperialist logic strikes many of us today as patently illogical, incoherent, and hypocritical. Yet in the minds of the vast majority of Americans of his time, the very fact of empire was our manifest destiny—ready or not. Savor, for example, this declaration by Whitman, bemoaning the wasted birthright of this destiny that if continued must lead to a moral and spiritual cancer—manifest destiny as pathological metastasis: "It seems as if the Almighty had spread before this nation charts of *imperial destinies*, dazzling as the sun, yet with many a deep intestine difficulty, and *human aggregate of cankerous imperfection*" (Whitman 1871, 67; emphasis added). See now how Whitman's "heroic" yet unknowing diagnosis/prognosis of US imperialism as a cancer sets and foresees the meme of *metastasis* that runs through *Breaking Bad*. Here is our exit and one way to return to Whitman's poem "When I Heard the Learn'd Astronomer" and its metastatic underwriting of the arc of *Breaking Bad*'s unparalleled treatment of US imperial selfhood.

First, Walter White is the future human aggregate of cankerous imperfection that Whitman most feared, but under his own imperial self-trajectory under the zeitgeist of manifest destiny, Whitman suffered its cancer, recovered, and advanced his own imperial selfhood as a "future human aggregate" of a more "democratic perfection." Second, in "Democratic Vistas" and throughout his periodic, self-imperializing proclamations through his metastatic editions of *Leaves of Grass*, we see that Walt Whitman's imperial selfhood was not intended to advance, in Harrison's (2004) important distinction, "an outward empire," for as Whitman makes clear, this outward expansionism had already proceeded apace, for better or worse. Whitman, despite his "breaking bad" phase as an "agent of empire," was all in and on for an "inward empire" of literary and "democratic perfection."

"How wonderfully transcendental," Walter White might be thinking, as he is shown reading the preface to Whitman's *Leaves of Grass* after his encounter with Gale Boettinger's recitation of "When I Heard the Learn'd Astronomer." But if he experienced any sort of epiphany in reading a passage from Whitman's 1855 preface, one that grants fundamental precedence to chemists and astronomers as "the lawgivers of poets," his epiphany would not be one concerned with "democratic perfection" or with himself as the "future human aggregate" of an "inward empire." Walter White's sense of "an inward empire" has already matured and metastasized in season 3 into one of the "snakes" Whitman says are gobbling up and taking the field that belongs to US manifest destiny. His imperial selfhood is not content with an inward empire. Harrison (2004) makes Walter White's "future aggregate" of an imperial self, one seeking an "outward empire," frighteningly distinct:

> In the context of American expansionism, the imperial self . . . understands his epiphany . . . as the authorization to run wild and set fires in Mexico or Central America. The imperial self does not dive deeply into itself only to emerge in the oceanic divine; rather, he plunges wildly into his monstrous sense of self (though he would not see himself as deformed or awful in any measure). . . . Look inward, but then look outward; the inward and outward empires, in the literatures and cultures of U.S. imperialism, are part and particle of an intertwining impulse to impose one's will and desires upon others. This imperial self . . . carries a gun, and knows his right to do so. (18)

Much can be parsed from this passage as we turn to our conclusion. First, although Harrison is profiling the imperial selfhood and arc of another "favorite W. W." (William Walker), we now understand that Whitman's imperial self as the arc of epiphanic omnipotence—the poet of US transcendental expansionism—is decidedly inward in his quest for a democratic-literary empire that would, over time, embrace Irish Americans, Mexican Americans, African Americans, and Native Americans through the outward (*meta-*) empire of his poetry as our national poetry.

Second, Whitman knew of, and even crossed paths with, William Walker in 1848 when Walker, "a founding partner in the New Orleans *Crescent*, employed an aspiring young poet named Whitman, as its editor" (Soodalter 2010, 24).[7] A stunning coincidence, is it not, as we reconsider the title of the present essay in light of such uncanny facts? How easy, also, to excuse a kind of interpretive overreach, and thus argue that Gilligan's revised ambition for *Breaking Bad*—a character who never resets to zero . . . going "from A to Z"—had designed the entire series as a remix, consciously or not, of all the elements of our "favorite" US zeitgeist.

Third, Walter White's imperial selfhood is a monstrous, metastatic arc that transcends Gilligan's own original teacher to gangster transformation. Yet Walt never considers himself, in Whitman's terms, a "monster" once he rationalizes his "deformed" decisions and "awful" actions within the twisted metastasis of inward and outward empires—those "snakes" that had already beset and transformed the arc of our "favorite W. W.": Walt Whitman.

Fourth, and finally, Walter White is no Walt Whitman; in his "Heisenberg" uncertainty, he is more "W. W"—now vastly (un)known as William Walker—America's repressed, unconscious, but always moving antihero: "a curious, and vicious, conquistador, [who] dwells restlessly in American letters; [yet] he keeps resurfacing, the imperial self as the ghost that cannot quite be forgotten (Harrison 2004, 5).[8] How else to read one of the most quoted lines from all of *Breaking Bad*, in the episode "Buyout" (season 5, episode 6)? (Note, too, Walter's repetition of "business" echoes Whitman's original reckoning and warning to America.) "You asked me if I am in the meth business or the money business. Neither. *I am in the empire business*" (emphasis added). "Buyout," indeed, as we close upon the poetic choice by Gilligan that might best integrate the "imperial selfhood" of Walt Whitman into the already metastatic poetry that is *Breaking Bad*.

Breaking Bad matters because it is a story whose moral lies deeply embedded in the US experience—we have always been an empire nation. Despite its discourses of rights and laws, US history—from the legal to the literary, from the constitutional to the cultural—is an arc of "breaking bad" in metastatic tension with its arc of "breaking good." The arc of *Breaking Bad* follows the method and pattern of a Whitman poem. With both expansively epic proportions and lyrically compressed intensities, it is a metastatic poem. Ken Egan (1987) calls this Whitman's "periodic structure" (an uncanny resonance with *Breaking Bad*'s credit sequence featuring the periodic table). Whitman's poetic arc is apparently unpredictable, yet it follows, Egan claims, an inevitably "alternating pattern," one that oscillates between "expansion and contraction of consciousness," one that relies upon an evolutionary process of push and shove, a truly "pulselike" development (2).

Egan then quotes Whitman to drive his point: "Most importantly, for Whitman the 'omniprevalent law of laws, the law of periodicity' is not simply cyclical, but dialectical, leading through an upward spiral to higher stages of consciousness. The rhythmic alternations in 'Song of Myself' move toward more ambitious projections of the Self" (8). And so Walter White, as a poetic character, is decidedly meta, but his arc is also replete with stasis, and in Whitman's own original coinage, "omniprevalent" with metastasis—"a more ambitious projection of the Self" that is unavoidably imperial.

As to Whitman's "When I Heard the Learn'd Astronomer," especially in light of Egan's uncanny use of metastatic properties to define Whitman's method and effect, note how Whitman distances himself ironically from dry academic expertise ("I became tired and sick") to embrace directly the transcendent reality of the stars "in perfect silence." And note how Kevin Eagan (2012) extends Ken Egan's assay of Whitman's poetic method into Gilligan's creative method. Eagan parses part of Whitman's poem:

> When I sitting heard the astronomer where he lectured with much
>   applause in the lecture-room,
> How soon unaccountable I became tired and sick,
> Till rising and gliding out I wander'd off by myself,
> In the mystical moist night-air, and from time to time,
> Look'd up in perfect silence at the stars.

To Eagan, "This concept of 'gliding out . . . off by myself' fits Gale as a character because his vision of freedom is of a spiritual transcendence. Walt Whitman's idea suggests moving *beyond* what the 'learn'd astronomer can teach, leaving human cares *behind*'" (Eagan 2012, 17; emphasis added). Note his pattern of metastatic references to capture this poem as perhaps the pivot upon which the entire series keeps moving—"going from A to Z"—*beyond* (meta) and *behind* (stasis). Notice too, that this concept of "gliding out" does not appear to fit the character arc of Walter White. Note, finally, the repeated reference of *gliding* within the series, pulled from two poems.

Yet in "*Leaves of Glass*: *Breaking Bad's* Whitman Fixation," Kera Bolonik (2013) ponders Gilligan's motivations. His fixation is, perhaps, on Whitman's imperialist, poetic legacy to radically extend the antiheroic, metastatic uniqueness of Walter White, and thus unite their "gliding out."

It may seem a cynical commentary on life in our time to compare a
man who . . . takes on as his life's work engineering the purest form
of something so poisonous and illicit as meth, with an American
bard . . . who took his cues from Transcendentalism. . . . And it is.
But that doesn't negate what they *share in common*: both are . . .
gliding out into the world, liberated from societal constraints.
(Bolonik 2013, 6; emphasis added)

As we marvel that Bolonik connotes the original meaning of *meta-*, we see
also that "gliding out" for Whitman meant something very different from
what it does for White. In "To Think of Time" in the final edition of
Leaves of Grass, Whitman says of the soul, "I swear I think now that everything without exception has an immortal soul! . . . . / And all preparation
is for it—and identity is for it—and life and materials are altogether for it!"
(Whitman 1892). Toward the end of *Breaking Bad*, Walter White rumi-
nates on the soul this way: "Once we've cooked through this methylamine
and made our money, there will be plenty of time for soul-searching" (season 5, episode 6). But that doesn't negate what they do share in common:
both are intellectual pioneers in their fields, their legacies—centuries
apart—demanding risk, casting them outside society, gliding out into the
world, liberated from societal constraints. Both strove for perfection in
their creations. However we understand "the arc of "W. W."—whether of
the soul, or of its "common share" of US manifest destiny's antiheroic
arc—*Breaking Bad*, as purveyor of "imperial selfhood," cooks up our
favorite imperialist psychopomp, Walt Whitman, adds trace elements of
our favorite imperialist psychopath, William Walker, whom Harrison
(2004) calls "the imperial self as the ghost that cannot quite be forgotten"
(5), to produce Walter White, "the most villainous character a television
show has ever dared us to root for" (Heller 2013). So say his name. He's our
favorite W. W.

Notes

1. The coinage is from Anderson (1971). The "imperial self" is a self-absorbed
   individual who embraces only what matters to him, accepting few, if any, of
   the influences that tradition or society may offer. See Anderson's chapter, "The
   Failure of the Fathers," and his commentary on Emerson and Whitman,
   whose "dreams of empire have had to do with imperial selves" (18).

2. Gilligan originally pitched *Breaking Bad* as "Take Mr. Chips and transform him into 'Scarface.'" He acknowledges the shortcomings of that character arc, describing his project in an interview with Terri Gross on *Fresh Air* this way: "A typical TV show is always about . . . taking the characters in any given hour as far as you can take them, but then resetting them more or less back to zero so at the beginning of the next week, they're still the characters you know and love. I wanted to make it a story of a character going from A to Z."

3. This woman turns out to be Gretchen Schwartz, a key character within Walter White's complex of rage, regret, and ultimate revenge—a complex arc not within the scope of this essay.

4. The *Oxford English Dictionary*'s entry on *metastasis* is endlessly suggestive for our purposes. The arc of its meaning is impressive: from rhetoric ("A rapid transition from one point or type of figure to another") to its present day medical and pathological connotations ("The movement of disease from one site to another within the body . . . as in many malignancies"). But the word's most ancient roots, when broken down to its integral terms, *meta* and *stasis*, push us back to an interactive binary. *Meta* carries "notions of sharing, action in common, pursuit, quest, and, above all, change (of place, order, condition, or nature)." *Stasis* as "inactivity; stagnation; a state of motionless or unchanging equilibrium." The now-general sense of the word came into being in the early nineteenth century—as in "transformation; change from one condition to another" (*OED*).

5. The edition that appears three times in the series—the 150th anniversary edition of the first 1855 edition—does not contain "When I Heard the Learn'd Astronomer" because it would not appear until the 1888 edition. (This is a minor "oops" for Gilligan and his otherwise supreme attention to detail.) But despite the ironic sense of its being "missing" from Walt's library edition and Gale's later, fateful gift, it heralds a truly new twist, turn, and abiding trope into the series, deep into season 3.

6. From *Wikipedia*: "a figure of speech in which a thing or concept is called not by its own name but rather by the name of something associated in meaning with that thing or concept. . . . from the Greek: 'a change of name,' with the prefix, *metá*, 'after, beyond'—thus, 'a name beyond a name.'"

7. Once again, the ghost, the *geist*, the zeitgeist of that "other favorite W. W.," William Walker, looms large here. Harrison documents the possibility that Walker and Whitman encountered each other as one was entering and the other exiting the job, but Harrison does not confirm what Soodalter is claiming.

8. Harrison is focused on the uber-imperial self of William Walker, whose memoir, *The War in Nicaragua*, is a criminal psychopath's poetry—his true account of creating an empire where slavery would be recognized in the

1850s. Whitman, like hundreds of thousands of Americans, certainly followed Walker's exploits until, having burned down Managua rather than surrender, Walker was overwhelmed, his face shot off by Nicaraguan nationalists, and he was buried in an unmarked grave.

References

Anderson, Quentin. 1971. *The Imperial Self: An Essay in American Literary and Cultural History*. New York: Knopf.

Bolonik, Kera. 2013. "Leaves of Glass." *Poetry Foundation*, August 6. http://www.poetryfoundation.org/article/246218.

Bowman, James. 2013. "Criminal Elements." *New Atlantis*, Winter: 163–73. http://www.thenewatlantis.com/docLib/20130507_TNA38Bowman.pdf.

Doherty, Thomas. 2012. "Storied TV: Cable Is the New Novel." *Chronicle of Higher Education*, September 17. http://chronicle.com/article/Cable-Is-the-New-Novel/134420/.

Douglass, Wayne J. 1981. "The Criminal Psychopath as Hollywood Hero." *Journal of Popular Film and Television* 8 (4): 30–39.

Eagan, Kevin. 2012. "'To My Other Favorite W. W.': Walt Whitman's Influence on *Breaking Bad* [Spoilers]." *Critical Margins*, September 19. http://criticalmargins.com/2012/09/19/to-my-other-favorite-w-w-walt-whitmans-breaking-bad/.

Egan, Ken Jr. 1987. "Periodic Structure in "Song of Myself." *Walt Whitman Quarterly Review* 4 (4): 1–8.

Gilligan, Vince. n.d. "Breaking Bad S01e03 Episode Script | SS." *Springfield! Springfield!* http://www.springfieldspringfield.co.uk/view_episode_scripts.php?tv-show=breaking-bad&episode=s01e03.

———. 2011. "*Breaking Bad*: Vince Gilligan on Meth and Morals." *Fresh Air with Terri Gross*. National Public Radio, September 19. http://www.npr.org/2011/09/19/140111200/breaking-bad-vince-gilligan-on-meth-and-morals.

Harrison, Brady. 2004. *Agent of Empire: William Walker and the Imperial Self in American Literature*. Athens: University of Georgia Press.

Heller, Chris. 2013. "*Breaking Bad* Returns: Is This Show Even about Walter White Anymore?" *Atlantic* online, August 11. http://www.theatlantic.com/entertainment/archive/2013/08/-i-breaking-bad-i-returns-is-this-show-even-about-walter-white-anymore/278552/.

Hutchinson, Gennifer. n.d. "Buyout." *Breaking Bad Wiki*. http://breakingbad.wikia.com/wiki/Buyout.

Klosterman, Chuck. 2014. *I Wear the Black Hat: Grappling with Villains (Real and Imagined)*. New York: Scribner.

Kreig, Joann P. n.d. "Walt Whitman and the Irish." Walt Whitman Archive. http://www.whitmanarchive.org/criticism/current/anc.00160.html.

Martin, Brett. 2013. *Difficult Men: Behind the Scenes of a Creative Revolution; From The Sopranos and The Wire to Mad Men and Breaking Bad.* New York: Penguin.

Mayerle, Judith. "Character Shaping Genre in *Cagney and Lacey.*" *Journal of Broadcasting and Electronic Media* 31 (2): 133–51.

Shiban, John. n.d. "Script for Breaking Bad Season 3 Episode 6: Sunset." *Scribd.* http://www.scribd.com/doc/181023748/Script-for-Breaking-Bad-Season-3-Episode-6-Sunset#scribd.

Smith, Henry Nash. 1947. "Walt Whitman and Manifest Destiny." *Library Quarterly Review* 10 (4): 373–89.

Soodalter, Ron. 2010. "William Walker: King of the 19th Century Filibusters." *HistoryNet*, March 4. http://www.historynet.com/william-walker-king-of-the-19th-century-filibusters.htm.

St. John, Allen. 2013. "Why *Breaking Bad* Is the Best Show Ever and Why That Matters." *Forbes Online*, September 16.

Walley-Beckett, Moira. n.d. "Bullet Points." *Springfield! Springfield!* http://www.springfieldspringfield.co.uk/view_episode_scripts.php?tv-show=breaking-bad&episode=s04e04.

Whitman, Walt. 1846a. "Annexation." *Brooklyn Daily Eagle*, June 6.

———. 1846b. "Our Territory on the Pacific." *Brooklyn Daily Eagle*, July 7. http://www.newspapers.com/image/50242670/?terms=our%2Bterritory%2Bon%2Bthe%2Bpacific.

———. 1871. "Democratic Vistas." Charlottesville: University of Virginia, American Studies program. http://xroads.virginia.edu/~hyper/Whitman/vistas/vistas.html.

———. 1892. "To Think of Time." In *Leaves of Grass*, no. 197. http://www.bartleby.com/142/197.html.

———. 1900. "Gliding over All." In *Leaves of Grass*, no. 271. http://www.bartleby.com/142/271.html.

———. 2005. *Leaves of Grass.* Edited by David S. Reynolds. Oxford, UK: Oxford University Press.

Contributors

Cordelia E. Barrera, an assistant professor in the Department of English at Texas Tech University, specializes in Latina and Latino literature, the US Southwest, and US border theory. Her publications have appeared in the *Quarterly Review of Film and Video*, *Western American Literature*, and *Chicana/Latina Studies*. Her work, which highlights the need to disrupt mythologies of the American West by incorporating border voices and identities, concentrates on the literature of social justice and the environment. Her current book project explores the literature of the US southwestern frontier through the lens of third-space technologies of the body and border theory.

Timothy Dansdill is an associate professor of English at Quinnipiac University in Hamden, Connecticut, who specializes in rhetoric and composition, with an abiding interest in nineteenth-century American literature. He teaches a diverse range of courses, including the History of the Personal Essay, Modern American Poetry, and the Rhetoric of the Digital Revolution.

Leonard Engel, a professor emeritus of English at Quinnipiac University in Hamden, Connecticut, was selected Outstanding Faculty of the Year in 1989 and received an Excellence in Teaching award in 2013. His edited collections include *The Big Empty* (1994); *Sam Peckinpah's West* (2003); *Clint Eastwood, Actor and Director* (2007); *A Violent Conscience:*

Essays on the Fiction of James Lee Burke (2010), and *New Essays on Clint Eastwood* (2012). He also has published numerous articles on American literature, Western film, and detective fiction and film.

Alex Hunt is a professor of English and the Haley Professor of Western Studies at West Texas A&M University. He has published numerous articles and books about western American literature, culture, and history. He is also editor of the *Panhandle-Plains Historical Review*.

Ian K. Jensen is a PhD candidate in English with a critical theory emphasis at the University of California, Irvine. His primary field is nineteenth- and early twentieth-century American literature and his scholarly interests include literary theory, continental philosophy from Kant to Levinas, ecocriticism, aesthetics, critical regionalism, and writing of place.

Brad Klypchak teaches courses in liberal studies at Texas A&M University–Commerce. A popular culture scholar, he earned his PhD in American Culture Studies from Bowling Green State University. Dr. Klypchak has taught and done research in music, film, theater, sport, performance, and mass-media studies. Recent publications include chapters in the edited collections *Heavy Metal: Controversies and Countercultures*; *New Essays on Clint Eastwood*; *Rammstein on Fire*; and *A Violent Conscience*.

George Alexandre Ayres de Menezes Mousinho is a PhD student at Universidade Federal de Santa Catarina, Brazil. He is currently interested in themes related to postapocalyptic and dystopian fiction in the Cold War era, Gothic fiction, film studies, and postcolonial studies.

Maria O'Connell is an assistant professor of English at Wayland Baptist University. Her research interests include systems theories, mythology, gender, and the role of stories in social construction, particularly in the Americas. She teaches English composition, world literature, and American literature. Recently she taught an honors course on wolves in American literature and a graduate course on posthumanist approaches to American nature writing. She has published on Cormac McCarthy and Jack London and is currently revising an article on Charles Bowden's nature writing. She was recently invited to submit an essay on *Blood Meridian* to *Critical Insights: Southwestern Literature*.

Brandon O'Neal is an independent scholar with a background in creative writing and classical history. A recent graduate of Ohio University, he resides in Lancaster, Ohio, with his daughter, Nola.

Glenda Pritchett received her PhD from the University of Chicago with a specialization in medieval English language and literature. She is currently an assistant professor of English at Quinnipiac University in Hamden, Connecticut, where she coordinates the first-year writing program; she serves as editor of the online journal of critical thinking and writing, *Double Helix*; and she teaches courses in early English, Irish, and Middle Scots literature, history of the English language, and composition.

Jeffrey Severs is an assistant professor of English at the University of British Columbia. He coedited (with Christopher Leise) *Pynchon's Against the Day: A Corrupted Pilgrim's Guide* (2011), and his articles have appeared or are forthcoming in *Twentieth-Century Literature, Modern Fiction Studies, Review of Contemporary Fiction*, and *Studies in American Fiction*. He is completing a book-length study of David Foster Wallace.

Matt Wanat is an assistant professor of English at the Lancaster regional campus of Ohio University, where he teaches composition, literature, and film. Wanat's scholarship examines intersections of narrative, genre, and culture in the areas of twentieth-century American literature and cinema studies, and his scholarly interests range from western American literature and film to Appalachian studies to localism and sustainability. Wanat has presented or published essays on Sam Peckinpah, Katherine Anne Porter, Wendell Berry, Jack Schaefer, Ann Pancake, Thomas Pynchon, Donald Siegel, and Clint Eastwood. Recently, his pedagogical interests have included coordination of campus-sustainability curriculum and events, including a campus vegetable garden worked by students, the produce from which helps to feed the hungry in Fairfield County, Ohio.

Index